PERSONALITY, POWER, AND AUTHORITY

PERSONALITY, POWER, AND AUTHORITY

A VIEW FROM THE BEHAVIORAL SCIENCES

Leonard W. Doob

Contributions in Psychology, Number 1

Greenwood Press
Westport, Connecticut · London, England

Library of Congress Cataloging in Publication Data

Doob, Leonard William, 1909–
Personality, power, and authority.

(Contributions in psychology, ISSN 0736-2714 ; no. 1)
Bibliography: p.
Includes index.
1. Leadership. 2. Interpersonal relations.
3. Personality. 4. Power (Social sciences) 5. Authority.
I. Title. II. Series.
HM141.D59 1983 303.3 83-1688
ISBN 0-313-23920-7 (lib. bdg.)

Library of Congress Catalog Card Number: 83-1688
ISBN: 0-313-23920-7
ISSN: 0736-2714

First published in 1983

Greenwood Press
A division of Congressional Information Service, Inc.
88 Post Road West
Westport, Connecticut 06881

Printed in the United States of America

10 9 8 7 6 5 4 3 2 1

To E. A. Bayne
suaviter in modo
fortiter in re

Contents

Acknowledgments

Usually unwittingly, sometimes wittingly, provocative friends at Yale University in the Institution for Social and Policy Studies, the Southern African Research Program, and Berkeley College have generously provided intellectual and practical assistance.

PERSONALITY, POWER, AND AUTHORITY

1

Prologue

No matter where we turn, power and authority greet or depress us. The words pervade ordinary speech and hence presumably serve a useful function. He has power, he is powerless, he is the power behind the throne, he seeks power, that party has or does not have power, this government is powerful or powerless—on and on, examples flow by. Also he is an authority, he lacks authority, he respects authority, he rebels against authority, he has an authoritarian personality.

In addition, a well-trampled tradition is encountered. Perhaps because the concepts of power and authority have been borrowed, respectively, from physics and belles-lettres,* they may have become challenging sources of inspiration in every social and behavioral science. Indeed, psychiatrists have not been able to escape them.[1] A high priest of political science once stated that his discipline is devoted almost completely to the study of power,[2] with the result that another distinguished writer in the same craft has wondered whether the

*Notes appear at the conclusion of each chapter; they are heralded with the usual superscripts. Four kinds of notes are employed:

1. They indicate the source of a quotation or paraphrase when the author's thought has been displayed or expressed, it is hoped, faithfully and accurately.

2. They also suggest the source when the original author wholly, partially, or microscopically has inspired the thought being communicated, even when his idea or research may have been distorted somewhat to serve the purpose of the moment. In these cases the note begins either with "Cf." or "E.g." to signal such usage. Grateful apologies are herewith extended to those authors. The reader, the gentle, curious reader, may thus be able to locate, if he chooses and has the patience, the original, the unexpurgated thought. In truth, the literature on power and authority is so heterogeneous, scattered, and voluminous that many of the critical strains can be brought together, it is thought, by means of this tour de force. It is quite possible, however, that numerous scholars and writers are not even honored with a superscript and a "Cf." or "E.g.". The cultural heritage on these two subjects is almost too rich; originality must often be, as someone has said, the ability to forget one's source.

3. A superscript usually after clauses or sentences beginning with the words "perhaps," "probably," or "possibly" signifies that the note provides not only the source but also a quick summary of research giving rise to the idea.

4. In a few instances a contention in the text is elaborated or illustrated at some length at the end of a chapter; the titles of these notes and the capital letter assigned are given in the text.

concept can be rescued from the "bottomless swamp" in which it has become submerged,[3] as he himself seeks frequently to avoid and yet to wade into that swamp. Authority, too, has an uncountable number of disciples ranging from Aristotle to modern politicians; the word itself reappears throughout the history of the Western world even under markedly different circumstances. No wonder, then, that the literature on both power and authority is staggeringly large and that often, though not always, it stresses seemingly petty distinctions whose progenitors hope thereby to increase their own power and authority.

Before unfurling my own distinctions, petty or otherwise, I have asked myself the question why I, foolishly or not, would also do battle with power and authority. Shall I not be increasing the prevailing chaos by offering a minor twist to themes already promulgated? Perhaps yes. Naturally, like anyone writing a book, I have had to convince myself that I may possibly have something new and helpful to say and that a few generous readers will agree with me. Or maybe not, and so I admit that, being excited by the interconnections of human thoughts and actions and the relevant scholarly disciplines concerned therewith, I find the problems of power and authority irresistible. They permeate all human relations, from the personal to the international, and hence they offer a stimulating challenge to try to bring together many of the contemporary ideas and problems in social science.[4] The critical word is "contemporary," for a rereading of classical treatises dealing with power and authority—such as Hobbes' *Leviathan*, published more than three centuries ago[5]—reveals insights as profound or more profound than any you and I can offer. Necessarily, however, those insights are expressed in the idiom of their period and hence are not always in tune with us and our concerns. Probably in the realm of political, social, and psychological ideas, as in philosophy, we do not progress appreciably; we simply express ourselves differently. On a personal level I have challenged myself to determine whether previous analyses I have made of related and seemingly unrelated topics—acculturation, communication, patriotism and nationalism, time, evil, personality, and peace—can be linked so that they contribute to the understanding of power and authority.

What follows, then, is an inventory of the problems and variables associated with power and authority. For easy reference they are lettered and numbered as they are divided into categories, subcategories, and sub-subcategories. When they are introduced, they are italicized and the exposition is briefly indented.

A *Definitions and Concepts*. Since I have had the fortune or misfortune to inflict upon myself numerous definitions of power, authority, and similar concepts provided by scholars in various disciplines and languages, by simpler human beings, and by dictionaries, I am well aware that proposed definitions limit the universe their originators can traverse. I know, too, that definitions are both boring and necessary. Let me, however, plunge slowly into the swamp and then as quickly as possible try to extricate myself.

On one point I think there is almost universal agreement: power and authority involve at least two or more persons who at a given moment can be arranged or who can arrange themselves along a *hierarchy:* one is
A.1 higher, stronger, more powerful, more authoritative than the other; one is superior in some respect to the other; or their statuses on some continuum are at different points. Asymmetry of this sort is inherent "in virtually all human relations."[6] The English language offers a rich vocabulary to describe such situations, as any thesaurus copiously demonstrates, but in this instance there seems to be no universally acceptable pair of words applicable to the relations along the hierarchy—and I prefer to avoid neolo-
A.2 gisms. I find the following *terminology* useful: I recommend it, and so for better or worse I shall use it throughout this book.

1. *Leader* and *follower:* the relation between persons at two points on a hierarchy is reasonably clear and recognized by them and perhaps also by others.
2. *Principal* and *subordinate:* the relation between persons at two points on a hierarchy is reasonably clear but not fully recognized by them nor perhaps by others.
3. *Participant:* the relation between two persons momentarily or indefinitely cannot or need not be arranged along points on a hierarchy.
4. *Controlling* and *controlled* force: in a hierarchical relation the member of a pair is an animal or plant, or is inanimate, and it affects or is affected by one or more participants.

The reasons for selecting the first terms applicable to human beings are given in note A, "Naming Powers and Authorities," at the end of this chapter. The justification for including forces is relegated to note B, "The Power of Forces." Here I would add only that relatively unobtrusive references to forces are made throughout this book to suggest that the analysis of power would be incomplete were forces to be completely ignored.

Back to the human terms. Assume that one individual *dominates*
A.3 another. If the two recognize the domination, then the dominating person is a leader, the dominated a follower. If either or both do not recognize the domination or if a third person believes that such recognition is lacking, the dominating person is a principal and the dominated one a subordinate. If these two persons are freely conversing and neither one has or has yet dominated the other, each is a participant. In simplified form:

HIERARCHY

Persons	*High*		*Low*
recognized	leader		follower
not recognized	principal		subordinate
uncertain		participant	
Forces	controlling		controlled

On the human level, a straightforward event can now be examined: *Two or more participants affect one another*. Even more simply it might be suggested that one person affects another person without being affected himself: a leader issues a command and a follower obeys. But there is likely to be some reciprocity (if you will or must), even when unacknowledged: the leader takes the follower's capabilities into account. The verb *affect* in the above proposition must be questioned: who is it who maintains that these persons affect one another? The participants themselves or someone else?

A.4 A proposition can stem from an objective report by an outside *observer* or investigator, or from a subjective report by a *participant*. The words "objective" and "subjective" refer not to the validity of the statement but to its source, a distinction that is often of crucial importance. Only the participant knows exactly how he himself feels, thinks, or judges, and this is one aspect of reality. Usually that participant, however, cannot possibly provide all the data that may or may not be relevant to his behavior. He may be unaware of the unconscious impulses within himself which a psychiatrist may help him discover; of the customs affecting him concerning which an anthropologist or a lawyer has adequate knowledge; or of the background of those customs which an historian might be eager or able to reveal. Scholars, investigators, scientists provide or attempt to provide the accurate formulations, although they too may be unwittingly handicapped by their own biases.

The next challenge is to elaborate what has transpired before the statement concerning the effect of the participants upon one another can be *fully* understood. Fully? Well, as fully as possible, or at least as power and authority are dissected by so many different persons and scholarly disciplines.

A.5 Two sets of variables are essential to suggest the *parameters* of an event; these constitute the framework in which the analysis will proceed as follows:

I. Background	1. Personality
II. Events	2. Perception
III. Ascription and Description	3. Judgment and Decision
IV. Actions	4. Behavior
V. Outcome	5. Personality

The pairs of these five variables are portrayed in the accompanying Guiding Figure to which frequent reference will be made hereafter since it serves as the overall guide to the analysis. On this figure:

a. The outer circles represent the variables characterizing the analyses by an observer, the inner circles are the subjective variables either noted by a participant or ascribed to him by an observer. For easy, distinguishable reference the outer circles are designated with roman numerals, the inner circles by arabic numbers.

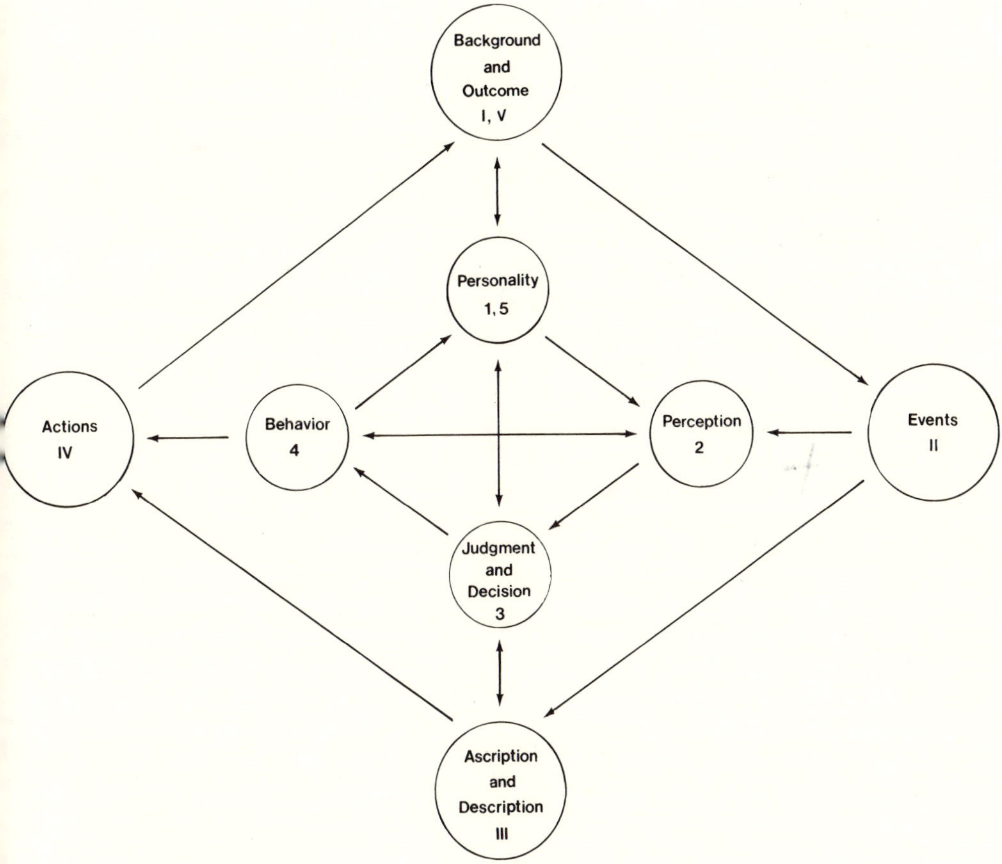

GUIDING FIGURE

b. The arrows symbolize causal or associational connections between the variables, double arrows an interaction between them.

In one large gulp, it is possible, I hope, to swallow the contents of the Guiding Figure and thus be fortified for the remainder of this book: out of a background (I) comes an event that is communicated (II) to participants whose interactions are ascribed and described by an observer (III), from those interactions emerges some form of action (IV) with possible consequences for the future (V). Also specific participants, whose personalities (1) affect their perception of the event (2), judge those events and make a decision about them (3) and hence behave overtly in some fashion (4) which may have some effect upon the way they respond in the future (5).

These roman and arabic numerals will be employed consistently in the inventory of the parameters of power and authority; they are indented as the variables each subsumes are identified. Within all of the five outer and inner circles, moreover, it would be possible to insert those subvariables and to suggest some of their relations. Indeed, before I ever evolved my own Guide, but unknown to me, a psychologist had offered a "map" which seeks to portray all the critical variables simultaneously; he has cut off segments into separate maps, presumably for the sake of providing step-by-step exposition. His map can be found with comments at the end of this chapter in note C, "The 'Map' of M. Brewster Smith." The similarities of the two designs, improbably a tribute to us both, demonstrates that psychologists think similarly when confronted with the vast problems of power and authority. I prefer to keep the Guiding Figure simple in appearance and therefore I have not included the subvariables and their relations; another device, that of guides explained below, seeks to cope with complexity.

A.6 After these fascinating and not easily digestible apéritifs, *power* may now be served. The competition among definitions, however, is keen. Before offering his own concept, for example, one writer has observed that "our day-to-day experience throws up a host of terms which describe a vast range of qualitatively different relationships: manipulation, guidance, counselling, pressure, hypnosis, suggestion, extortion, blackmail, coercion, advising, instructing, commanding, demanding. Similarly, we possess a sophisticated repertoire of concepts which outline appropriate responses to these initiatives: acceptance, agreement, obedience, capitulation, resistance, opposition, and so on."[7] It is not easy, therefore, to attempt to distill sagacious definitions from existing conceptualizations; out of deference to the sages and for the benefit of the conscientious a few illustrations of the semantic struggle are provided in note D at the end of this chapter, "The Definition Jungle." And so:

> *Power:* the actual or potential ability of one or more participants (or forces), according to the true or false conviction of an observer or a participant, to have affected or to affect the specified, significant actions of one or more other participants (or forces); or the principal or leader possessing or evoking this conviction (i.e., the power or power holder).

I leave to note E, "The Selected Definitions of Power and Authority," the defense of the definition, specifically, the use of "power" to refer to the power holder, the prominence of the word "conviction," and the nature of "specified, significant actions."

A.7 The concept of *authority,* like that of power, has not been neglected by political philosophers and social scientists and hence definitions also abound.[8] It is useful, I think, to consider authority a special adjunct to power:

> *Authority:* the repeated, true or false conviction that the hierarchical position of the principal or leader (when he is the referent for the conviction concerning

power) had, has, or will have the consent of the one or more participants whose specified, significant actions have been, are being, or will be affected; the principal or leader possessing or evoking that conviction.

Again the note "The Selected Definitions of Power and Authority" calls attention to "consent" (a synonymn for *legitimacy*) and other concepts within this definition.

Scholars and writers have often illustrated their definitions of power and authority by concocting various combinations of the two, whether or not they have used exactly the same terms.[9] It is tempting to propose a heuristic 2×2 table in which a "powerful authority" is someone with both power and authority (a top government official elected to office in a democratic society); a "powerless authority," an authority with little or no power at his disposal (a theoretical scientist in a university); a "despot," a principal with power but no authority (a dictator in a fascist society); and a "cipher," a nobody with neither authority nor power (an alienated tramp). Such a schema, however, is only flashy and can be misleading. Like any typology it would ignore degrees of power and authority. Also in terms of the present approach it would fail to specify the views of different persons. Hitler may have been considered a powerful authority by himself and his most ardent followers, but a despot by most outside observers and by some, perhaps many, Germans and Austrians. Indeed, the classification of a participant depends upon his role in the situation when a classification is plastered upon him. At home a gentle middle-class husband in Western society may be a powerful authority, at work a despot, a powerless authority vis-à-vis a friend, and as a passenger on an airborne plane a cipher. No, I conclude, no typology, no fancy labels.

Finally, one other concept requires definition. *Sovereignty* is the
A.8 belief of leaders that they have supreme authority and power over
the affairs of a group and its territory and that outside interference must be resisted; their power and authority thus conceived is accepted by some or all of their followers and the outsiders. Officials of a nation-state, for example, believe their power and authority cannot be "abrogated" by someone else:[10] "a Commonwealth without Sovereign Power is but a word, without substance, and cannot stand."[11] In modern governments and large corporations the powers with sovereignty are concealed behind so many administrative layers that only infrequently can they be identified or located by their necessarily obedient followers.[12] Possibly a bright light: according to an eloquent view, national sovereignty that engenders the possibility of nuclear war and the extinction of millions must cease unless mankind is to be annihilated.[13]

This section ends, as other sections sometimes end or are interrupted, not with a summary but with an aphorism or guide which would pinpoint the analysis. These guides are simple sentences that would salvage from the previous discussion the insight that conceivably might be useful as future power and authority are encountered.

✓ *Guide:* Power and authority may be more or less precisely defined at the outset of a treatise or by a speaker, but thereafter everyday or alternative connotations cling to the definitions and dilute or pollute them.

B

Whole vs. Parts. I return, not reluctantly, to the Guiding Figure in order to anticipate and possibly gainsay some of the doubts such an analysis perforce provokes. The figure provides an eclectic view not only of the whole but also of the parts. If for whatever reason a specific participant is of interest—and only he—then attention is riveted upon the variables indicated by the inner circles of the figure; but if the political system is puzzling, one or more of the outer squares suggests the variables to be taken to account. As anyone except a narrow specialist or a publish-or-perish theorist must agree, a ''complete'' analysis of behavior requires that both the individual and the institutions or events having impact upon him be considered either simultaneously or eventually.

Since power and authority cover a vast multitude of phenomena, it must follow that the variables in the figure are very abstract. Indeed, a psychologist once asked, ''Isn't it merely a careless use of terms to speak of the power structure of both a nation and a summer camp?''[14] His reply and one given here must be a flat *no*. On some level of abstraction any two referents in the universe can be subsumed under an abstraction, just as it may be declared—crudely, to be sure—that a saint and a terrorist or, for that matter, a barrel of beer, are similar because the saint and the terrorist are both human beings and all three can be weighed on a scale like other objects. Abstractions, however, should not be arbitrary if they are to serve a useful purpose. It is contended, therefore, that the two pairs of five variables displayed on the Guiding Figure are applicable to a nation, a summer camp, a political campaign, workers in a quarry, or a strong wind, in short, to situations in which one participant or force affects another participant or force. The apparently heterogeneous set of phenomena is thus brought, it is hoped, within a single universe or discourse.

Observers, especially when they are scholars or social scientists, prefer to concentrate upon a manageable though incomplete portion of the power-authority or any other universe. Political scientists and sociologists, particularly Americans, for example, are often enamored of a fascinating empirical question: in specific communities, who governs, by whom are the critical decisions made and how are they executed? The replies of the various schools of thought to this challenge to what somewhat impishly can be called the whodunnit approach range from elitist to pluralistic theories; they will be considered in a later chapter. In contrast, psychologists eager to probe, by means of the most fruitful ''systematic positions'' within the discipline,[15] the depths of participants in order to ascertain whether they seek or avoid power, concentrate upon the predispositions of their subjects and consequently make only passing reference to matters of concern to political and other social scientists.[16] In either case, barely a portion of the process is thus examined.

Some investigators deliberately and explicitly avoid viewing the whole and maintain in effect that a glimpse at the part is sufficient. A behavioral scientist states bluntly that "The power measures developed in this book are intended to gauge actors' objective influence upon outcomes, not their *subjective* feeling of power or powerlessness."[17] A legitimate segment of power is thus singled out for consideration, but for what reasons should the "objective influence" be considered more important or significant than the "subjective"? Perhaps, it could be argued, such influence is critical from a political or pragmatic standpoint, for then political or social change is investigated. The analysis, nevertheless, would be more complete or more robust if aspects of the individual participants were also taken into account. Not surprisingly a psychologist in a review entitled "Power as a Personality Construct" takes the opposite viewpoint: "Only expressed feelings of individual power and readiness to apply [the production and implementation of power] is brought into focus" in the account. And yet the same writer concludes his survey by suggesting that "perhaps . . . a theory of power can serve as an integrative principle within psychology and for social science as a whole."[18] A messianic theory can achieve such a noble goal only when the context is known in which a personality is examined or in which a laboratory experiment is performed and not, as is often the case, when a context is merely assumed.

Both approaches are essential; hence the Guiding Figure has inner and outer circles. Certainly it is important to know who the leaders are, who possess wealth in a society, and how power and authority are distributed. Equally significant are the individuals who view power and authority in that society. When they receive a communication, how do they react to its contents? Is it stored in short- or long-time memory?

What seems to happen when investigators cling to a part of the analysis is that they swing back and forth between considering individuals as the dependent or the independent variable while attempting to explain their own and others' reactions to authority and power. Usually, except when the aim is to determine the ways in which they do or do not influence principals and leaders, subordinates and followers are treated as if they were dependent variables: these persons are affected by institutions and events. Principals and leaders in turn are believed to be the independent variables, affecting subordinates, followers, and events, particularly when they are great men or when great men generally are invited to be the molders of human destiny. According to the fashion of the age or the prejudice of the theorist, however, they may also be labelled products of their time and hence dependent upon the milieu in which they happen to acquire power or become authorities. Such arguments are endless; let us end them for the moment and continue the quibbles in note F, "The Guiding Figure," at the end of this chapter. But not without an important dictum: in many situations, the two sets of variables interact so that they can be considered both dependent and independent. They have a *Spiral Relation.*[19]

B.1 The principal objection to the Guiding Figure and the mode of analysis can be that they do not deal adequately with *groups*. True, the focus is upon *individuals* within the inner five circles. Participants are affected by events and they affect the institutions and events studied casually by journalists and carefully by social scientists. As individuals they change or do not change over time, whether attention is paid to their life spans or differences from generation to generation. Their roles are evaluated, improved, or damaged. The view is often expressed that people die but institutions survive. Nonsense, institutions survive after the death of some persons because other persons carry on. Some but not all scholars have a penchant for considering only outstanding leaders when they probe the topic of "personality and politics," which of course is their privilege. The conviction behind the Guiding Figure, however, is that it may be important very frequently to have predispositions or personality refer to ordinary citizens who also participate in the political process.

With firmness, however banal, it has been said that "in one sense there really is only one 'unit' of analysis—the individual" and "all larger units are made up of individuals."[20] This view is satisfactory if the observer can locate and actually observe all the participants, and if a participant from his subjective private standpoint can do likewise. An objection: when reference is made to the authority or power of a group, it may not be possible to uncover all the participants. Precisely, and therefore the schema challenges the observer or the inquiring participant to specify just what he means. He may be referring (a) to the modal status of the group's members or (b) to the status of the group's leaders or representatives. If he means (c) the group's overall status as compared with other groups, he should reveal who is making the comparison or who is being compared, viz., the leaders or the members of the two groups. Thus a "powerful" club within a community may be composed of members from the upper stratum of the society, may have a charismatic person as a leader, and may evoke respect from nonmembers in that community.

B.2 The arrows in the Guiding Figure suggest that power and authority are being viewed within a *temporal frame* of reference. It is not sufficient to know that a parent or chief remains the authority and retains power over the child and follower for long or short periods of time. Each event and each perceived communication has some kind of impact which may be undetected in spite of many repetitions but which eventually can lead to change and rebellion. To catch the reasons for the stability or the change, the greater sweep embodied in the figure is essential.

Having plead the case for the whole, I now admit that the whole is never attainable. Each analysis striving to be complete must be incomplete for a very compelling reason: every situation and every person is unique and therefore empirical investigation is always necessary in order to weight relevant variables. If the weight of an object at a given distance from the fulcrum determines whether it will balance or upset the system, that object must be weighed beforehand in order to predict its effect on the system. The weight in turn is affected by the quantity of the material from which the object is made, whether platinum or grass. The classical equation does not and cannot specify what the material will be; at this point empirical investigation is required. The metaphorical materials being weighed may be numerous, but they are finite in comparison with the infinite ways in which weights must be provided for the variables affecting power and authority. Little wonder, then, no matter how strenuously we seek to grasp the whole, we may have to settle for a part. It is well, however, to recognize the limitation.

> *Guide:* No aspect of behavior can be thoroughly analyzed without exploring its ramifications; people cannot be cut into segments except for the convenience of an investigator or a discipline. At a minimum it is useful to specify the parameters before and after research is concentrated upon a compelling if arbitrary detail.

C *Research.* First, a warning. This section is included because research is unavoidable if power and authority are to be systematically comprehended; but the reader may avoid it without fear of treading too far down a primrose path. Whether the approach to power and authority concerns observers or participants, principles inevitably appear. Nothing mysterious is implied. The observer who is a scholar or a bystander seeks to understand what transpires, and his understanding results from past experiences and gives rise to generalizations applicable to the present and future. The leader or principal carries within himself principles through which he seeks to affect followers or participants who in turn have principles which help them cope or try to cope with the situations in which they find themselves. And principles in turn require data gathered, when possible, by means of standardized methods. This situation is not the least bit peculiar. Investigations of most phenomena, especially those concerned with behavior of human beings, try to adduce generalizations transcending the particulars at hand without neglecting their uniqueness. You are like me and all other persons in some respects; fortunately, you also differ from me and them in other respects.

C.1 Most generalizations concerning hierarchies are little more than assertions surrounded by a necessarily limited *sampling* of selected data. For decades psychologists and sociologists have been conducting laboratory studies under controlled artificial conditions and, more often than not, with college or university students as subjects. As all honest investigators admit, the emerging generalizations, even when replicated in other laboratories, are restricted in scope as a result of the culture of the subjects, of the experimental task through which an aspect of power or authority has been assessed, and of the frame of reference guiding the research. In like manner, the erudite, more or less exact descriptions of governments in general, of a particular government, or of specific leaders are just that: descriptions that necessarily are confined to the chosen topics and usually do not pretend to transcend them. Clearly, for example, there is no reason to anticipate that political and lay authorities function similarly in traditional, democratic, fascist, and communist countries.

Every experimental or empirical study in the social sciences, in short, necessarily must rely upon a limited sample of human beings and situations. No experimenter or investigator is omniscient or omnipotent, he must perforce confine his attention to a selected sample which he tries to explore as thoroughly as possible. What emerges, then, is some kind of generalization of restricted applicability, a fact readily acknowledged by all honest researchers.

C.2

Other *limitations* of research can be easily located. Whatever happens on this planet has been influenced by previous events, hence an impossibly thorough analysis would go back to remote ancestors. But nobody has the patience, the time, the energy, or the knowledge to provide a full account of a sneeze or a prejudice, and therefore at some point there must be an *Arbitrary Limitation*[21] in tracing, respectively, the genetic and sociological origin of those two events.

Then generalizations are incomplete or faulty because the data are not at hand even when an Arbitrary Limitation is explicitly admitted. Seldom if ever is anyone in a position to collect all the information likely to be relevant, especially when participants interact informally. The give-and-take accompanying momentous decisions, especially on a national and international level, may be recorded, but may not be immediately or ultimately available. Memories later reflect the selective biases of the participants or the recorders; for example, the thoughts, feelings, and behavior of subordinates and followers may be less interesting and hence may be abbreviated or ignored. In many countries the latter are now quizzed by pollsters but, as will be stressed below, surveys have their own difficulties which include sampling and instrumental errors connected with the wording and order of questions, the rapport between interviewer and respondent, and the salience of the issues for which they are designed. In the absence of imperfect data or even in the presence of far better data, it is in effect impossible to comprehend exactly or fully how and why a person has passed judgment concerning the power he has or the goals he would seek. We are, as I keep repeating to all who will listen, solipsistically encased. Those who are outside of us can never quite know how we feel; we are doomed to make risky inferences from the stimuli we know or believe we know are having effects upon those we would comprehend.[22]

Finally, as already proclaimed, one result of the ubiquity of power and authority in social science is the inclination of scholars, with notable exceptions, to bite off manageable chunks within their own disciplines and to avoid stressing the interconnections between themselves and their neighbors. The philosophically inclined, however, make veiled references to various fields of knowledge, but unsystematically and usually as declarations rather than as documented statements. The customary Arbitrary Limitations in one sense are legitimate. It is sufficient for a psychiatrist to diagnose a man as prone to depression and characterized by a feeling of powerlessness whenever he is faced with seemingly insoluble problems. In his own area of competence that diagnostician is not expected to be able to forecast when and for what reasons an economic recession will arise which will create bread-and-butter difficulties for the patient. If the man's family or he himself wishes a realistic prognosis, therefore, a combination of psychiatric and economic wisdom is required. The analogy is seemingly appropriate: segmental propositions concerning hierarchies, however valid within a limited frame of reference, are likely to be incomplete guides to understanding the complicated interaction between or among participants. The Guiding Figure, I deliberately repeat, for this very reason tries to embrace all relevant variables, even while heaping heavy responsibility upon actions (IV) and behavior (4).

C.3 As a result of reviewing such a dismal outlook, it is to be anticipated that no *theory* of hierarchies as a guide to research has become more powerful or authoritative than its rival; alas, no theory has been received with universal acclamation except by its originator and his or her devoted adherents. However deplorable this situation may be, it is inevitable. Although we strongly crave an all-embracing theory, we are doomed to fall short of the goal. After their own laborious, laudable investigations of power and authority, some but not all scholars bluntly acknowledge the limitations of their own generalizations.[23] The proponent of the most widely publicized theory of elitist power in the United States forces himself to admit that "no general answer is sufficient" to the crucial power-related questions as to whether the elite he believes he himself has identified are "role-determined" or "role-determining."[24] Although sometimes experimenting social psychologists seem almost to convince themselves that their hypotheses transcend their own findings—and hence they write as if their limited discoveries are applicable to mankind ever since the time of Adam and until the Second Coming—one of them has admitted in a respectable scholarly journal that his discipline is "primarily an historical inquiry" which "deals with facts that are largely nonrepeatable and which fluctuate markedly over time."[25] The numerous revisions and addenda that have been and are being continually proposed in order to establish the validity of perhaps the most sweeping and embracing of all theories concerning power, viz., Marxism, indicate its theoretical and practical limitations. Even Marx himself in one of his most quoted passages qualified and then tried, with a touch of somewhat tricky metaphysics, to rescue his doctrine of determinism: "Men make their own history, but they do not make it just as they please; they do not make it under circumstances chosen by themselves, but under circumstances directly encountered, given, and transmitted from the past."[26] As social science, justifiably named a "soft" rather than a "hard" science, develops, it is to be doubted—yet without complete certainty—whether patches to any single theory will eventually give rise to a radically different and more valid theory in the manner of a Galileo whose revolutionary, iconoclastic conception of the universe enabled him to overcome the tortuous additions required to have the Ptolemaic conception conform to newly discovered astronomical data. Anticipate, then, no miracles in the foreseeable future.

Why does it appear impossible or difficult to evolve a single, comprehensive theory concerning hierarchies? The reasons are numerous and they are common, if unacknowledged, in the social sciences and psychiatry. In part they can be traced to human frailties: the theorists perforce are enamoured of their own theories, so that, consciously or unconsciously, they seek out and select supporting rather than contradicting facts. A few pursue academic immortality for themselves not only, as I have already said, by formulating fancy definitions, but also by coining striking phrases or neologisms with which their names may possibly be associated forever after. Some would be original by concentrating upon factors their predecessors, they maintain, have avoided—and indeed new insights are thus often but not always obtained.

Then, if it is agreed, as our definitions implore, that power and authority involve actual or potential interaction among participants of varying statuses, it must follow that individual differences which cannot be glibly or easily subsumed under an embracing principle must always be anticipated. Surprises occur as a result of the uniquenesses of personality and the emergence of group products not always encompassable by considering only the parts of their sum. It is all very well to assert, as many historians do when they defend the practical utility of their discipline, that we must learn from the past, but truer seems to me to be their other platitude that history never repeats itself and consequently that "the political experience of one age is never precisely the same as that of another" and hence even a "modification in the categories of political philosophy" is necessary.[27] History, moreover, is unavoidable; within the confines of single communities the relation of the participants can or should be examined not at a single moment but over time.[28] Persons and situations, in short, are sufficiently unique, so that facile generalizations are to be avoided—when possible, I say with a sigh. Little wonder, then, that a strict empiricist, indeed a political scientist, advises that "nothing categorical can be assumed about power in any community."[29]

Besides affecting what he himself does, a theorist's theory can affect others as well as events. If he is an educator, he has students who may try to absorb what he has to say. If he writes articles or books—again the name of Marx inevitably must be mentioned—some of his readers will be influenced by what he has written. If he is a leader, he may have some effect upon his followers and other leaders. Here is a variant of the slippery self-fulfilling hypothesis: Predictions concerning the future in some instances may be valid in part or in whole because they have been made or believed, and also appropriately affected the very events they have predicted.

C.4 Having expressed profound skepticism concerning the state of the art, I would now quickly emphasize the *utility* of theories and data. They should be gratefully received for two principal reasons. If the theories are well established and the data are convincing, at the very least they can be employed to anticipate the future on an actuarial basis within their own frame of reference. For example, a careful investigation of the contacts between community organizations and the local offices of the United States Training and Employment Service substantiated, among other hypotheses, the following: "The lowest frequency of interaction between two organizations will occur when neither organization perceives benefits from interacting."[30] There is no way of knowing whether this unstartling generalization is universally valid or useful as the power relations of other organizations are examined; yet for the local office and the service the proposition may well have pragmatic utility when it is desired to improve or increase contacts between the groups.

Then, secondly, accurate knowledge of any kind should always be added to an investigator's kit with the aid of which some relevant person or situations are investigated in the future. Just as it is useful to know that productivity on the floor of a factory sometimes but not always may be markedly affected by illumination and ventilation, however, so new factors may arise that are utterly unrelated to those previously associated with power and authority in the past. Thus a microscopic study of the power structure of one city, as has been reported twice for the City of New Haven, Connecticut, is enlightening,[31] but the emerging details, impressive as they seem, are not likely to be identical, no matter how similar, in other communities closeby, elsewhere in the United States, certainly not in non-Western cities in the Orient, and indeed not in New Haven a decade or less later. But it is good to have the details established in spite of these reservations, for they contribute to a theory of perhaps limited scope. We use a specific drug for a particular set of illnesses, but we do not anticipate that it will be a panacea for all illnesses. Perhaps all that one can achieve is to select an analogy from the past which seems to fit the present in as many details as possible, even though the similarity may be little more than a metaphor.

> *Guide:* Solidly determined, if limited, chunks of knowledge from the past are valuable but can be only cautiously utilized in the present and future.

C.5 To document or counteract intuitive assertions concerning power and authority and to evaluate laborious methodological techniques, research *criteria* must be utilized. Indeed modern scholars pride themselves on their careful methods. Sometimes, however, the method wags the problem. Bold behaviorists among political scientists, for example, have selected what they believe to be objective and hence laudable techniques: by their actions shall all participants be known since those actions and not their internal states are supposed to be directly measurable. This view, however, is somewhat delusional, inasmuch as errors may be committed by the investigators themselves before they publish their findings. They must collect the data, which means interviewing decision-makers and followers and examining documents; they must synthesize these experiences and draw conclusions. At each step, wittingly or not, they may trip.

Valid assertions or theory, in brief, require valid data; those data must be assembled, and their assembly demands some kind of measurement and implied quantification. Only the techniques are being considered here, not their statistical manipulation. For the discipline of statistics requires a tome in its own right. In the present context, therefore, its current sophisticated descriptive and inferential procedures cannot be outlined.[32] Suffice it to point out that statistics is concerned with central tendencies (means, medians, modes), deviations from those tendencies (ranges, standard deviations), fluctuations resulting from random and nonrandom sampling (in popular language, the margin of error), the relations between or among variables (correlations, analyses of variance, factor analyses), and the bases for assuming that obtained differences are or are not due to chance (tests of significance). Since these statistical procedures are dependent upon valid data, no amount of statistical manipulation can make invalid data valid except in a spurious or misleading sense. Very conventional criteria must be invoked to evaluate the methods that are or can be employed to measure power and authority: validity, reliability, and objectivity.

C.5.a A method is *valid* if it succeeds in measuring what it purports to measure. If a man says he does not seek power and soon afterwards strives to be elected to public office or to become leader of a social group, his statement in retrospect must be considered false, and thus the method of questioning has produced invalid data. The criterion of validity in this instance, however, applies only when his subsequent behavior is used as the validating criterion; at the time of the interrogation he may have been telling the truth as he consciously perceived his own strivings, and unforeseen circumstances may have changed his intentions. Or that method of asking him outright might be considered valid if the goal of the questioner has been to determine from his public utterance whether or not he is a liar. The problem of validity, therefore, cannot be approached until a criterion is explicitly formulated: whatever information is acquired may serve some useful purpose and in that sense be considered valid.

C.5.b *Reliability* on a verbal level usually refers to the consistency with which information is elicited from an informant either to a variety of questions pertaining to the same topic or to the same or similar questions after the lapse of time. An individual who replies inconsistently to similar questions during a conversation or interview or who replies differently to the same question a short time later may be called unreliable or the method may be so branded. Different questions, however, though apparently similar, may tap different responses: and a different reply on a second occasion may result from an actual change in the interim. Reliability, therefore, cannot be easily ascertained: and the difficulty increases when the individual's behavior rather than his verbal responses is of concern.

C.5.c The third criterion, *objectivity,* refers to the interaction between the investigator and the participants: a method may be called objective when the elicited information is not appreciably affected by the investigator or by the particular conditions under which that information is obtained. In the United States it was once demonstrated that more respondents expressed anti-Semitic sentiments when the interviewers did not look Jewish, did not use a Jewish name, or both, than when the reverse was true;[33] and it has been known for decades that on certain political questions blacks tend to respond differently when the interviewers are black or white,[34] so that "interviewer effects" of this kind may be greater than changes ascertained over a period of time.[35] Nonobjective data, however, cannot be summarily dismissed even though their value for the stated purpose of the investigation at hand may be challenged. Perhaps it is important to know that the reply of an individual is partially or wholly a function of the interviewer's race or ethnic group: something about him may thus be validly revealed through a procedure that does not satisfy the criterion of objectivity.

C.5.d The three research criteria are the same as those described in any elementary textbook: they are *applicable* to conventional academic investigations, and therefore they are or should be employed, formally or informally, both by the observer of power and authority who seeks to make a notable or diminutive contribution to knowledge as well as by participants who would comprehend one another. They merit acclaim, not disdain. They are or should be also applicable to any kind of empirical labor, whether performed by a psychiatrist, a detective, a diplomat, anyone associated with the intelligence services of a corporation or government, or an ordinary citizen. Spy thrillers and detective stories largely devote themselves to the theme of data hunting. When once the data have been procured by hook, crook, ingenuity, deception, or luck, they must be evaluated by means of the same stale, academic criteria.

The problem of the participants who require or receive information about one another will be dutifully explored in Chapter 8. There it will be evident that the same criteria appear, but even more informally. Informality, however, is no excuse for sloppiness, as competent leaders must know if they are to hold their posts and sensible followers must realize if they are not to lose their heads literally or figuratively. To snap the methodological monotony, let a character fashioned by a gifted novelist hold forth: "Well," he continued, "what is it you know about Kamensky?" "Why, nothing more than I have told you," I said. "Then you're guessing," he said. "You should never do that. One mustn't guess if one is a revolutionary, one must draw logical conclusions from observed facts, for revolution is a science and revolutionaries must work by scientific method."[36] The criteria, in brief, are the scientific substitutes for guessing, however easy and attractive guessing and its twin, intuition, appear to be.

Finally, the individual, regardless of his hierarchial position, possesses a self-concept, the validity of which he may never question even though the relation of that concept to reality, however defined, may have an important bearing on his well-being or on his judgments as a participant. To meet the challenge of knowing thyself, again the same trio of criteria must be applied. Do I really wish to attain that goal, do I believe I can attain it, do I feel friendly or hostile toward the peers whose cooperation is essential, do I in fact have the skill to reach the goal? Questions such as these, as will also be emphasized in Chapter 8, occur with relation to power, and may also be relevant to an authority who has or does not have confidence concerning the position he occupies. Insight into oneself is so frequently and glibly assumed that the professions of psychiatry, especially psychoanalysis, and counseling flourish in Western society.

These stern strictures, although they must be taken seriously, do not disallow flashes of comprehension enabling the observer or the participant to obtain valid, reliable, and objective information concerning the problem at hand. The power behind the throne may suddenly be discovered; verification may be equally swift. It is a pity, however, that shortcuts to knowledge are seldom available. And so the discussion returns to formal methods of investigation, not because they lead inevitably to perfection or salvation but because they can function as models to evaluate shortcuts.

C.6 A fuzzy line can be drawn between measures that directly or indirectly secure information about power and authority. When *direct measures* are utilized, the participant is fully or somewhat aware that an observer or another participant is collecting data, whereas with an indirect method he is less aware or not aware at all. Obviously an investigator never reveals his purpose completely, no matter which approach he employs, perhaps because he fears a respondent cannot comprehend it, perhaps because he himself may not be able to anticipate exactly what he himself will do with the data after they have been collated and fed into a computer. In face-to-face situations, however, those being interviewed at the very least suspect or guess the purpose of the conversation or the questions. In recent times investigators have been compelled by their consciences, and especially by American governmental agencies supplying the research funds, to obtain what is called informed consent from their subjects. Often there is a conflict for the researcher or his donor between the potential psychological damage to subjects and the concealment required by the research if the technique is to be effective.

C.6.a The most direct approach of all is to confront a participant via an *interview* or a *questionnaire* and to ask him, for example, (a) whether in some or many situations he believes he possesses power or authority, (b) what his attitudes toward power and authority are, or (c) whether he generally feels powerful or powerless. The question can be vague and open-ended or concrete and closed. In passing it is important to note that the relationship itself between interviewer and respondent may involve authority and power. The interviewer is the authority or the power since the queries come from him; the respondent is the participant who decides whether to respond or not, or to express what he "really" thinks, believes, or knows. In research, but not in many police interrogations, however, the interviewer may have little if any power over the respondent except for the probability that his very presence may require the person to be somewhat polite. An interviewer conducting a conventional survey secures cooperation by suggesting that the responses of participants are valuable, by pledging anonymity, by displaying his credentials, and possibly by offering a material reward. Under these circumstances it is possible to determine whether a respondent has grasped a question; to probe more deeply, when necessary, with follow-up questions; and to make note of nonverbal forms of communication like facial expressions and subtle verbal clues like the speed of the reply and the tone of the voice. There is always the danger, however, that respondents, in an effort to present themselves in a favorable light, will falsify their opinion. Canadian adults, to avoid appearing ignorant in front of an interviewer or that person's confederate, once fabricated opinions about nonexistent events especially when they were made to believe or they themselves believed they should be knowledgeable.[37] Since memories fade and participants ordinarily do not keep adequate records or any records at all of the interplay with others, investigations of past decisions almost always must rely upon interviewing; often, particularly when documents are lacking, so frequently the case in Africa, the technique is given the dignified, provoking title of "oral history." On occasion deeper interviews precede or follow more shallow written questionnaries.[38]

Questionnaries distributed to a group (as in a classroom) or through the mail have the advantage of standardizing the items that evoke the responses but, even when the items have been carefully pretested in oral form, there is no certain way of knowing precisely how individuals will respond as they allegedly indicate something about themselves and their activities. At a minimum this direct method may produce clues to some predispositions, at a maximum to all phases of the power-authority process, especially the reasons for the decisions and the outcomes. A panel of 672 American consumers was asked to indicate how important they considered 36 different values, among which they ranked "social recognition" at the very bottom of one hierarchy and being "obedient" similarly next to the bottom on another scale.[39] Should they have been believed? We do not know, for possibly—as in an interview—their pride may have led them to falsify their beliefs even under conditions of anonymity. It seems likely, however, that they were thus revealing something of unknown significance about themselves since otherwise they would not have responded, truthfully or falsely, consciously or unconsciously, as they did. Perhaps they considered it important to construct a devil-may-care façade for the benefit of the investigator.

In general, if validity is defined as the degree of correspondence between replies to a questionnaire or in an interview or conversation on the one hand and the behavior in real life on the other hand, abundant research has demonstrated only that the relationship fluctuates between a fairly close one (for example, voting intention and the actual vote, at least in Western countries) to one close to zero (for example, adherence to ethical beliefs by some politicians and their actual behavior in public office). Here arises for the first time the problem of the relation between predispositions and behavior, a topic to be considered at great length as beliefs, attitudes, and the behavioral outcome are appraised in subsequent chapters.

Reliability of data obtained from interviews can sometimes be determined less convincingly not by repeating the same question but, as indicated above, by including similar questions pertaining to the same topic; then the degree of consistency among the replies can be ascertained. On the surface a questionnaire might appear to be very objective, except that the replies may be affected by the circumstances under which it has been administered. Replying in a classroom may produce an effect different from that pervading the home in which a mailed questionnaire is filled out, and filling out a schedule in the home may be affected by the presence or absence of other persons.

No quantitative tabulation is available, I believe, but I have the impression that direct interviews have been employed more frequently and extensively in assessing power and authority than any method other than intuition or consulting historical records. Two quick examples: members of the United States Forestry Service were once interviewed to determine whether the authority of the federal rule book or their own professional values affected their decisions;[40] "power and the relation" among psychiatrists, psychologists, and social workers were investigated by asking them directly a variety of questions ranging from how they felt about the admiration and esteem they had been receiving from nonmembers of their own profession to their willingness to communicate with those outsiders.[41] In the first study, it would have been impossible to observe the foresters as they made their decisions, although perhaps those decisions, if recorded, could have been compared with the rule book. In the second, the area of research was completely subjective; overt behavior would have revealed very little, if anything, about internal predispositions.

C.6.b Many of the problems being described in this section on research do not arise in connection with controlling or controlled inanimate *forces* since adequate standardized, objective procedures are available to measure their power. The horsepower of an engine can be calibrated by a competent technician, the energy released by an erupted volcano is assessed on the Richter scale, rainfall is accurately measured by determining its depth in inches or centimeters on a gauge. Problems arise, however, when the attempt is made to forecast the impact of these forces. Adequate data may be lacking: too few weather stations report the progress of a low pressure system across the country. Or the data may be too complex to analyze: information suggests that a gathering storm may go out to sea or may sweep across a land mass, depending upon prevailing winds and temperature when two weather systems meet. Similarly animals can be appraised. The load beasts of burden are able to carry and the probable ferocity of a wild animal coming in contact with a human being can be anticipated. But intraspecies variability must be taken into account as well as the circumstances under which an animal's power is utilized or experienced. Additional complications occur in the case of contagious diseases; thus it may be directly and unequivocably clear to a physician or the patient himself that a child has a cold or has been brought down by an identifiable virus, but it is difficult or impossible to anticipate to whom the malady will spread or whether an epidemic will ensue.

C.6.c *Laboratory experiments*—experiments in the strict sense—have been extensively employed to study power and authority. From one standpoint this method approaches perfection: the investigator controls the variable being investigated; he may obtain a measure before and after the manipulation by means of an observation, an interview, or a questionnaire. In addition, experimental subjects may be selected because they have attributes related to the investigation, such as their position in some profession, occupation, or educational hierarchy; they may be observed during the experiment itself to note how in fact they do behave under varying conditions of power and authority that have been determined by the experimenter. Finally a control group—equivalent to the experimental group in as many respects as possible except for the manipulation, or randomly selected from the same populations as the experimentals who also are selected through the same method—may be similarly measured. Thus it seems probable, if not certain, that whatever changes occur or are observed in the experimental group are due not to extraneous or chance factors but to the experimental manipulation. As indicated at the outset of the present section, however, the experimental subjects are seldom a representative sample of human beings or even of their own society: too often in the United States conveniently obtainable students are dragooned to participate. In addition, subjects are usually aware that they are being observed and that their behavior is being recorded; hence under these artificial conditions they perforce perform differently from the way they might in real life. The emerging generalizations, limited as they are, at least provide a first approximation of generalizations that may or may not be valid in situations transcending the laboratory.

For that very reason, frequent references throughout this book are made to illustrative experiments. In order not to clutter the text with details concerning these experiments and empirical investigations, I have sometimes relegated relevant information to footnotes. The research is usually heralded in a precautionary manner with an adverb at the start of the sentence—*probably, possibly, perhaps*—and the usual superscript at its end indicates where the details can be found at the end of the chapter. Those details, when not provided in the text, are as follows: the country where the research was conducted, since cultural and temporal factors often affect the outcome; the number and kinds of persons who were the subjects or respondents; the method or technique; the results; sometimes a comment; and of course the location of the reference. Such an outline provides sufficient coverage of each investigation; and simultaneously one of the adverbs in the text warns the reader and this writer that the finding is limited and may not be valid. Such a warning is especially necessary in connection with the gap between behavior in the necessarily artificial conditions created by psychologists in their laboratories and actual behavior in the rough-and-tough situations of real life.

Inferences, risky or otherwise, always accompany *indirect mea-*
C.7 *sures*. Statistical data and other information from documents that have been originally collected for one purpose may later be utilized as indices of hierarchies. According to a social psychologist, "evidence for the 'power' of a ruling class can be found" in various "indicators," such as whether or not specified participants possess "a disproportionate amount of wealth and income" as compared with other groups in the society, whether they are more fortunate with respect to infant mortality and education, whether they control the principal social and economic institutions of the state, and whether they dominate the government.[42] Statistical data concerning wealth, health, and schooling are usually available and in Western societies are likely to be sufficiently, though imperfectly, reliable and objective; but their significance as indices require explicit operational definitions before the relevant data can be collected or supplied.

Indirect methods par excellence include those unobtrusive techniques enabling data to be collected either when the persons are unaware that they are being investigated or else when they can neither know nor imagine the precise purpose being served by the investigation.[43] Children, for example, may be observed unobtrusively at play; those who are dominant can be compared with those are submissive with respect to data gathered from their parents concerning demographic attributes or the child-rearing methods to which they have been subjected; the children cannot possibly appreciate their potential contribution to the lofty goals of serious science.

More or less similarly, if it is known that participants change a belief or their behavior after receiving a communication from a communicator (whether an investigator or a principal), if all other things in their lives are irrelevant—as they seldom are—*and* if a comparable control group not receiving the communication does not appreciably change, the inference may be drawn, perhaps, that the communicator or his communication is more powerful or has more authority than members of his audience.[44] Distributors of products can thus be said to have power over consumers when their sales increase in one market where they have widely advertised and remain roughly the same in another comparable market where they have not advertised their wares. If an elected official changes his stance in the direction of the latest public opinion poll, it may be "plausible" to attribute power to the poll or the sample on which it is based.[45] In this instance the temporal sequence—previous view, poll, changed view—is impressive, provided some other event has not occurred at the same time and provided only the incident itself is appraised. When no Arbitrary Limitation is imposed, as one usually is for practical or expedient reasons, the power relation between the public official and the poll may also require a consideration of why he was suggestible in the first place and why the respondents to the poll expressed themselves as they did. One final illustration of the unobtrusive approach, perhaps its reductio ad absurdem: it has been seriously maintained that "the system" of power within the office of a business or company can be "fairly easily" mapped by observing who talks to whom in informal situations (coffee breaks, lunch, Christmas "parties") or who rides together in the same car pool.[46] Such indices, it must be admitted, however, have been used with high reliability and objectivity, particularly when more than a single investigator makes the inference. But they remain inferences—risky stimulus inferences—that may be unavoidable when other methods cannot be employed.[47]

When social scientists, particularly psychologists, use so-called projective methods, the subjects know they are being tested, measured, or whatnot, but they cannot fathom the technique or even the goal of the investigator. In the scholarly literature on power and authority the biggest splash during recent decades has been made by observers administering a version of a Thematic Apperception Test (TAT) originally designed courageously and immodestly to tap many, if not most of the unconscious motives with which mankind is gifted and plagued. Individuals are shown somewhat ambiguous drawings or photographs and are then asked either to indicate what the characters there portrayed are doing or to compose a story in which those characters play a role; what the subjects say is recorded and later coded by means of the investigator's categories which he believes to be symptomatic of the presence or the absence of a power motive, or somewhere in between. TATs have been employed to try to determine a person's sense of power or powerlessness, a sense he may be unable or reluctant to express to someone else when questioned bluntly or directly. The claim is made that the data thus obtained "lay out more or less explicitly in words the cognitive systems which the members of a culture are supposed to share."[48] Certainly the protocols often but not always can be reliably and objectively scored; the main challenge concerns their validity when validity is assessed by behavior in real life or by the relation of "inner experience" to other personality traits.[49] The TAT method of inference, therefore, is risky and imperfect, as will be subsequently emphasized, but it cannot be cast aside if only because there is no royal pathway to comprehending what takes place consciously and unconsciously in the subjective reactions of human beings. Like almost any seemingly arbitrary, methodological technique employed by psychologists, preliminary hypotheses can usually be squeezed out of TAT data, provided enough persons agree to submit to the test so that statistically significant differences emerge. But how can such differences be interpreted?[50]

Projective techniques have also invaded questionnaires and interviews. The following is an item at some distance from reality but it is not as far away as a conventional TAT: "Suppose a major project were before the community, one that required decision by a group of leaders whom nearly everyone would accept. Which persons would you choose to make up this group—regardless of whether or not you know them personally?''[51]

Occasionally investigators employ direct and indirect methods in the same research. They gather data from interviews, questionnaires, and observations from the same or different samples of individuals; they also make inferences about them on the basis of past and present behavior. Traditionally, anthropologists depend upon a variety of methods, although they tend to concentrate upon observation, participant observation (data secured by living with the peoples being studied and participating as much as possible in their everyday existence), and informal interviews. In all instances they seek to become as unobtrusive as possible: after a period of time, it is hoped, their strange accents, clothes, manners, and appearance as well as even skin color will fade somewhat into the indigenous society so that their presence no longer disturbs or distorts the very existence they are seeking to investigate. The power structure of a small Dominican community and the precipitating causes of changes in their economy were once ascertained by an anthropologist who lived in that community for eighteen months and thus in his opinion he obtained a ''view from the bottom.''[52] To be able to claim, as another anthropologist does concerning African societies in general, that ''members of a society who have power at their disposal hold it, and exercise it through several networks'' requires the synthesis of innumerable observations and informal interviews.[53]

Guide: Errors in seeking to comprehend participants in any respect are always to be anticipated but are also often assessable.

NOTES

A. Naming Powers and Authorities. The choice of names for the participants who interact in power and authority relations is very arbitrary. We could label one cheese and the other caviar, provided we were to attach to the two foods appropriate definitions and provided we then perhaps capitalized them or enclosed them in quotation marks. The greatest temptation is to call one C (controlling unit) or A, and the other R (responsive unit) or B, a system employed by many worthy scholars.[54] There is no real objection to A, B, C, R, or any other letter of any available alphabet except that the letters are aesthetically unappealing and, more important, give the spurious impression that we have achieved the heights of algebraic abstraction. Nowadays many scholars are addicted to the word ''actors'' which I reject not only because I dislike fashionable, oft-repeated words and clichés but because it has the explicit connotation of the theater in which men and women portray not themselves but fictitious characters and hence behave differently according to the roles they assume. Power and authority also require role playing, but the interacting persons are almost always responding to real events, or at least they consider them real.

Perhaps I express the bias of a democratic society, but words such as superior, superordinate, and stronger to refer to the upper persons and inferior, dependent, and weaker to refer to lower persons have elitist connotations I would avoid. Even upper and lower are generally disliked, so that blue-collar persons claim to belong not to the lower class but to the working class. I shed a tiny tear as I disregard these words because they are abstract—superior with respect to what, for example?—without sounding hollow like A and B. ''Party'' has a respectable lineage especially in legal terminology; but again the term, applicable as it is to both the plaintiff and the defendant who are in conflict, requires an adjective to designate the hierarchical relation.

I am not altogether happy with my conventional choice of leader and follower. The terms are satisfactory in many power- and authority-relevant situations except when one person does not acknowledge the other's status. For this reason the detached concepts of principal and subordinate are almost always employed, even though subordinate is unavoidably and admittedly somewhat demeaning. Participant is neutral: the individual is interacting with others or with forces, and the hierarchical relation has not become clear.

B. The Power of Forces. The nonhuman forces refer to many aspects of the environment influencing or influenced by human beings: animals, plants, objects, physical features of the environment (e.g., mountains, oceans), natural phenomena (weather, climate, gravity), organs of the human body, metaphysical beings such as gods. Why include them in the present discussion, especially when it has usually but not always been the custom to excommunicate them from analyses of power and authority?[55] In passing, I find it impossible to resist citing a description of ''primitive'' marine coelenterates: ''When two individuals of the same species are placed in close contact, the smaller of the two will always begin to disintegrate. It is auto-destruction due to lytic mechanisms entirely under the governance of the smaller partner. He is not thrown out, not outgamed, not outgunned; he simply chooses to bow out.''[56] While it is true that the behavior of these coelenterates may throw no light on power and authority, the significant changes in evolutionary theory within the last few decades and especially the emergence of sociobiology, controversial as that subject is, at the least suggest the possibility that some of the human tendencies related to interactions may have a genetic basis which, however, continues to require extensive exploration.

There is, moreover, a perfectly straightforward, psychological reason for welcoming forces to the universe of power: both the lash of a tyrant from whom one cannot escape and that of crashing lightning a few yards away evoke fear, although their origins, if not the ensuing misery, are quite different. Whoever disagrees with this decision should read a chapter in an elegant, delicate French treatise titled ''Les Commandements de la Nature.''[57] Like the unmentionable Evil one, I could also quote Scripture, whether at the outset of the Old Testament (''and God made a wind to pass over the earth'') or toward the end of the New Testament (''four angels standing on the four corners of the earth, holding the four winds of the earth''),[58] to allow forces to enter the present framework. Finally, it is interesting if not altogether relevant to note that the term ''power'' as employed by engineers indicates a force ''under human control and available for doing mechanical work,''[59] in different words capable of being controlled.

For these reasons, I cannot agree with many writers who arbitrarily exclude forces from an analysis of power: the presence of human beings interacting with forces is compelling. It should be clear, however, that human beings usually play a role even when forces control their actions. Lightning strikes, but the damage is avoided when someone has installed a lightning rod on the building, or most persons are not harmed because they take cover as the storm approaches. In 1972 the dam supporting Buffalo Creek in West Virginia collapsed and resulted in deaths and the destruction of communities and personal relationships. But this tragedy is explained by a reference not alone to the heavy rains, which were only the immediate cause, but to human factors: the dam had been poorly built and refuse had been thoughtlessly dumped into the waters which it held. In addition, reactions to the catastrophe began as people tried to save themselves from the rushing water, and eventually their traditional habits and not the flood itself affected the ways in which they tried to adjust to the event.[60]

Other forces of nature are or can be controlled by principals. Simple weeding may facilitate the growth of plants. The erosion of soil resulting from overgrazing in many parts of Africa and elsewhere or from the use of chemical fertilizers in the United States and other countries demonstrates how the soil and crops can be disastrously affected by human intervention. As we too slowly realize, the natural resources of this planet are being depleted at an alarming rate.

C. The "Map" of M. Brewster Smith. The map is herewith reproduced. It is modestly offered as "a heuristic device" and is "not a theory." On the map it can be seen that the variables are grouped into what the author calls five panels connected by solid arrows to suggest the various relations and by dotted arrows to indicate "feedback loops." The similarity between this map and the Guiding Figure is striking. Panels I and II are called, respectively, "Distal Social Antecedents" and "Social Environment as Context for the Development of Personality and Acquisition of Attitudes" and correspond to what is called in the Guiding Figure "Background" (I and V) and in part "Observer's Depiction" (III). Panel III refers to "Personality Processes and Dispositions" and represents the individual's "Predispositions" (1 and 5) and part of his "Judgment and Decision" (3). Part IV, "The Situation as Immediate Antecedent of Action" is the same as "Events" (II). Panel V is the actual "Political Behavior" and includes "Behavior" (4) and especially "Actions" (IV).[61] The question may be legitimately asked: since the two schemas are so similar, why do I not use the map? Hopefully I cannot be accused of trying to stake out a claim for mine just because it is mine; I believe I have valid reasons. First, the map appears in a short article and is not elaborated; one of its keenest admirers has commented upon it and has tried to improve it,[62] but his interests, much as I respect them, are different from mine. Second, throughout this book I have tried to show some of the relations among the variables in a theoretical sense. Third, I think the map does not clearly distinguish between the outside observer and the participant. Otherwise, in the usual academic tradition, I could quibble and say that there is no need to have two separate panels for I and II, an insufficient number of variables are included in panel III, etc. These points, however, are trivial and unimportant: Smith offers a provocative schema worthy of contemplation.

D. The Definition Jungle. There may be only one certain way to avoid squabbling over definitions and that is to abandon the concepts of power and authority completely. Two German writers have indeed tried to extricate themselves from the swamp by proposing that *Herrschaft* (domination) serve as a substitute for *Macht* (power);[63] but, if I may continue the metaphor, they have succeeded only in jumping out of that swamp into a bottomless pit. The squabbling in my view raises two questions: should "power" be limited to certain kinds of action and behavior, and what is the relation between "power" and "authority"?

Regarding the first question I would contend that distinctions are possible, but they are arbitrary and hence fail to include in a single frame of reference phenomena possessing common attributes and differing not qualitatively but quantitatively. A political scientist cites an illustration from one of his colleagues who suggests that the odds are much greater that an instructor is more likely to induce students to read a particular

C. The "Map" of M. Brewster Smith

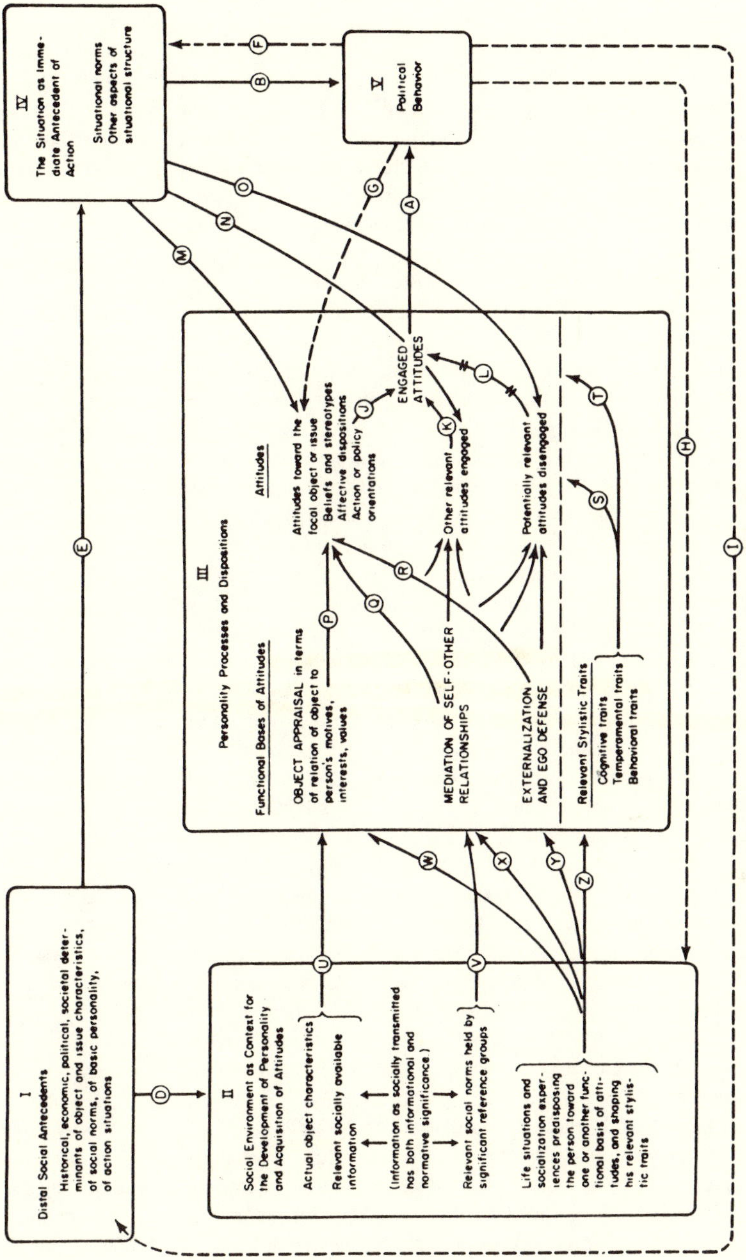

Source: M. Brewster Smith, A map for the analysis of personality and politics. *Journal of Social Issues*, 1968, 24, no. 3, 25. Reprinted by permission.

book by threatening to give them a failing grade in the course if they do not do so than by merely mentioning or recommending the book. The polite suggestion "constituted an attempt to 'influence' " the student, whereas the "explicit threat to invoke a sanction constituted . . . a power relation."[64] This distinction between influence (defined as "a communication intended to affect the action" of another person "in the absence of sanctions") and power (defined as "a certain relationship" in which one person "presents" another person "with an 'offer' to which is attached a contingency in the form" of a reward or promise or of a penalty or threat)[65] rests, respectively, on the presence or absence of explicit sanctions, viz., a direct threat concerning a grade vs. a suggestion concerning a possible sanction or a lower or higher grade by, respectively, not reading or reading the book. Similarly the same writer also claims that to "forewarn of a 'threatening situation' is not the same as to make a threat," so that he does not think "the weatherman" should be called a " 'powerful' person," although "the information he provides often has a considerable 'influence' on the plans of millions of people."[66] Whether one chooses to say that the weatherman as well as the terrorist with a gun have the power to influence people is a matter of taste, even while admitting that the resources of each and the changes each facilitates are quite different. As here defined, I agree by and large that the weatherman possesses the authority which the terrorist lacks and that the terrorist has the power which the weatherman lacks. This is true, however, for most but not all participants. You and I may choose to follow the implied advice of the weatherman who forecasts a severe storm, but on the basis of the same information the captain of a small fishing boat may conceive of no alternative other than to remain in port.

Power has been called "the ability to compel obedience, either through the use or the threat of force."[67] Certainly power frequently involves force, but other devices—bribes, compliments, even logic—may prove equally effective in the absence of force. I see no good reason to concentrate on one technique and to exclude others. Other phrasing has been employed to draw a distinction. Obedience and not compliance, for example, occurs in response to an authority;[68] hence a bandit evokes not obedience but compliance. Ah yes, but the bandit is nevertheless a principal who affects the behavior of his victim.

That bandit, however, lacks authority as here defined, and thus we are led gently to another squabble, the relation between power and authority.[69] Close colleagues engage in footnoted disputes concerning whether it is more useful to assert that power may be exercised by virtue of authority or for some other reason, rather than to consider authority a form of power.[70] Many writers make the same distinction here advocated in providing definitions: authority is considered to be "a form of institutionalized power"[71] or "legitimate power."[72] The consensus seems to be that two concepts are needed: "the regulation of behavior may or may not involve reference to authority."[73] That bandit again has power over his victim who does not, however, consider him part of a recognized hierarchy. It may be said that governments in general have authority among their citizens, but with varying degrees of power. During the energy crisis in the United States, for example, the federal government under President Nixon had the legal authority to decree a speed limit of 55 miles per hour for automobiles; but its agents, the local police, were unable completely to enforce the regulation. Any military clique can plan a coup without legal authority, although it may claim moral authority; but if it is successful and remains in control, it exercises power and acquires, or tries to acquire, legal or pseudolegal authority. In democratic countries the political party in control of the government has power (through patronage, the police, perhaps the courts, the mass media, etc.) and has authority until the next election; then, if it is voted out of office, it loses much of its power and authority.

E. The Selected Definitions of Power and Authority. There seems to be no simple, adequate word to refer to the person who possesses power and hence in the definition I resort to "power" all by itself. I have no enthusiasm for this decision since in some contexts the word sounds awkward; but it is sanctioned by a standard unabridged dictionary[74] and in American English "the power behind the throne" and "the powers that be" are idiomatic.

The word "conviction" is given such prominence in the definition of power in order to emphasize that the hierarchical position of an individual must be judged by someone, whether the judge is an observer or a participant; and the judgment may be true or false. The basis for the conviction is to be found in one or more of the objective and subjective variables displayed in the Guiding Figure. An observer, for example, may be convinced that an individual is a leader, as a result of what he himself has observed in the society or in the course of an event; or the observer may ascribe leadership to him after observing some of his actions. A leader may be convinced that he himself has the ability to affect his followers on the basis of his experience in the past, of what he perceives at a given moment, of a rational judgment concerning the alternatives facing him, etc.

The phrase in the same definition, "specified, significant actions," is deliberately vague in order to permit the observer and the participants to supply their own referents. Leaders in democratic states, for example, determine the taxes citizens must pay and the ways in which some industries are regulated, but they do not claim, or at least they do not directly claim to affect the kind of poetry poets write or the precise hour at which a family eats its evening meal. The word "significant" is included ostensibly to exclude trivial interactions between participants (yes, the person who never heeds the weatherman). The robber threatening a victim with a gun affects him significantly since presumably money, valuables, or a life is at stake. The driver of an oncoming car whose bright headlights cause pedestrians or other drivers to blink or flinch, although affecting them in that respect, is not thought to be exercising power; yet, if blinking or flinching for whatever reason is considered significant, then power would be ascribed to the inconsiderate driver.

Or should we shrewdly conclude that a customer "technically imposes his will upon the jeweler when he makes him surrender a diamond ring by paying for it"? We are warned not to confuse this situation "with that of the gangster who forces the jeweler to hand over the ring at the point of the gun."[75] Why not? The two situations are different of course, yet the same variables are involved: a resource in the form of money or a gun, an action that would not have occurred in the absence of the resource. The aim always is to discover basic similarities in situations that seem diverse and therefore the judgment concerning significance dare not be glibly passed. For similar reasons it seems desirable to reject or at least to challenge the proposal to "narrow" a conception of power by confining it to "relations in which severe deprivations are expected to follow the breach of a pattern of conduct":[76] severity is not easier to define than significance. Since forces have conviction only in an anthropomorphic sense, their role with respect to power must be referred to human beings: an observer or a participant is convinced that a force is controlling (an avalanche can crush a village) or is not controlled (a rider whips his horse).

The key to the definition of authority is the notion of consent: someone is convinced that affecting actions is legitimate, correct, or justified. If the individual is a principal or leader, he believes he has or should have the right—morally, legally, or what not—to exercise power. If he is a subordinate or follower, he believes another person has or should have that right, or he thinks that he himself has or should have it. An observer may have a similar conviction concerning any of the participants.

To be noted, too, is the word "repeated" in the definition of authority which implies not only the conviction or acceptance by one or more participants but also continuity. The reference to "hierarchical position" calls attention to the phenomenon that an authority is likely to exercise power and to induce obedience among followers in a hierarchy, no matter who happens to occupy the position.[77] From some moral standpoint, a principal with power but without authority does not have the right to exercise that power or command obedience, whereas a principal with authority believes he is "entitled" to have those lower in the hierarchy obey him whether or not they find his actions "acceptable or desirable."[78]

F. The Guiding Figure. Petty and semiprofound illustrations are offered in a partial defense of the Guiding Figure. Should a housewife boil or bake potatoes for the evening meal, should a leader institute a boycott so that the leaders of another country will introduce domestic reforms? Whether it be a housewife or a cabinet official, a decision is made that expresses a power relation and that may involve authority. If we examine the potatoes rather than the boycott and assume that the woman selects boiling, a host of nonfascinating questions can be raised. Why did she make the decision? Does she herself prefer boiled potatoes, does she think that boiled potatoes are preferred by one of her children whom she favors or her husband rather than another member of her family; is she expressing her housewifely power because she knows her family must eat what they are served; is she trying to demonstrate her power for any number of trite reasons that can be discovered, for all we know, only by analyzing her, including her childhood experience with potatoes? How will her family react to the decision since they are subordinates and not the principals in the decision? This cosmic illustration has convincingly demonstrated that a psychological analysis of a mundane decision involving power and authority requires a complicated set of concepts (1–5).

Potential rather than actual power resides in the participants' predispositions (1), perhaps awaiting events (II) to be activated. Actuarial reasoning is embodied in the past experience of a scholar or politician (I). When it was once demonstrated, for example, that the composition of local school boards in the United States affected the power they exerted in their local communities,[79] an observer might legitimately if tentatively conclude that future decisions would be similarly affected (V). The activities of a complicated organization such as NATO involve the decisions of leaders who interact with one another. Their action has been and is being affected by decisions within their own governments. Those decisions in turn also are variously influenced to some extent by the decisions of individual citizens (2 and II). I emphasize again that the Guiding Figure may be entered at any point in order to study a segment of the problem of power or authority, but it serves the function of reminding the observer, the participant, or the reader that only a segment has been or is being examined. A decision of NATO can be analyzed in its own right, without making a psychological study of all the representatives, however relevant the additional data would or might be.

Why such an elaborate figure? For three reasons. First, power and authority have been explored by so many different investigators and they are of interest to human beings in such varied ways that it is necessary to consider a large number of factors if all their investigations and interests are to be included in the present analysis. Second, as already indicated, both the individual participant and the observer are taken into account; hence the need to have, respectively, the inner and outer circles. Then, third, the participant is treated not only behavioristically (i.e., in terms of observable behavior) but also subjectively (i.e., in terms of his conscious and unconscious tendencies). There is nothing especially original or startling in this latter approach which is now current in social psychology. The assumptions behind a very excellent book which summarizes theories and research in what is called cognitive social psychology are said by the author, in his own words, to be the following:

1. The individual is an active processor of information.
2. The interpretation of a stimulus depends both on attributes of the stimulus and on the perceiver's prior expectations and standards of comparison.
3. The individual tries to organize his experience: such organization typically involves selection and simplification.
4. The function of such an organization is to provide a guide for action and a basis for prediction.[80]

On the figure the first assumption above refers to the participant's judgment (3), the second is designated as perception (2) and refers to the combination of events (II) and the predispositions (1), the third again involves judgment (3), and the fourth is the reaction (4) and the actions (IV) which become part of the background in the future (V).

1. Kenneth B. Clark, *Pathos of Power*. New York: Harper & Row, 1974. P. 75.
2. Harold D. Lasswell and Abraham Kaplan, *Power and Society*. New Haven: Yale University Press, 1950. P. xiv.
3. Robert A. Dahl, The concept of power. *Behavioral Science*, 1957, 2, 201–18.
4. Kenneth B. Clark, Problems of power and social change. *Journal of Social Issues*, 1965, 21, no. 3, 4–20.
5. Thomas Hobbes, *Leviathan* (1651). New York: Dutton, 1950 edition.
6. Harry Eckstein and Ted Robert Gurr, *Patterns of Authority*. New York: Wiley, 1975. Pp. 9–10. Also Sanford M. Dornbusch and W. Richard Scott, *Evaluation and the Exercise of Authority*. San Francisco: Josey-Bass, 1975. P. 32.
7. David V. J. Bell, *Power, Influence, and Authority*. New York: Oxford University Press, 1975, P. 7.
8. Robert L. Peabody, Authority. *International Encyclopedia of the Social Sciences*, 1968, 1, 473–77.
9. E.g., Seymour Martin Lipset, *Political Man*. Garden City: Doubleday, 1959. P. 81.
10. Guy E. Swanson, *The Birth of the Gods*. Ann Arbor: University of Michigan Press, 1960. P. 20.
11. Hobbes, op. cit., p. 306.
12. James S. Coleman, *The Asymmetric Society*. Syracuse: Syracuse University Press, 1982. P. 50.
13. Jonathan Schell, *The Fate of the Earth*. New York: Knopf, 1982. Pp. 186–88.
14. Dorwin Cartwright, A field theoretical conception of power. In Dorwin Cartwright (ed.), *Studies in Social Power*. Ann Arbor: Research Center for Group Dynamics, 1959. Pp. 183–220.
15. John Schopler, Social power. In Leonard Berkowitz (ed.), *Advances in Experimental Social Psychology*. New York: Academic Press, 1965. Vol. 2, pp. 177–218.

16. Cartwright, op. cit.

17. Jack H. Nagel, *The Descriptive Analysis of Power.* New Haven: Yale University Press, 1975. Pp. 157–58, italics his.

18. Henry L. Minton, Power as a personality construct. In Brendan A. Maher (ed.), *Progress in Experimental Personality Research.* New York: Academic Press, 1967. Vol. 4, pp. 229–69.

19. Leonard W. Doob, *Patterning of Time.* New Haven: Yale University Press, 1971. Pp. 66–68.

20. Bell, op. cit., p. 70.

21. Doob, op. cit., p. 10.

22. Leonard W. Doob, *Patriotism and Nationalism.* Westport: Greenwood, 1976. P. 17.

23. Robert E. Agger, Daniel Goldrich, and Bert E. Swanson, *The Rulers and the Ruled.* New York: Wiley, 1964. P. 687.

24. C. Wright Mills, *The Power Elite.* New York: Oxford University Press, 1956. Pp. 24–25.

25. Kenneth J. Gergen, Social psychology as history. *Journal of Personality and Social Psychology,* 1973, 26, 309–20.

26. Karl Marx, The eighteenth brumaire of Louis Bonaparte. In Emile Burns (ed.), *Handbook of Marxism.* New York: International Publishers, 1953. Pp. 116–31.

27. Sheldon S. Wolin, *Politics and Vision.* Boston: Little, Brown, 1960. P. 25.

28. Agger, Goodrich, and Swanson, op. cit., p. 62.

29. Nelson W. Polsby, *Community Power and Political Theory.* New Haven: Yale University Press, 1963. P. 112.

30. Stuart Schmidt and Thomas A. Kochan, Interorganizational relationships. *Administrative Science Quarterly,* 1977, 22, 220–34.

31. Robert A. Dahl, *Who Governs?* New Haven: Yale University Press, 1961. Polsby, op. cit.

32. Frank M. Andrews et al., *A Guide for Selecting Statistical Techniques for Analyzing Social Science Data.* Ann Arbor: Survey Research Center, 1981.

33. Duane Robinson and Sylvia Rohde, Two experiments with an anti-Semitism poll. *Journal of Abnormal and Social Psychology,* 1946, 41, 136–44.

34. Hadley Cantril, *Gauging Public Opinion.* Princeton: Princeton University Press, 1944. Pp. 115–16.

35. Howard Schuman and Shirley Hotchett, *Black Racial Attitudes.* Ann Arbor: Survey Research Center, 1974. Pp. 39–52.

36. Rebecca West, *The Birds Fall Down.* New York: Popular Library, 1966. P. 162.

37. Sheldon Ungar, The effects of others' expectancies on the fabrication of opinions. *Journal of Social Psychology,* 1981, 114, 173–85.

38. Cf. Trevor R. Hadley and Theodore Jacob, The measurement of family power. *Sociometry,* 1976, 39, 384–95.

39. Robert E. Pitts, Value-group analysis of cultural values in heterogeneous populations. *Journal of Social Psychology,* 1981, 115, 109–24.

40. Andrew S. McFarland, *Power Leadership in Pluralist Systems.* Stanford: Stanford University Press, 1969. Pp. 66–67.

41. Alvin Zander, Arthur R. Cohen, and Ezra Stotland, Power and the relations among the professions. In Cartwright (ed.), op. cit., pp. 15–34.

42. G. William Domhoff, *The Powers That Be*. New York: Random House, 1978. P. 12.

43. Eugene Webb et al., *Unobtrusive Measures*. Chicago: Rand McNally, 1966.

44. William A. Gamson, Power and probability. In James T. Tedeschi (ed.), *Perspectives on Social Power*. Chicago: Aldine, 1974. Pp. 34–60.

45. Cf. Jack H. Nagel, *The Descriptive Analysis of Power*. New Haven: Yale University Press, 1975. P. 48.

46. Michael Korda, *Power!* New York: Random House, 1975. P. 90.

47. Cf. Webb et al., op. cit., pp. 182–83.

48. David C. McClelland, *Power: The Inner Experience*. New York: Irvington, 1975. P. 125.

49. Cf. David G. Winter, *The Power Motive*. New York: Free Press, 1973. E.g., p. 141.

50. Cf. Abigail Stewart and Zick Rubin, The power motive of the dating couple. *Journal of Personality and Social Psychology*, 1976, 34, 305–9.

51. Robert Presthus, *Men at the Top*. New York: Oxford University Press, 1964. P. 57.

52. Kenneth Evan Sharpe, *Peasant Politics*. Baltimore: Johns Hopkins University Press, 1977. P. 221.

53. Jacques Maquet, *Power and Society in Africa*. New York: McGraw-Hill, 1971. P. 27.

54. Robert A. Dahl, Power. *International Encyclopedia of the Social Sciences*, 1968, 12, 405–15.

55. Cf. Marc Augé, *Pouvoirs de Vie, Pouvoirs de Mort*. Paris: Flammarion, 1977. Arnold Bergstraesser, *Die Macht als Mythos und als Wirklichkeit*. Freiburg: Romach, 1965. Elias Canetti, *Crowds and Power*. New York: Viking, 1962.

56. Lewis Thomas, *The Lives of a Cell*. New York: Bantam Books, 1974. P. 9.

57. Thomas Lemaitre, *L'Art de Commander et L'Art d'Obéir*. Avignon: Editions Aubaniel, 1969. Pp. 15–24.

58. Gen. 8:1; Rev. 7:1.

59. Encyclopedia Britannica, *Power*. Chicago: William Benton, 1962. P. 390.

60. Kai T. Erikson, *Everything in Its Path*. New York: Simon & Schuster, 1976.

61. M. Brewster Smith, A map for the analysis of personality and politics. *Journal of Social Issues*, 1968, 24, no. 3, 15–28.

62. Fred I. Greenstein, *Personality and Politics*. New York: Norton, 1975. Pp. 25–32.

63. Manfred Hennen and Wolfgang-Ulrich Prigge, *Autorität und Herrschaft*. Darmstadt: Wissenschaftliche Buchgesellschaft, 1977.

64. David V. J. Bell, op. cit., p. 114.

65. Ibid., pp. 21, 24.

66. Ibid., p. 25.

67. Robert Paul Wolff, *In Defense of Anarchism*. New York: Harper & Row, 1970. P. 4.

68. Thomas McPherson, *Political Obligation*. London: Routledge & Kegan Paul, 1967. Pp. 13–16, 31–33.

69. Carl J. Friedrich, *Tradition and Authority*. New York: Praeger, 1972. P. 49.

70. Gene W. Dalton, Louis B. Barnes, and Abraham Zaleznik, *The Distribution of*

Authority in Formal Organizations. Cambridge: Harvard University Division of Research, 1968.

71. William W. Meissner, *The Assault on Authority*. Maryknoll: Orbis Books, 1971.

72. Sanford M. Dornbusch and W. Richard Scott, *Evaluation and the Exercise of Authority*. San Francisco: Josey-Bass, 1975. P. 37. Hans Gerth and C. Wright Mills, *Character and Social Structure*. New York: Harcourt, Brace, 1953. P. 195.

73. Glenn Negley, *Political Authority and Moral Judgment*. Durham: Duke University Press. P. 7.

74. *Webster's Third New International Dictionary,* 1963. P. 1779, definition 4.

75. Peter M. Blau, *Exchange and Power in Social Life*. New York: Wiley, 1964. Pp. 115–16.

76. Harold D. Lasswell, *Power and Personality*. New York: Viking, 1962. P. 12.

77. Bertrand de Jouvenel, *The Pure Theory of Politics*. New Haven: Yale University Press, 1963. Pp. 100, 104.

78. Fred J. Abbate, *A Preface to the Philosophy of State*. Belmont: Wadsworth, 1977. Pp. 23, 31.

79. Ralph B. Kimbrough, *Political Power and Educational Decision-Making*. Chicago: Rand McNally, 1964.

80. J. Richard Eiser, *Cognitive Social Psychology*. London: McGraw-Hill, 1980. P. 8.

2

Background

Both the observer and the participants possess what they consider to be knowledge and theories concerning the setting in which power and authority are, respectively, observed and experienced. Who has political power in a particular society? The observer may point to a particular group: his pointing constitutes his knowledge, whether true or false. In addition, he may also seek to explain why and how they have such power: the explanation constitutes his theory, again whether true or false. Participants within the same society may also believe they know which clique has power and they may likewise subscribe to some kind of explanation to account for that clique's status; the information similarly may be true or false. The terms "true or false" have been deliberately stated quite glibly although establishing the truth or falsity of knowledge and theory is usually a laborious process. The observer's knowledge or theory may be considered true or false by another observer, whether a contemporary or the member of another generation, or by the participants who in turn may draw their conclusions concerning the observer's generalizations or explanations.

More often than not the distinction between knowledge and theory becomes fuzzy. For the language in which knowledge is formulated may have implicit theoretical implications. When it is known, for example, that a particular person is a Zulu or an American, a fact is thus stated, but that fact immediately suggests other alleged facts, actually so many that whoever possesses the knowledge may believe that merely on the basis of nationality he has insight into the person's values and behavior.

The background or setting of power and authority is of interest to observers and participants. To "explain" these phenomena the social scientist and the laymen must assume that events do not spring from Jove's whims but arise as a result of circumstances in the milieu. Each participant makes a similar assumption when he seeks to comprehend other participants. Those participants have a private, subjective background of their own to be considered in the next chapter: the observer seeks to understand their predispositions, and again the participant usually shows some concern for the predispositions of other participants. But first the general background.

I.A *The Past.* The competent observer knows that nothing ever happens completely de novo. Even the most brilliant discovery, composition, or painting contains elements from the past of both the society and the creator. Ordinarily, therefore, the observer and the participant functioning as an observer of other participants resemble historians who try to account for what has transpired in the more immediate past that has impact upon the present or future. Deep delving, however, as suggested previously, is usually impossible or impractical: an Arbitrary Limitation looms. If either observer or participant is a Marxian and has found Marxist theories adequate to explain power-related events in the past, he will surely invoke those theories again; but he and we in turn need not account for Marx's insights. Or if a leader has exercised his authority successfully in various situations in the past, it may be assumed that, unless there is some vast change in his milieu or in him, he will probably follow similar procedures in the future. Possibly the immediate experience of participants suffices to predict their behavior or their relation with others.[1] The reputation of a person by definition stems from his past behavior as perceived by others, so that professionals with high prestige are likely to be heeded by participants when functioning in their normal professional roles[2]—and often their opinions on nonprofessional topics receive similar respect. As a form of self-fulfilling prophecy, the reputation for power may be "one source of power, just as the reputation for wealth may be a help in obtaining a favorable credit rating—if only in default of more precise information."[3]

I.A.1 It is extremely useful, if banal, ever to be reminded that any aspect of human relations can be affected by past *experience.* Previously successful modes of resolving conflict, whether between individuals or nations, may continue to be employed, especially when reinforced by cultural norms. Among the Burmese the possession of power is reported to be one of their highest values which even has a "physical dimension." Leaders must demonstrate "with every move that they can handle authority with skill and a light touch." At the same time, however, they also emphasize another value which inhibits this power motive and makes them sensitive to the needs of others.[4] Experience that is transmitted from generation to generation is usually referred to as tradition, because those individuals who have had the experience cannot be completely identified, nor can the reasons for their influence be fully explained.

In a crude sense the power of forces is known from their effects in the past. The atomic weight of elements has been empirically ascertained; other specimens, it can be assumed, must have identical weights. The owner of a dog knows whether the animal has been vicious or gentle and hence treats him accordingly.

I.A.2 As an unavoidable precaution it is also necessary to emphasize that *present or future* situations differ from those in the past from which experience has been gained. The child who has used ingratiation to exercise power over adults may discover as an adult that this tactic no longer is rewarding or that it must be drastically modified. It comes as no surprise to learn from a quantitative study of eighteen nations in North America and Europe and an equal number in Latin America that between 1816 and 1966 there was a decrease in the number of monarchs functioning as heads of state or as effective executives and an increase in the number of presidents and the size of cabinets.[5] The authorities and the powers to whom ordinary citizens reacted and the number of available high political positions toward the upper end of the hierarchy thus fluctuated with the changing political structure prevailing at the year of their birth. Or it might have been argued on the basis only of past experience and their philosophy that all Israeli families in a kibbutz would continue to follow the rule of having their own infants and very young children sleep at night not in their parents' home but in age-graded houses, inasmuch as all families save one had followed that tradition. In 1973, however, returning war veterans did not approve of the practice, especially because they feared the childrens' houses were inadequately protected; since they had gained prestige as a result of their accomplishments in battle, within a year they were able to break the tradition and bed all children in their own homes.[6] Again pressure in the present altered past practices.

Guide: The past, however defined, has some but a varying effect on the present.

I.B. *Culture and Society*. At the very least every observer and participant knows something about the culture and society in which power and authority are exercised, and he also has a theory concerning their importance. If correct, such knowledge is valuable: experience occurs within a social context which affects the hierarchical status as well as the attitudes and beliefs of each participant. Of relevant significance here is the sociopolitical structure. Each person is enmeshed in a culture (the traditional ways of thinking, evaluating, and behaving transmitted from generation to generation) and a society (the rules and customs governing human relations in a specific area). The society's structure reflects the culture and determines the distribution of power and authority. In traditional societies it is usually difficult to distinguish between the social and political structure since the two are so intertwined: principals with high status are powerful in both spheres. In modern societies, on the other hand, power may not be so concentrated; as a result, political leaders emerge from groups or classes possessing varying degrees of authority. Attached to the political, economic, and social institutions are traditional ways of thinking and acting.

I.B.1 Just as they are ever present among the higher and some of the lower animals, hierarchies are *ubiquitous* in every human society or group and therefore reflect and produce differences in power and authority. Men are "rule-following animals," it has been said.[7] There are differences between those who give and those who receive orders. The ubiquity is simple to illustrate by recalling only a few of the bipolar terms that frequently appear in English:

power: strong vs. weak
authority: commanding vs. obedient
legitimacy: recognized vs. ignored
sovereignty: respected vs. violated
family: parents vs. children
government: statesmen vs. citizens
occupation: employer vs. employee
industry: foremen vs. workers
Marxism: capitalists vs. proletariat
social class: upper vs. middle vs. lower
planes: pilot vs. passengers
domestic service: master vs. servant, slave
religion: clergy vs. congregation
restaurant: head waiter vs. waiter vs. bus boy
military: officers vs. enlisted men
sex: males vs. females

The list is not only incomplete but also somewhat misleading. Few modern women would agree that males are dominant, or at least that they should be. Then more than a dichotomy separates the high and the low in many instances. The Pope of the Catholic Church is at the top of a hierarchy, but there are gradations below him—cardinals, archbishops, bishops, and priests—before the laity is reached, and they, almost from the inception of the Church, have had their organizations that have raised profound challenges to the dicta of the Vatican.[8] Many hierarchial relationships shift from situation to situation. The pilot of a plane has the authority to order passengers to fasten their seat belts, an edict he also has the power to enforce through flight attendants; but on the ground his political opinions on subjects unrelated to aviation may be impolitely ignored or rejected.

I.B.2 Why, then, are hierarchical arrangements *inevitable?* Ultimately or originally—the adverbs scarcely differ—the reason can be traced to the fact that men are not born genetically equal and they are not raised equally. They live under conditions of inequality; they follow differing models of authority. In short, their destiny is a function of both biological and social factors. At the outset the child is less powerful than his parents: he cannot fend for himself, he requires them as the potent authorities from whom he gradually—hopefully—frees himself, for better or worse, as he matures and as circumstances in his environment permit. Some persons are taller than others as a result of their inheritances: they themselves and the milieu in which they have lived undoubtedly have had little influence upon their heights; and height may facilitate the power that tall men and sometimes tall women acquire or expect. So-called higher powers appear necessary in any society to explain man's existence; and to these gods are "attributed both omnipotence and permanence."[9] The very concept of "horsepower" suggests the differences among forces that affect people whose own strength, knowledge, or skill enable or do not enable them to cope with those forces. Similarly human beings can or cannot control some or all of the actions of animals which, among themselves, have their own hierarchies traceable to genes or, less often, experience.

If human beings are to function effectively as they live and work together, they must belong to a society with attending rules. An organization, whether temporary like an ad hoc committee or a more or less lasting one like a government, in turn requires that a select few or even a single individual has the authority and power to lead, to enforce the rules enabling it to function as it would and must, and perhaps to punish the disobedient.[10] In ethnocentric terms, but in principle applicable everywhere, the justification for such universality rests on an appeal to common sense: "What an utter chaos human life would be—it could not long endure—if every day we had to settle by family debate or authoritarian decision how many meals we would eat *this* day, at what hour of the day or night."[11] Unless the powers possess some authority in the opinion of the subordinates, as Gandhi suggested, they may be disobeyed and eventually overthrown.[12] The legitimacy accorded those with power or authority, as will be emphasized subsequently, depends upon the ensuing benefits and deprivations,[13] and hence is related to the goal being sought by the subordinate who passes judgment.[14]

Whether a society has a common culture or, in pluralistic societies, several cultures, whether the society is nomadic or complex,[15] organizations help participants to resolve the problems of power and authority arising in connection with morality, communication, decision-making, and leadership. As a result some form of inequality is both necessary and desirable, even when participants within the system do not explicitly recognize the need for the stratification or comprehend in detail the way it functions.[16] "Desirable"? The observation is not meant as a hymn of praise to power as such or in any philosophical sense: the degree and distribution of power in a society is another problem which must be avoided until the very end of this book. I continue: elite principals and leaders always emerge, whether their hierarchial status is confined to particular situations or embraces the most significant activities of the society and whether or not that status has been inherited or acquired. Passing reference must be made to the relation between the two sexes because almost everywhere men have tended to be more powerful than women in some respects;[17] some of the differences stem from physical strength and others from culturally determined discriminations which are now being acknowledged, evaluated, and slowly changed—even in traditional societies.[18]

Guide: Hierarchical differences in virtually every situation are inevitable and always serve a relevant function.

I.B.3 Like any other aspect of cultures and societies, hierarchies exhibit extreme *variability*. Ascending the throne as king in some traditional African societies has been restricted to persons belonging to specified "closed" social groups, whereas in others the privilege has been "open to almost all members of the society."[19] From one standpoint, governments function between two extremes, one form tends to preserve the status quo so that citizens must cooperate with one another to achieve or maintain the values they treasure, the other tends to change the structure in behalf of new values.[20] Either tendency implies an assignment of authority and power which, every school boy and girl must learn,[21] means the extent to which the high-status authorities and powers, the minority in the society, are influenced by the less authoritative and less powerful majority. The authority evoked by institutions—or, more accurately expressed, the authority exercised by leaders and by symbols attached to institutions—changes over generations, the precise reasons for which are seldom easy to locate. If it be true that in the West there is now "a reaction against conventional religion" and that "irreligion has become democratised and is being incorporated into the cultural and social establishment of many Western societies,"[22] the shift has not occurred overnight, but has gradually emerged as a result of multidimensional factors including the policies and actions of churches, the development of science, the diffusion of education, the increased participation of individuals in their own affairs, and the contrary philosophies embodied in fascism and communism.

I.B.3.a The emergence of various forms of power and authority cannot be traced to a single explanation or theory, however alluring or elegant *monism* appears to be. Contrary to Marx's own prediction—and he is so important that reference to him must always be made in any serious dissection—modern communism did not first arise in a highly industrialized society. A full reply to almost any historical question requires the inclusion of a host of factors beginning with the land's topography and natural resources and ending with the personalities of particular leaders, including all interacting factors so complex that they must be subsumed under the almost meaningless category of "chance." Other theories also abound. Perhaps, for example, political centralization occurs when governments undertake new activities requiring central coordination, when a threat exists from the outside such as war, when the old forms no longer seem adequate, and when an absolute monarch or his equivalent seeks additional control within the society.[23] According to a sophisticated political philosopher, the role of authority "must inevitably increase as the body politic grows in size, complexity, and heterogeneity."[24] Such factors cannot be squeezed into a monistic jacket.

I.B.3.b The broadest perspective, as usual, is supplied by *anthropology* which sometimes seeks to classify societies with respect to power or authority patterns and then to search for correlates with the typology. Various typologies have been devised and various relations have emerged from their studies, but no sweeping, all-embracing principles are apparent. For example, among thirty-nine traditional societies (including, however, ancient Egypt), a strong but imperfect association between the types of sovereign groups and a high god has been noted: the greater the number of types, the greater the probability that a high god is recognized.[25] Only on the basis of utter speculation might it be guessed that an all-powerful god has been needed to produce harmony among the groups. Additional studies are reported at the end of this chapter in note A, entitled "Anthropological Classifications." Out of the sweeping, anthropological research, perhaps only one unastonishing proposition is salvageable: although people resemble social insects to a greater extent than they do the higher mammals with respect to "complex social coordination, division of labor, and self-sacrificial altruism" and their behavior in these respects must have some genetic components, such behavior is not programmed genetically; perhaps it depends upon "culturally evoked indoctrination which has had to counter self-serving genetic tendencies."[26] During socialization, therefore, selfish, power-seeking impulses are curbed; the innate capability for acquiring altruistic ones may be realized.

> *Guide:* The origins and developments of hierarchies are as varied and diverse as their scope and content.

I.B.3.c *Groupings* also vary, but everywhere, it seems, individuals perforce are members of and participate in more than one group. The hunting-and-gathering !Kung (Bushmen) in the Kalahari desert traditionally live in small bands varying in size from fifteen to sixty-five persons; membership therein depends in part upon the family or kin group to which they also belong.[27] The Baganda in Uganda have had a complicated structure, at the top of which there was once a king whose power and authority were clearly acknowledged over the individual clans and subclans as well as over administrative-political groupings (corresponding, in a British translation, roughly to counties, subcounties, and parishes). He could delegate the power to members of his court and to chiefs, but ultimately it came from him and from him alone. For clans such delegated power concerned religion, for the other groupings it pertained to immediate activities prescribing the possession and cultivation of land in a patron-client relation.[28]

Modern governments structure authority in one of three ways. Authority may be separated as in the American system of checks and balances. It may be apportioned to different groups as in the federal system of Switzerland. Or it may be delegated when a leader strips off one of his prerogatives and assigns it to a committee which becomes responsible to him but which operates more or less independently of him unless a crisis arises.[29]

In Western society reference groups are numerous, as a cursory allusion to family, church, government, schools, political parties, clubs, and associations is sufficient to suggest. The existence of many different groups is likely to raise the problem of legitimacy. Who, for example, is the authority concerning a woman's right to have an abortion and under what conditions? In recent times judgments about abortion have been passed by the Pope, other religious leaders, governments, pressure groups, physicians, families, and the women themselves. What must be emphasized here is, first, that participants who accept or reject the communicated recommendations have acquired knowledge of and attitudes toward these groups as they are socialized, so that as adults they do or do not recognize their legitimacy. Then powers change; for example, in the United States both the federal government and the individual states have altered their regulations concerning abortion. Finally, new groups continually arise, especially those of an informal sort, either because an organization is required to take care of needs not previously experienced or because participants change in some respect by moving to another area or neighborhood or as a result of being socially mobile. Many of these groups are informal cliques whose demands upon individuals may be almost as pressing and perhaps more salient than those of the formal institutions within the society.

> *Guide:* Power and authority are embodied in and expressed through the groupings within a society.

I.C *Socialization*. The concept of human socialization is being employed here not to refer to the common attributes of mankind, which are genetically programmed and which develop as the organism matures, such as motor skills, language, dramatic changes in morphology and in basic and other drives during adolescence. Attention instead is paid exclusively to the distinctive variations of such attributes and the distinctive traits developed or facilitated in each society and in the strata therein. The fact that this aspect of socialization transmitted through relevant child-rearing practices affects later predispositions and behavior is indisputable, but the precise relation between those practices and what happens later cannot be clearly delineated. Observers seeking to comprehend the background of participants, and participants seeking to comprehend other participants or themselves have their own theories concerning the importance of infancy and early childhood. Let me immediately smuggle in the thought that those theories of theirs and indeed their approach to power and authority in turn have been determined in whole or in part by the ways in which they themselves have been socialized. This thought is essential to mention in order to pay homage to the sociology of knowledge which maintains that the theories and beliefs of an age can be traced primarily to the social and economic positions of the individuals within the society and only secondarily to their experiences as children.[30]

Socialization, consequently, is not the magic key that unlocks the mysteries of adult personality; child-rearing practices do not produce mirror images of the socializers. As the individual matures, he retains his mother tongue, but his pronunciation may differ somewhat from that of his parents as a result of later associations. For example, at home he may learn a dialect which he will never forget but which he will not employ in situations requiring the "proper" pronunciation of the language. Character traits and other aspects of his personality similarly are likely to deviate from those of his parents, likewise because of influential outside forces. Even Freud never traced all adult tendencies back to childhood in an unequivocal straight line: each of his patient's experiences while being socialized he appraised with respect to their unique attributes and aftereffects.

The reasonable assumption would seem to be, therefore, that of a Spiral Relation between changes in socialization practices and changes within the society. In stable societies, if there be such, parents rear their children more or less as they themselves have been reared; to a varying degree this way of all flesh continues even during periods of rapid change. But parents as powers and authorities do not or cannot only reproduce their kind: their experiences give them an outlook different from their own parents', some of which spills over into the techniques they employ in their homes. A prominent, competent pediatrician like Dr. Spock has reflected and then tremendously affected many persons in their parental roles throughout the Western world. In the United States a strong relation between the authoritarianism of parents and their children appeared in studies conducted between 1963 and 1975; then in the early 1980s one investigation revealed no relation whatsoever, perhaps because attitudes toward authority and accompanying beliefs tended to be influenced by persons outside the family.[31]

Undeniably children learn the *language* of their parents and, even
I.C.1 though nuances of differences may appear between generations,
they thereby acquire fairly distinctive forms associated with aspects of the power and authority favored by the society. Ordinarily the speakers of a language are not aware of its tendencies in these respects because from their standpoint it is perfectly "natural" to use their mother tongue to express themselves in any way they wish. The significance of language is more likely to become evident to them and to us only when an utterly different society is experienced. A political scientist who has done field work among the Somalis believes that, although these people have great pride in themselves and their culture, they are basically egalitarian in outlook. He reports, for example, that in the school in which he taught no one thought it strange for the school's bus driver and cook to participate in meetings concerning the curriculum and other problems associated with the school. The Somali language reflects this cultural tendency. It has "few honorific titles and no words for 'Mr.,' 'Mrs.,' or 'Sir.' Everyone from the nomadic child to the President of the Republic is called by his first name, often by a childhood nickname, and a person's name is almost never preceded by a title." When the author induced students in his school to role-play a conflict between a teacher and a headmaster, references to authority

and to the power of authorities appeared significantly more frequently when the players performed in English than in Somali. Speaking English rather than Somali, he concludes, "makes authority considerations more relevant."[32] The language may have grown out of the culture but, when established, it presumably affects a speaker's attitudes toward authority and power.

Within recent years those struggling for women's rights have caused most of us to be aware of the use of the masculine pronoun in English when the reference is to both sexes ("Everyone should brush his teeth twice a day"). The power men have or have had over women, however, still pervades the language in subtler ways and on an unconscious level. A sociolinguist, for example, points out that the sentence, "Mary is John's widow," is correct and idiomatic, but that the reverse, "John is Mary's widower," may be correct but is not idiomatic. John dominates Mary after his death, a condition not attributed to a deceased Mary.[33] Also embedded in the language, as Hobbes wrote, are the "Titles of *Honour,* such as Duke, Count, Marquis, and Baron"; they are "honourable," for they signify "the value set upon them by the Soveraigne Power of the Commonwealth."[34] Authorities have streets and towns named after them or they acquire nicknames (Ivan the Terrible, Catherine the Great).[35]

I.C.2 The *repercussions* of socialization practices have been stressed, perhaps overstressed by one psychoanalyst, Alfred Adler, whose system of analysis almost always returned to the individual's motive to be more rather than less powerful. Every very young child, he indicated, must perforce observe that he is subordinate to adults since it is clear to him that he is "weak and small, incapable of living alone; he does not trust himself to do those simple tasks that one thinks him capable of doing, without mistakes, or errors, or clumsiness." The compensatory drive to become superior, that is, to be "greater, and better, and more glorious, than all others in his environment" lingers on, sometimes in a normal and acceptable form, sometimes in a manner that must be considered pathological.[36] This broad outline of the development of power has been modified and improved by some writers,[37] and popularized virtually beyond recognition by others.[38] A serious study can be cited to suggest the kind of difficulty that arises when a simplistic explanation in terms of a power motive is invoked in parallel with socialization. The delinquency rate (as measured by vandalism, truancy, stealing and shoplifting, smoking narcotics, and lying) is reported to be higher among Hausa boys in Nigeria coming from polygynous than from monogamous families.[39] It seems unlikely that the difference can be attributed to a power motive. Perhaps the father in a polygynous family is less of an authority since he rotates the time he spends with his cowives and hence provides less paternal supervision; perhaps material comforts are fewer in larger families. Additional research, as outlined at the end of this chapter in note B, "Socialization of Power Strivings," supports the view that socialization plays an important but not an invariable role in relation to power and authority.

Modal socialization practices may have repercussions upon the political system of a society[40]—or vice versa. The assumption here is that the adult feels more comfortable and is more satisfied when his role as an adult in a group resembles the one he was forced to perform as a child. But then again the training adults receive as members of groups may affect the ways in which they socialize their children. In any case, the participants themselves are not always constantly aware of all the background events that have led them to adopt some of their practices regarding authorities. One morning in the South Tyrol, for example, I listened at breakfast to a group of adults addressing one another in a mixture of German and Italian. They were being friendly and polite; those with German as their mother tongue were undoubtedly not recalling at the time the fact that they knew Italian because more than sixty years ago England and France had offered Italy this section of what was then Austria as a bribe to induce Italian leaders to enter World War I on the side of the Allies rather than that of Germany and Austria-Hungary. During their childhood they had no choice but to learn some Italian since their land was still part of Italy; and as adults they had no objection to using this second language as this early-morning occasion demanded.

Children everywhere are provided with reasons for the existence of authorities, a topic to be considered as beliefs are discussed in the next chapter. The source of an authority must be appreciated if that authority is to be considered legitimate. Parents have authority, the very young child must intuit, because they provide the means of satisfying basic needs such as food, comfort, and affection. For adults gigantic superstructures evolve through the ages. According to one Muslim scholar, for example, Islam's "code of Divine guidance in all spheres of human activity" (*Din*) is "from its very nature . . . the source of political authority" since its principles are based on "Divine Revelation"; that authority, therefore, is "delegated and exercised under its prescribed limits, developed for the unity of mankind and realized for the spiritual end of human society."[41] When the legitimacy of authority is challenged anywhere, social change is likely: children mature and disobey their parents, radicals or rebels try to overcome a regime peacefully or violently.

Weaning at some point from parents, literally and figuratively, is
I.C.3 virtually inevitable for most human beings. A degree of independence from the original authorities and a release from this power is attained. Even when weaning is unwelcome, it occurs eventually when parents die; and either then or when detachment from parents is achieved, substitute parents may be found. The modal tendency, however, remains: freedom is sought and realized. In the past there may have been a wisp of similarity between the desire of the leaders of colonial peoples and that of their followers to rebel against their European masters, and thus to achieve the power and authority accompanying adult, independent statehood. They were motivated, however, by more than a rejection of paternal rule in this psychological sense: they sought to avoid the humiliation and exploitation resulting from their less powerful positions.

I.C.4 Mankind has faced a specialized, challenging problem before and since Plato's time, the *rearing of powers and authorities* sufficiently capable to perform their duties more or less effortlessly and justly.[42] Among animals, such as chickens and monkeys, a pecking order emerges on the basis of an attribute such as strength or sexual prowess. The relationship is likely to be linear: in a group of animals, one of them dominates all the rest, the second in line dominates the others, the third the remainder, etc. A somewhat similar relation may exist among very young children who play together. Soon different children become leaders in other situations, yet perhaps they emerge "consistently" from one subgroup. Later on, moreover, they must adapt their techniques somewhat to the demands of their followers.[43]

Leaders whose status is ascribed by reason of their birth or social class, rather than achieved as a result of their own efforts, are destined to assume positions of power and authority within the society almost regardless of how they have been socialized, although the competence they display may well be affected by their experiences as children. For achieved status we must rely on the compelling platitude that leadership depends in part upon circumstances existing within the society, in part upon the personality and capability of the individuals—and it is these latter attributes that can be influenced during socialization. A gentle or harsh childhood may incline one person to seek power, another to avoid it; and here again the choice depends on the particular kind of gentleness and harshness and upon the opportunities within the society. It is probable that no one can be completely trained to exercise authority, hence some "discontinuity" is likely to be experienced when the principal first assumes a role possessing authority; what he does perhaps, it has been speculated, is to "turn to the models of the exercise of authority which he has himself experienced."[44]

Guide: As the human twig is bent, so shall the individual grow, but in ways difficult, sometimes impossible to foretell.

I.D *Temporal Potential.* Every person, yes every person, judges time. These judgments, a supremely human capability, are very complex, even as complex as judgments concerning power and authority. In the "Temporal Figure," note C, provided at the end of this chapter, the parallels are evident: against a background (total potential) a stimulus that is perceived induces the individual to make some kind of judgment (primary judgment) which upon reflection he may revise or express in a manner intelligible to his peers (secondary judgment). Of specific concern here is the total potential: the temporal motives which affect the allocation of time, information about time, and orientation or perspective. That potential, therefore, is another background variable which the observer or the participant can or must note when he would comprehend, respectively, the event or other participants.

I.D.1 All the factors associated with past experience have implications for the ways in which participants may or must *allocate* their time. Both metaphorically and literally it is clear that time is limited: part of every day must be given over to sleep, and death is eventually certain. Every participant, therefore, knows or comes to know how much time is devoted to particular activities, and often when those activities are supposed to occur; and the observer whose knowledge includes the allocation of time by participants may thus gain insight into the ways in which power and authority affect their existence. I would summarily dismiss the contention that the concept of power should not be applied to "a single instance of influencing a decision," regardless of its importance,[45] because that instance has its experiential background and consequences, hence a temporal dimension.

To the extent that socialization affects the immediate and eventual behavior of an individual, it also influences his temporal potential. Devoting time to one activity diminishes the time needed for other activities. The amount of leisure time at the disposal of an adult may be traced in part to his parents who once inspired, inclined, or compelled him to fit into a particular occupation and thus forced him to spend his days and years discharging its temporal obligations. Compulsory school attendance in the West or rites de passage in traditional societies have obvious temporal implications. And it must also be added that parents, especially mothers from the very outset, devote huge amounts of time to their children; they are usually powerless to do otherwise.

The structure of the society regulates to some degree the ways in which participants apportion their time. In the West, for example, labor unions bargain with employers concerning the length of the work week; and virtually all enterprises specify the age at which men and women must retire. Governments possess numerous temporal powers.[46] Citizens may exercise the privilege of voting only on specified days or occasions. They must reach a statute-determined age before they may be elected to office. They may have to spend a trivial, if annoying, amount of additional time to reach their destinations as a result of one-way streets. Young men and sometimes young women are forced to endure critical years in military service, they and their families make temporal judgments concerning plans when that service begins and ends. The time of imprisonment in jails and penitentiaries is almost completely allocated; and the ultimate sentence—capital punishment—prescribes the time of death.

The culture which is embodied in and sustains the social structure imposes restrictions on the temporal aspects of drive satisfaction. Meals occur three or four times a day according to custom, but the drinking of water is not regulated. Love-making for the young in the West is supposed to be postponed until they are "of age," and, in the past and even now for some, until marriage. After obtaining a marriage license, some authorities require that weddings be delayed a specified time. Divorces cannot be immediately obtained. Within the limits of their occupations, participants may choose the amount of time they spend with their families or associates, but they may be obligated to tolerate their company on particular occasions such as birthdays and anniversaries.

Possession of ample and relevant resources may enable the individual to spend less time earning a living or acquiring prestige than is his lot when he has access only to scarce or irrelevant resources. The force of climate determines in large part both when and how long workers may cultivate crops. The weapons of a ruling elite, such as the Europeans in South Africa, prevent that elite from being overthrown and hence prolong their period of domination.

There is likely to be a relation between temporal allocation in some respects and other aspects of power and authority within a society. If time is money, then those with money have the power to regulate how others may spend their time, and the subordinates in turn demand monetary compensation. In some traditional societies murder is avenged without delay by the aggrieved; in others, punishment is delayed until guilt has been determined by an authority such as a chief or a court. In contrast with societies dispensing with an authority who determines guilt or administers justice, those utilizing such an authority tend to delay other activities in their existence. They are likely to obtain their food from agriculture and husbandry which demand patience and toil rather than from a more immediate source such as hunting, fishing, and collecting. They probably attain political integration through an organized state rather than through a more or less autonomous community or the family. They may approve of men having property rights in women. They have a penchant to exert strong rather than weak pressure upon children during socialization and to prohibit rather than to permit free premarital sexual relations.[47] Warning: such characterizations are correlations, and therefore do not reveal causal connections; and exceptions are numerous.

I.D.2 Allocating time and passing temporal judgment requires *information* about time which can be derived from a variety of sources ranging from consulting a timepiece or viewing the angle of the sun to a deliberate choice between an immediate and a future gratification. The process is thus similar to what occurs when participants respond in situations involving power or authority: their temporal judgments are affected by their personalities, previous experience, the precipitating event, perception, and so on. And Arbitrary Limitation prevents a detailed consideration here of these judgments; reference again is made to note C, the "Temporal Figure," at the end of this chapter and to the analysis on which it is based.

I.D.3 Socialization also influences the individual's temporal *orientation,* the direction—past, present, or future—toward which generally or in a given situation he turns his attention. A participant anywhere is compelled at some point to be oriented in all three directions: the traditional cultivator, who lives in the present most of his existence because his rewards and punishments are immediate, must also think of relatives and ancestors now dead and he must contemplate the harvest of the crops in the future. Future orientation inevitably is part of planning: we do something now, we obey an authority because later we shall achieve the goal we really seek. The simplest contract requires some deferred gratification, as does education. Differences between societies or persons represent, consequently, differences in emphasis with respect to perspective.

> *Guide:* Tempus fugit during the experiencing and observation of power and authority.

I.E. *Resources.* Among the significant background data noted by observers, and likely to be known in part and certainly sought by both principals and subordinates, are the resources that have been employed in the past and hence can also be employed in the present and future. Included are nonhuman forces, like the strength of a beast of burden, or natural resources, such as mineral deposits or waterways, which provide their possessors with actual or potential wealth. Under this heading, consequently, are all the "bases" of power, ranging from materials to what is vaguely called charisma or sex appeal.[48]

In the West reference is usually made to the resources of the public and the private sector, and sometimes to the relation between the two. For the public sector there are statistics on the number of police and other armed forces at the command of government officials, as well as their equipment, their location, and their loyalty to the government. International resources may be similarly measured, although here—particularly in cold wars—the striking power of the weapons is mentioned as well as the diplomatic skill of leaders and their representatives in dealing with other states.

I.E.1 Previously I had the temerity to suggest—good naturedly, to be sure—that some political and other social scientists adhere to the *whodunnit* tradition in their research: in specific communities or countries, they ask, who are the principals or leaders with power or authority, who makes the critical decisions affecting subordinates and followers? In reply, various schools of thought pay tribute to their own perspicacity in the scholarly journals and in learned books. For present purposes, two extreme schools are contrasted. One brave set of writers indignantly and polemically attributes power to a small number of elite who are said to amass various benefits for themselves not only within each community but also throughout the country: to these capitalistic barons are attributed interconnecting links enabling them to reign nationally in a country like the United States.[49] Another group calls itself pluralistic since its empirical findings in designated communities suggest that the nature of the issues determines who the decision-makers are likely to be; their data demonstrate, they think, that stratification is not as rigid as elitist theory suggests.[50] In either case, money or its equivalent as well as the authority wealth commands are the instruments of power usually mentioned. Money, no matter how sophisticated or crude the monetary system, is a major resource, for whoever has a swollen bank account or a vast collection of cowry shells may not achieve all his earthly goals, but he is likely to have power or command authority in one or more hierarchies of the society. It is no coincidence, therefore, that one side of a coin in Western societies usually contains the portrait or silhouette of a powerful ruler, past or—in nondemocratic states—present.[51]

The widely proclaimed elitist hypothesis for the United States is that there is a small group of powers and authorities who "in the economic, the political, and the military domains" have profound effects upon the lives of most citizens: they make the decisions "having major consequences," they have become "self-conscious members of a social class" with all the organization and esprit that entails. The criteria justifying the postulation of an elite include their ability to affect the decisions of government, the homogeneity and unity of the members, the self-perpetuation of their power through the recruiting of replacements from a small segment of the society, and above all "the social similarities and psychological affinities" that prevail among them and hence make them feel comfortable in one another's company and provide them with a fairly common set of values[52]—and prejudices. As a result they are proclaimed to be "essentially autonomous."[53] The broad view that the capitalist or ruling class has the resources to exercise control must be refined in such a way that the affected phases of existence can be specified; presumably even the most avid determinist does not include coughs and sneezes in the sphere of activities affected by the modes of production. But should the theory be invoked, the devil's advocate must ask, when the effects of industrial pollution on the throat and nasal membranes are considered?

Securing an empirical measure of the resources and hence the power of a group, elitist or otherwise, is by no means a simple task. Both before and after liberation from Britain, the Creole elite in Sierra Leone, constituting about 2 percent of the total population, exercised their power not through the control of business, agriculture, or political leadership but through the ownership of property and the domination of the professions, especially the civil service. Their status, consequently, has not been based on the economy but on a subtle series of symbolic actions ranging from ceremonial or social events, kinship, and the Anglican Church to forms of etiquette, types of dress, and a mystique concerning death.[54] Or consider the mass media in the West. Their financial resources increase the probability that they can reach and affect extremely large numbers of listeners, viewers, subscribers, or readers. A quantitative study of the press in thirty-two countries during the late 1960s suggested, by means of an index, the degree of concentration of daily press ownership. In the United Kingdom, Japan, and Canada, that concentration tended to be high, in the United States low; the trend toward concentration was stronger in developing than in developed countries.[55] The index, though objective, did not reveal the relative influence of the newspapers within their countries or how they fared in comparison with other mass media. In addition, we must remind ourselves, access to information even in societies permeated by mass media and advertising is not automatic, for usually only powers in control of the media have the objective facts at their disposal, the selection and communication of which are affected by their own policies, prejudices, or goals.

In more general terms, the challenge to elitist theories is to demonstrate that resources in fact are controlled by fewer and fewer persons. Writers on the left are convinced that in capitalist lands power is centralized among the principal exploiters by means of interconnecting links.[56] Undoubtedly such assertions are at least partially true. In Western countries, connections exist between big business and government, bankers may be influential in local communities, and some clergymen identify themselves with the social classes from which the powers come. What used to be called muckraking reappears when journalists tear apart the power structures of medical services, unions, the press, commerce, etc.[57] And certainly in authoritarian countries centralized government tends to control most of the significant institutions and associations.

In the West, the pluralist approach to power is probably more valid than the elitist or monistic alternative. As societies and hence their structures become more complex, it is virtually impossible for a small group to accumulate the resources enabling them to obtain and retain absolute or complete control.[58] The complications stem from scientific and technological innovations as well as from an enormous expansion of industry and education, with the result that resources may be more widely distributed.[59] Owners of large industries cannot be foremen: they delegate power and authority because they have neither the time nor the skill to supervise the details. It may be argued, nevertheless, that the very remoteness of government from most participants in a highly industrialized state enables it to acquire "an independent life of its own."[60] When the critical decisions in a small western town in the United States were once examined, it was found that the power had been transferred from a small group, whose goals had been to preserve and to protect the community's "historical heritage," to diverse groups concerned with business, real estate, politics, and the mass media.[61] There was little evidence that those interest groups had been neatly woven into a single association with sufficient resources to merit the label of a stratified elite.

In some situations, nevertheless, a combination of pluralistic and elitist theories seems to fit the facts. According to a perspicacious economist, the United States has a "bimodal system." At the top is pluralism: power is diffused in large corporations since the crucial decisions stem not from directors but from management. Small enterprises, on the other hand, can be called elitist in organization: on farms and in professional groups and construction firms power is concentrated in the owners or in those performing the services. On a national level, moreover, elitism again appears. The large corporations are of greater economic significance than the small enterprises: "around 1,000 or 2,000 firms" a few years back contributed "about half of all economic products"; 50 of the 13,687 commercial banks in 1971 possessed 48 percent of all assets. As a result of their economic power, the giants affect both political decisions and the mass media: their views are believed to be more authoritative than those originating in the small enterprises.[62] There is thus pluralism within corporations, elitism within small enterprises and for the country as a whole.

The conception of how society's resources are distributed affects assumptions concerning the way in which principals and leaders are allegedly selected or select themselves. A staunch advocate of an elitist theory once believed that the United States lacked "a truly common elite program of recruitment and training," although he suspected that attendance at a private preparatory school, at a prestigious college in the East, or at one of the major law schools was the route by means of which "the metropolitan 400" acquire the resources enabling them to exercise power.[63] Pareto asserted that revolutions and coups are likely to occur when those considered to be the elite no longer have the resources to be able to circulate freely into positions of power.[64]

In every society, then, powers possess varying personal and social resources. They may utilize available resources, modify them, or create new ones. During catechism classes Catholic priests once taught more or less powerless peasants in a Dominican village effective methods they could use to obtain more money from the coffee they grew.[65] Leaders may have authority to exercise power, but they will not be effective unless they have resources enabling them to reward or punish those lower in the hierarchy.[66] Obviously, "no matter how much academic dispute there may be over the meaning of 'power' . . . no one denies that the authority of the revolver is a basis of 'power.' "[67] That statement, alas, is not an idle metaphor: governments and gangs can retain authority and exert power by stockpiling lethal weapons to be employed by available, cooperating subordinates.

Guide: The actual powers and authorities relevant to events are not always obvious, they may also be difficult to specify.

I.E.2 Powers possess *guns and symbols*. The power of guns and other forms of violence is obvious, even for those unconsciously seeking death or wishing to gamble with their existence. The resources much subtler than weapons and money in any society are nonverbal symbols which, according to one observer, tend to persist "longer" than the social arrangements regulating interpersonal relations.[68] In a rural setting of South Tyrol a priest once bitterly complained to me about a private dwelling that had been recently built next to a small chapel atop a hill. That chapel had formerly been visible from all directions, but was now hidden on one side by this secular house. "This shows," he said, "that for these people God is no longer the power." Buildings generally may symbolize the power relations between participants. Those that are larger, more ornate, and—in the West—located in particular neighborhoods communicate the greater prestige and power of their owners. Clothes can perform a similar function, whether they conform to the latest style, carry an expensive label, appear casual like jeans, or are conventionally formal like uniforms. The insignia displayed by all soldiers and sailors communicate their ranks and hence the scope of their authority.

Languages provide distinctive features that can be invoked as a resource. Unlike present-day English, which no longer uses its familiar grammatical form of *thou, thee,* and *ye* except in prayer and among sects such as the Friends, this mode of address in other languages—the formal *vous* and the informal *tu* in French—suggests the hierarchical relation and degree of intimacy between the speakers or writers.[69] The need for the form in English, moreover, is so great that English speakers employ titles, first names, and sometimes even grammar (the third person instead of the second in addressing high officials and judges) as substitutes to achieve the same purpose.

The right to vote in government or industry accords participants a role in decisions affecting themselves, however remotely, and therefore the exercise of that right influences the distribution of power and authority. Domestic and foreign lobbies are formal organizations exerting pressure upon policy makers in behalf of their clients who believe that through these paid or unpaid representatives they can achieve their goals. In the United States such pressure is legally recognized: lobbyists must register and thus at least reveal their identities to some government officials. The tactics of pressure groups range from bribery and skullduggery to moral and intellectual persuasion.

The resources of those groups and lobbyists are similarly employed in nonpolitical spheres, as when shops, industries, organizations are boycotted in behalf of particular causes.[70] Forms of pressure available to subordinates rather than principals are considered in Chapter 9. Producers and other principals potentially have the resources to achieve a literal or symbolic monopoly. A literal monopoly enables an industrialist to have more or less complete control over a commodity or service. A symbolic monopoly depends on the attitudes participants ascribe to some referent as a result of indoctrination from communications. Beer drinkers may prefer one brand after enduring its claims through advertising, even though they may be unable to distinguish different brands in a well-conducted blindfold test. Or patriotic citizens may believe their country unique or superior, a view not necessarily shared by outsiders.

> *Guide:* The resources of powers and authorities are finite and more or less measurable.

***

Equipped with some knowledge concerning the relevant culture and society as well as specific aspects thereof—the socialization process, the temporal potential, and the resources—the observer, this chapter has suggested, is or should be in a favorable position to anticipate how participants will react to power and authority. And again the other standpoint: as a result of his experiences in his society, his socialization, his temporal potential, and his knowledge of the resources at his disposal and at the disposal of others, the individual participant himself is predisposed at any given moment to react to authority and power in general or in specific ways. For in the past he has been gratified or frustrated, or his experiences have been uncertain. Obeying his parents has enabled him to be treated well rather than shabbily according to his lights. These experiences of his are stored within him, and hence are about to be considered in the next two chapters.

NOTES

A. *Anthropological Classifications.* In an older tradition anthropologists produced interesting classifications of political systems and hinted at associational sequences. One influential symposium examined eight African societies. In their introduction the editors emphasized that kinship was important in all societies but its political function varied. In "very small" societies, they stated, the "largest" political unit included people "united to one another by ties of kinship," in other societies a lineage structure was coordinated with the political system but remained "distinct and autonomous in its own sphere," and in still others "an administrative organization" was based on territorial groupings and kinship served "merely to cement" the relations within the political units. In their view, political development was related to the size of a population, but not to its population density nor to the ways in which food was accumulated.[71]

Anthropologists as well as others have sometimes noted that the organization of some societies has been designated as "loose" ("individualistic and expressive"), others as "tight" ("rigorously formal and orderly"). One anthropologist has arranged twelve attributes along a continuum from loose to tight: three at the loose end are the "mere presence" of a recognized political authority, the "legitimate use of force," and "political authority differentiated within the community"; three at the tight end are "some corporate control" of "stored food" and of "incorporeal property," with the tightest of all being a "theocracy." Then he systematically appraised thirty haphazardly selected societies in these respects (all traditional except for the Hutterites in North America and the kibbutzim in Israel). Those scaled as tight in terms of these twelve attributes, in contrast with those scaled as loose, tended to have kin groups that were unilateral rather than bilateral; contrary to the African study cited above, they also tended to place a high reliance on food crops and to be densely populated.[72] This second study is more impressive than the African one because it is based on a larger number of societies.

Among two dozen traditional societies a positive association of some magnitude has been found between economic development (as assessed by a reference to the importance of agriculture) and political development (as indicated either by the number of different types of political officials or the size of the territory within the jurisdiction of government); community size was also significantly related to the number of political officials.[73] Not unexpectedly in ninety-nine preindustrial societies a positive if not a perfect relation seems apparent between technological differentiation and the number of authority levels within a society, presumably because individuals can be expected to perform efficiently only in a limited number of groups and hence an authority structure is needed to keep their performance efficient.[74]

B. *Socialization of Power Strivings.* Numerous investigations have sought to establish a connection between distinctive socialization practices and the power strivings of children and adults. The connection turns out to be not an invariant one, even though the studies have almost exclusively been confined to persons in the Western world, particularly in the United States. A favored method has been to match scores of parents and their children (an omnibus measure of socialization if ever there be one) on a readily available paper-and-pencil test modestly named "Machiavellianism" (a tendency to manipulate others) and to be discussed a bit more extensively in the next chapter. A low but positive association was once demonstrated between parents' scores on this questionnaire and their sixth-grade children's success at deceiving others in a bluffing game but not in detecting the deception of others; the fathers' scores were related to the children's scores on a modified, simpler version of the same test, but the children's own scores were not related to their actual behavior in the game.[75] Another American study revealed no overall relation between the Machiavellian scores of parents and their ten-year-old children. After a statistical squeeze the investigator was able to find an inverse (not a direct) relation between the children's scores and their mothers' but not their fathers' scores; and the scores of both parents were dimly related—again inversely—to the children's manipulative behavior in a contrived situation.[76] Such unsatisfactory, contradictory results are not surprising because the attitude toward deception and its use—allegedly measured by the Machiavellian scale—may also be affected by the age and sex of the child and, as also demonstrated in Japan, by his or her birth order within the family.[77] In addition, it is quite possible that parents can function as positive or negative Machiavellian models for their children who may want to be either like a successful father or unlike an unsuccessful one, however success and failure are defined by the child as he observes his parents.

In addition to conforming to or rebelling against their parents, children's power striving may be influenced by peers and teachers outside the home. During socialization, the tactics of children may change; more older than younger Canadian girls, for example, indicated that they would use diplomacy rather than simple requests or strong pressure to persuade their mothers or best friends to stop looking at television and play a game with them.[78] Whether or not an adult strives for a position of power or authority by becoming a formal or informal leader in his society, however, depends upon existing circumstances in his society as well as upon his experiences as he moves from childhood into adulthood.

Experience with authority or authority-related techniques occurs during socialization. Fairly typical American and Japanese mothers have been carefully interviewed concerning what they imagine they would do in six situations in which their child required some kind of discipline: if the child were to refuse to eat vegetables, to swallow medicine, or to brush his teeth or if he were to throw a block at another child, to disrupt shopping, or to paint a picture on a wall. Overall, 18 percent of the Japanese and 50 percent of the American mothers said they would use "authority" to curb the child, with authority being cognitively defined as demanding compliance and offering "neither a rule nor a reason to the child verbally." The percentages who would be inflexible and demand immediate compliance without offering an alternative were, respectively, 58 and 68. The investigators believe that these and other data from the same investigation illustrate the possibility that "early socialization in Japan relies on close interpersonal ties and a climate of affection and interdependence leading to identification with the goals and values of the group," whereas in the United States "socialization is accomplished through more direct instrumental processes with greater reliance on explicit rewards, punishments, and techniques of control in encouraging behavior.''[79] The percentages above of course indicate only modal tendencies in the two samples, but they suggest perhaps that in later life the reactions to authority may be affected by these early experiences.

An analysis of practices in eighty-eight traditional societies reveals that by and large girls tended to be socialized ''more easily'' than boys; greater pressure had to be exerted upon the boys but they complied to a greater degree than the girls.[80] The reasons for these differences are obscure, but again it seems legitimate to imagine the probability of some carry-over into adult behavior. Perhaps authorities need to exert less pressure on women to have them conform, but may one believe that men conform to a greater degree?

Children slowly develop beliefs concerning authorities with prestige, presumably as a result of their socialization experiences. In a sensitive study of over one-hundred white South African children between the ages of six and thirteen, it was found that 41 percent of the youngest children considered God or Jesus ''the most important person in my country'' and 30 percent named a parent, personal acquaintance, or political leader; among the oldest of these children, 89 percent named a political leader, 7 percent a parent or personal acquaintance, and only one child (or less than 3 percent) God.[81] According to one summary of the research on political socialization a decade or so ago, by and large American children initially acquired an ''image . . . of political authority'' that was highly benevolent as well as powerful, even in aggrieved and depressed subgroups of the population, such as urban blacks (but evidently not in similarly less powerful groups, for example, poor whites in Appalachia).[82] Perhaps the most reasonable view is to assume that children and adolescents continue to retain somewhat submissive attitudes toward authorities, but that the reasons they supply either to themselves or to others change as they and their language become more sophisticated.[83]

On the basis of replies to semiprojective questions in the 1960s by a total of 266 adolescents between the ages of eleven and eighteen in England and the United States and between the ages of thirteen and eighteen in Germany, it appears that ''authoritarianism'' decreased with age: younger children tended to believe that governments exist to enforce the law and to ''curb wickedness'' and that obedience is essential, whereas older children were skeptical about laws and were convinced that they should be abandoned or revised when they were seen not to serve the common good. These cross-national trends were discernible in spite of the fact that attitudes toward the legitimacy of law also varied from country to country.[84] Similarly there are changes in the way in which the instruments of power are conceptualized. At first the child may attach no value to money: it is another object in his environment or another vocal vibration to which his parents and his older peers refer. Gradually he appreciates the goods and services it can command and hence places value upon its possession.

1. U.S.A.: forty male undergraduates. *Method:* in a laboratory, a fictitious peer allegedly solving ''dull'' arithmetical problems was strictly or only slightly monitored. *Results:* the previously strict monitors then monitored more strictly the peer performing a second set of the same problems, trusted that peer less, and considered him less dependable than did the previously lax monitors. Lloyd H. Strickland, Surveillance and trust. *Journal of Personality,* 1958, 26, 200–215.

2. Cf. Dorwin Cartwright, Power: a neglected variable in social psychology. In Dorwin Cartwright (ed.), *Studies in Social Power.* Ann Arbor: Research Center for Group Dynamics, 1959. Pp. 1–14.

C. Temporal Figure

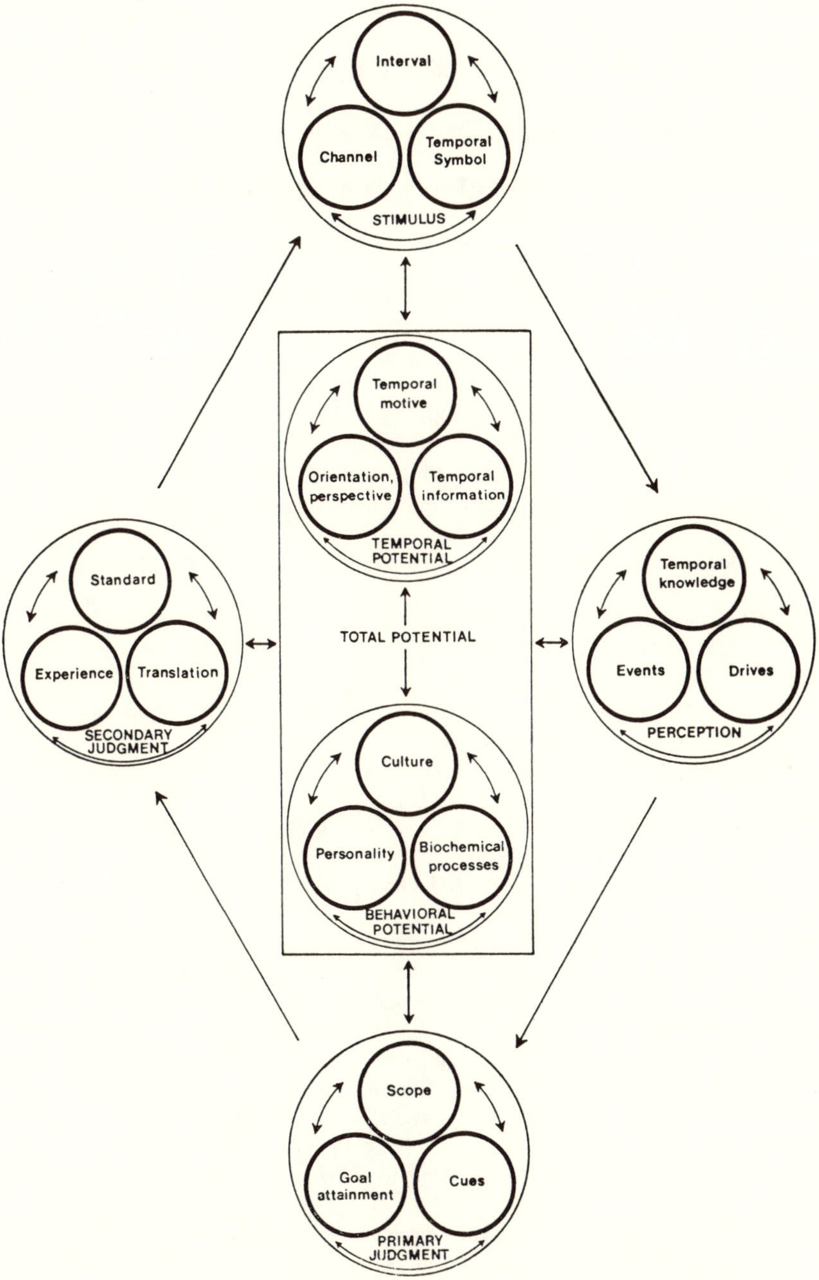

Source: Leonard W. Doob, *Patterning of Time*. New Haven: Yale University Press, 1971. P. 31. Copyright © 1971 by Yale University. Reprinted by permission.

3. Roderick Martin, *The Sociology of Power*. London: Routledge & Kegan Paul, 1977. P. 45.

4. Lucian W. Pye, *Politics, Personality, and Nation Building*. New Haven: Yale University Press, 1962. Pp. 146, 148.

5. Arthur S. Banks, Political characteristics of nation-states. *Journal of Politics,* 1972, 34, 246–57.

6. Shimon S. Camiel, Some observations about the effect of war on kibbutz family structure. *Family Coordinator,* 1978, 27 43–46.

7. Richard Peters, *Authority, Responsibility, and Education*. New York: Eriksson-Taplinger, 1960. P. 14.

8. Jean-Guy Vaillancourt, *Papal Power*. Berkeley: University of California Press, 1980.

9. Cf. Kenneth B. Clark, The pathos of power. *American Psychologist,* 1971, 26, 1047–57.

10. Cf. Richard H. Stephens, *Wealth and Power in Peru*. Metuchen, N.J.: Scarecrow Press, 1971. P. 22.

11. A. W. Green, *Sociology*. New York: McGraw-Hill, 1956. P. 75, italics his. Cf. Andrew Czartoryski, *Education for Power*. London: Davis-Poynter, 1975. P. 14.

12. Noted by John M. Swomley, Jr., *Liberation Ethics*. New York: Macmillan, 1972. P. 226.

13. Cf. Czartoryski, op. cit., p. 116.

14. Arnold A. Hutschnecker, *The Drive for Power*. New York: M. Evans, 1974. P. 11.

15. Cf. Harold Garfinkel, Conditions of successful degradation ceremonies. *American Journal of Sociology,* 1956, 61, 420–24.

16. Jacques Maquet, *Power and Society in Africa*. New York: McGraw-Hill, 1971. P. 151.

17. Amaury de Riencourt, *Sex and Power in History*. New York: David McKay, 1974.

18. Cf. Martha Mueller, Women and men, power and powerlessness in Lesotho. *Signs,* 1977, 3, 154–66.

19. Peter C. Lloyd, The political structure of African kingdoms. In Michael P. Banton (ed.), *Political Systems and the Distribution of Power*. London: Tavistock, 1965. Pp. 63–112. Cf. Robbins Burling, *The Passage of Power*. New York: Academic Press, 1974. Pp. 46–52.

20. Cf. Robert M. Carmack, Power in cross-cultural perspective. In James T. Tedeschi (ed.), *Perspectives on Social Power*. Chicago: Aldine, 1974. Pp. 255–309.

21. Cf. David A. Durfee, *Power in American Society*. Boston: Allyn and Bacon, 1976.

22. Colin Campbell, *Toward a Sociology of Irreligion*. London: Macmillan, 1971. P. 142.

23. Barrington Moore, Jr., *Political Power and Social Theory*. New York: Harper & Row, 1958. Pp. 2–3.

24. Bertrand de Jouvenel, *The Pure Theory of Politics*. New Haven: Yale University Press, 1963. P. 143.

25. Guy E. Swanson, *The Birth of the Gods*. Ann Arbor: University of Michigan Press, 1960. P. 65.

26. Donald T. Campbell, On the genetics of altruism and the counter-hedonic components of human culture. *Journal of Social Issues,* 1972, 28, no. 3, 21–37.

27. Lorna Marshall, Sharing, talking, and giving. In Richard B. Lee and Irven DeVore (eds.), *Kalahari Hunter-Gatherers.* Cambridge: Harvard University Press, 1976. Pp. 349–72.

28. Augustine Kobina Ebow Mensah, *Autoritätskonzept und Autoritätswandel in Ghana, Nigeria, und Uganda.* Munich: Kurfürsten-Druck, 1970.

29. David V. J. Bell, *Power, Influence, and Authority.* New York: Oxford University Press, 1975. Pp. 86–87.

30. Karl Mannheim, *Ideology and Utopia.* New York: Harcourt, Brace, 1936. Pp. 237–80.

31. David F. Bush, Bernard J. Gallagher, III, and Wendy Weiner, Patterns of authoritarianism between generations. *Journal of Social Psychology,* 1982, 116, 99–105.

32. David D. Laitin, *Politics, Language, and Thought.* Chicago: University of Chicago Press, 1977. Pp. 29, 194–207.

33. Robin Lakoff, *Language and Woman's Place.* New York: Harper and Row, 1975. Pp. 34–35.

34. Thomas Hobbes, *Leviathan* (1651). New York: Dutton, 1950 edition. P. 77, italics his.

35. Pitrim A. Sorokin and Walter A. Lunden, *Power and Morality.* Boston: Porter Sargent, 1959. Pp. 15, 47.

36. Alfred Adler, *Understanding Human Nature.* New York: Greenberg, 1927. Pp. 65, 70–76.

37. E.g., Uriel G. Foa and Edna B. Foa, *Societal Structures of the Mind.* Springfield, Ill.: Charles C. Thomas, 1974. Pp. 98–101.

38. Roderick Gorney, *The Human Agenda.* New York: Simon & Schuster, 1968.

39. Daniel I. Denga, Juvenile delinquency among polygynous families in Nigeria. *Journal of Social Psychology,* 1981, 114, 3–7.

40. Harry Eckstein and Ted Robert Gurr, *Patterns of Authority.* New York: Wiley, 1975. P. ix.

41. Muhammad Aziz Ahmad, *The Nature of Islamic Political Theory.* Karachi: Ma'Aref, Pp. 1, 12, 14.

42. Lord Radcliffe of Werneth, *The Problem of Power.* London: Secker and Warburg, 1952. Pp. 8–9.

43. Cf. Barry E. Collins and Bertram H. Raven, Group structure. In Gardner Lindzey and Elliot Aronson (eds.), *Handbook of Social Psychology.* Reading: Addison-Wesley, 1969. Vol. 4, pp. 102–204.

44. William W. Meissner, *The Assault on Authority.* Maryknoll: Orbis Books, 1971. P. 152.

45. Peter M. Blau, *Exchange and Power in Social Life.* New York: Wiley, 1964. P. 117.

46. Cf. Leonard W. Doob, *Patterning of Time.* New Haven: Yale University Press, 1971. Pp. 86–87.

47. Leonard W. Doob, Time: cultural and anthropological aspects. In Tommy Carlstein, Don Parkes, and Nigel Thrift (eds.), *Making Sense of Time.* London: Edward Arnold, 1978. Pp. 56–65.

48. Harold D. Lasswell, *Power and Personality.* New York: Viking, 1962. Pp. 27–30.

49. C. Wright Mills, *The Power Elite*. New York: Oxford University Press, 1956.

50. Cf. Robert A. Dahl, *Modern Political Analysis*, 3d ed. Englewood Cliffs: Prentice-Hall, 1976. Pp. 74–78.

51. Philippe D'Arcy, *L'Argent et Le Pouvoir*. Paris: Presses Universitaires, 1976. P. 17.

52. Mills, op. cit., pp. 3–29, 269–97.

53. Robert D. Putnam, *The Comparative Study of Political Elites*. Englewood Cliffs: Prentice-Hall, 1976. Pp. 1–5.

54. Abner Cohen, *The Politics of Elite Culture*. Berkeley: University of California Press, 1981. Pp. 41–59, 114–15.

55. Raymond B. Nixon and Tae-youl Hahn, Concentration of press ownership. *Journalism Quarterly*, 1971, 48, 5–16.

56. E.g., Herbert Marcuse, *Counter-Revolution and Revolt*. Boston: Beacon Press, 1972. Especially chap. 13.

57. Morton Mintz and Jerry S. Cohen, *Power, Inc*. New York: Viking, 1976. G. William Domhoff, *The Powers That Be*. New York: Random House, 1978.

58. Geraint Parry, *Political Elites*. London: Allen & Unwin, 1969. P. 65. Cf. Nelson W. Polsby, *Community Power and Political Theory*. New Haven: Yale University Press, 1963.

59. Tatu Vanhanen, *Political and Social Structures*. Ann Arbor: University Microfilms International for Finnish Political Science Association, 1977. Pp. 118–19.

60. Bertrand Russell, *Authority and the Individual*. Boston: Beacon Press, 1960. P. 19.

61. Ritchie P. Lowry, *Who's Running This Town?* New York: Harper & Row, 1962.

62. John Kenneth Galbraith, The bimodal images of the modern economy. *Journal of Economic Issues*, 1977, 11, 189–99.

63. Mills, op. cit., p. 295.

64. Cf. Parry, op. cit., p. 57.

65. Kenneth Evan Sharpe, *Peasant Politics*. Baltimore: Johns Hopkins University Press, 1977. P. 213.

66. Cf. Abner Cohen, *Two-Dimensional Man*. Berkeley: University of California Press, 1974. P. 77.

67. William Ker Muir, Jr., *Police: Streetcorner Politicians*. Chicago: University of Chicago Press, 1977. P. 286.

68. Cohen, op. cit., p. 36.

69. Rolf Kroger, Ken Cheng, and Ishbel Leong, Are the rules of address universal? *Journal of Cross-Cultural Psychology*, 1979, 10, 395–414.

70. Cf. William J. Wilson, *Power, Racism, and Privilege*. New York: Macmillan, 1973. Pp. 15–16.

71. M. Fortes and E. E. Evans-Pritchard, *African Political Systems*. London: Oxford University Press, 1940. P. 36.

72. Pertti Pelto, The differences between "tight" and "loose" societies. *Trans-action*, 1968, 5, no. 5, 37–40.

73. Melvin Ember, The relationship between economic and political development in nonindustrialized societies. *Ethnology*, 1963, 2, 228–48.

74. Stanley H. Udy, Jr., *Work in Traditional and Modern Society*. Englewood Cliffs: Prentice-Hall, 1970. Pp. 50–51.

75. Robert E. Kraut and J. Douglas Price, Machiavellianism in parents and their children. *Journal of Personality and Social Psychology,* 1976, 33, 782–86.

76. Dorothea Braginsky, Parent-child correlates of Machiavellianism. *Psychological Reports,* 1970, 27, 927–32.

77. Brian Sutton-Smith and B. G. Rosenberg, *The Sibling.* New York: Holt, Rinehart & Winston, 1970. Pp. 36–38. Dora Shu-Fant Dien and Hitoski Fujisawa, Machiavellianism in Japan. *Journal of Cross-Cultural Psychology,* 1979, 10, 508–10.

78. Gordon E. Finley and Carolyn A. Humphreys, Naive psychology and the development of persuasive appeals in girls. *Canadian Journal of Behavioral Science,* 1974, 6, 75–80.

79. Mary Conroy et al., Maternal strategies for regulating children's behavior. *Journal of Cross-Cultural Psychology,* 1980, 11, 153–72.

80. Michael R. Welch, Barbara Miller Page, and Lynda Lane Martin, Sex differences in the ease of socialization. *Journal of Social Psychology,* 1981, 113, 3–12.

81. Meredith Aldrich Moodie, The development of national identity in white South African schoolchildren. *Journal of Social Psychology,* 1980, 111, 169–80.

82. David O. Sears, Political behavior. In Gardner Lindzey and Eliot Aronson (eds.), *Handbook of Social Psychology.* Reading: Addison-Wesley, 1968. Vol. 5, 315–458.

83. Cf. Sheilah R. Koeppen, Children and compliance. In Samuel Krislov et al. (eds.), *Compliance and the Law.* Beverly Hills: Sage, 1972. Pp. 161–80.

84. Joseph Adelson and Lynnette Beall, Adolescent perspectives on law and government. In Krislov et al. (eds.), op. cit., pp. 151–60.

3

Personality: Motives and Beliefs

This chapter and the succeeding one concentrate upon participants' predispositions, upon their personalities. An observer, as already noted, can make only inferences concerning those internal tendencies. Their relation to one another is so complex that the present analysis is confined to those features related to power and authority; otherwise virtually all of psychology and psychiatry would have to be considered. Why is it important to focus upon participants' personalities? Phenomenologically or existentially it is desirable and necessary to know why they act as they do as a result not only of the pressures upon them but also of their own desires and feelings. Even when subordinates comply, for example, with the violent commands of a leader, they acknowledge the compulsion to themselves and select the course they judge to be the better part of wisdom. Or they hope it is the better part. Their ability to decide plays a role on some level, consciously or unconsciously. The internal processes, furthermore, are literally the stuff that gives meaning to existence. It may and can be noted that the foreign office of a modern nation seeks power on the international arena, but the cliché—accurate as it is for journalistic purposes or even for predicting what will happen in the future—takes on additional meaning when and if insight is gained into the personalities of the officials in that office and also into the various strata throughout the country. That such psychological information is difficult to obtain cannot be gainsaid, but is no reason either to avoid acknowledging the gap in information or not to salvage whatever crumbs are available.

Power and authority play a role in many conceptualizations of human predispositions. In Freudian terms, for example, the superego or conscience exerts authority over the ego and the id, both of which on occasion (whether in dreams or in waking life) seek to rebel against its authority. Two careful commentators on Freudian psychology suggest that "the superego commands, corrects, and judges the ego in a wholly parental fashion."[1] A non-Freudian may simply recognize that the individual is experiencing a conflict in which authority or power may or may not be at issue. Another example: the lay concept of self-control fits the definition of power being employed here, except that only a single person is involved: one part of him, as it were, does or does not exercise power over another part. He would down yet another drink, but he does not do so because he knows he must drive home afterwards. He thus controls the desire for the drink in behalf of another motive, viz., to remain alive while driving or not to be arrested for driving while intoxicated.

And so on: an arbitrary choice among concepts must be made. Psychologists and others, however, as is well known, possess the gift of tongues as they find or invent words to refer to behavior and its underlying predispositions. Only the gods on Olympus could persuade them to adopt uniform terminology, but then those gods would begin to quarrel among themselves concerning the appropriate symbols. An arbitrary selection, therefore, must be made—without resorting to neologisms. Motives and beliefs are discussed in this chapter, attitudes and skills in the next chapter. It must be understood, however, that the combination, organization, and integration of predispositions, the individual's unique personality, is thereby somewhat neglected for a simple reason. Even with the Faustian aim epitomized by the Guiding Figure, a dissection of power and authority cannot include the subtle analysis required to grasp completely a single individual's personality. Aspects of personality, nevertheless, are not overlooked as the four variables are examined, if only in passing, especially in connection with leaders.

> *Guide:* Participants' predispositions play some role—whether overwhelming or humble—in power and authority relations.

It is obviously inappropriate to ascribe predispositions to inanimate forces, but their potential or actual power will be mentioned. Animals, however, have predispositions affecting their cooperation with one another and the manner in which they group themselves into strata.[2] They must be treated in the way that observers deal with those human beings who cannot be interrogated and whose internal experiences must be inferred; and the animals' tendencies almost always contain a more significant genetic component than those of their human descendants.

1.A *Power Motives.* The first, and frequently the most important, of the variables intervening between events as they are perceived and the participant's judgments that are stored as part of his general background is that of motive. The basic assumption of anyone concerned with human behavior, whether he be a psychiatrist, a social scientist, or a layman, is that behavior is goal-directed, which is another way of maintaining that men and women, no matter how aimless their actions appear, are driven by internal urges. When a psychologist defines social power as "the ability or capacity" of one person "to produce (consciously or unconsciously) intended effects on the behavior or emotions of another person,"[3] he is making an indirect reference to the individuals' motives, perhaps also to their skills.

Motives can be examined from so many diverse standpoints that an Arbitrary Limitation must immediately be invoked so that the analysis can be confined largely to what might be called the power motives. Unquestionably those motives play a significant role in man's thinking about man. Human beings may be considered only as one of the higher animals but more fruitfully, too, they must be appraised as social, economic, and political beings. In their political role, it is said they have "a strong tendency, sometimes, to seek political power" over their contemporaries.[4] A philosopher once proposed that there are six "ideal types" of individuals, by which he meant not that such persons in fact exist, rather that participants—presumably in Western society—can be comprehended in terms of the ways in which their principal motives and values are organized: theoretical, economic, aesthetic, social, political, and religious.[5] The "political man," as summarized by a competent admirer, is ". . . interested primarily in *power*. His activities are not necessarily within the narrow field of politics; but whatever his vocation, he betrays himself as a *Machtmensch*. Leaders in any field generally have high power value. Since competition and struggle play a large part in all life, many philosophers have seen power as the most universal and most fundamental of motives. There are, however, certain personalities in whom the desire for a *direct* expression of this motive is uppermost, who wish above all else for personal power, influence, and renown."[6]

The six types have been operationalized in a questionnaire asking, for example, "Which of the following branches of study do you expect ultimately will prove more important for mankind: (a) mathematics, (b) theology?"[7] Not unexpectedly in the earlier 1930s over a thousand American males in schools and colleges scored higher with respect to the political values and lower with respect to the aesthetic ones than a comparable sample of females; and eighty-one salesmen scored higher on political values than did eighty missionaries.[8]

One of the most widely used measuring devices, the semantic differential, which successfully provides a significant clue not only to the meaning of concepts and communications but also to attitudes in a wide variety of societies, demonstrates again and again that respondents' appraisals can be approximately or appropriately designated by means of three factors called activity, evaluation, and potency. The last is clearly related to power and has been illustrated in the original monograph by the following power-oriented continua: large-small, strong-weak, heavy-light, and thick-thin.[9]

It seems useful and necessary, therefore, to postulate the existence of power motives, but it is also essential to comprehend the nature of those motives within the personality. At this point the honored distinction between primary or basic and secondary or instrumental drives must be mentioned or recalled. The former refer to universal needs, such as those for food, water, comfort, shelter, sexual satisfaction, etc.; the latter to those that may not be universal but can be acquired as a result of learning and experience. Secondary, instrumental drives, however, can become as strong or as compelling as primary, basic ones: hunger strikes may be motivated by political ideals.

Power motives belong in the instrumental category. They are not biologically basic, although they may play a significant behavioral role in conjunction with other motives or experiences of the individual. It is rare that one may speak of a power motive as such—power for the sake of power—since usually power is sought or avoided in the service of some other drive or motive. According to one summary, for example, classical psychoanalysts, including Freud, hold the view that participants strive for power as compensation for previously endured frustrations. Such persons then allegedly display the following reactions: they are unwilling to share their positions or possessions, they are reluctant to consult other persons or to take advice from or give information to them, they dislike delegating responsibility, and they would "devise and impose orderly systems" upon their contemporaries "in the political arena."[10] When or if such a syndrome exists, a power motive toward the specified ends has emerged.

The assertion by an angry writer that "the urge to have power is inherent in man"[11] is correct in the sense that participants have the potential to acquire a power motive but only when conditions in their milieu or in their personal lives encourage its development. Psychologists and psychiatrists postulate the existence of a trait when characteristic or similar reactions, whether internal or external, are exhibited in a variety of situations. Among the twelve personality factors appearing most frequently as items on numerous tests employed in the West is that of "dominance,"[12] obviously closely related to what is being called here a power motive. Just as nobody is completely consistent, so few individuals ever seek to be dominant in every situation.

Within recent years American social scientists, especially psychologists, have been chasing evidence to demonstrate that all persons can be categorized in terms of their power strivings. They have collected tons of paper-and-pencil data concerning responses which for better or worse they have grouped together under the eye-catching heading of Machiavellianism. Their definition of the underlying predisposition "revealed by the content of the scale items designed to measure this variable," is the following: "an amoral, manipulative attitude toward other individuals, combined with a cynical view of men's motives and of their character."[13] Let us leave aside the question as to whether the memory of the brilliant, frustrated Italian civil servant and author is being maligned and quote two of the items that "should convey the flavor of the scale":

> Never tell anyone the real reason you did something unless it is useful to do so.
>
> Generally speaking, men won't work hard unless they are forced to do so.[14]

This slick, repetitive scale can be effortlessly administered and scored in order to label respondents high or low in "Mach," or somewhere in between. As already indicated in note B, "Socialization of Power Strivings," in Chapter 2, the Mach scores are related inconclusively to socialization experiences. Investigations of Americans suggest that those with high scores on such an easily manageable instrument derive almost as much or more satisfaction from the means they employ to achieve goals as they do from the goals themselves—or at least they show no compunction to resort to so-called Machiavellian tactics.[15] A secondary instrumental motive may thus develop, as is supposed to occur within the hypothetical miser who treasures money for its own sake rather than for the goods and services it does or could provide. Power for such persons, if a view be falsely drawn out of context, has "an absolute quality possessing comparable utility regardless of the situational context in which it is involved."[16]

The *expressions* of the power motives are most varied,[17] which
1.A.1 certainly is an understatement. One person may feel a sense of power from winning an argument, whether trivial or profound. Another may assist a participant and bestow genuine benefits upon him, part of the motive for which is not only altruism but also a desire to dominate the recipient. And yet another may resort to alcohol or drugs, so that at least in his fantasies he becomes an approximate king of some universe.

Immediately, however, the temptation must be resisted to employ the concept of power motive too broadly as a form of explanation. The assertion is often made, for example, that tyrants have risen to power because of their craving for power. Each dictator probably has had motives other than power throughout their careers. Mussolini, ambitious as he was during his youth, genuinely sought at first and later to a lesser degree to improve the lot of his countrymen, the evidence for which are his early writings that were grounded in a kind of international socialism and not in the horrors of the nationalistic fascism he eventually developed.[18] Perhaps the power motive may function significantly differently in the two sexes, at least in Western societies; the culturally determined attitudes of men and women toward each other may mediate different reactions.[19]

So much depends upon the operational definition assigned to the power motive in a given situation. Possibly high-status participants may seek to express the power associated with that status by contributing to the good of a group.[20] According to one psychiatrist, the power motive becomes gratifying in its own right as a result of the rewards it brings, and the feeling of powerlessness leads to neurotic or even psychotic tendencies.[21] Here, perhaps, is one of the reasons why human beings commit evil deeds.[22]

The various analytic attempts that have been made to describe the power motive would require more than a ponderous volume to be reported and evaluated adequately. "In surveying the list of more or less generic interpersonal trends," a psychologist once stated, "it became clear that they had some reference to a power or affiliation factor." He emerged with sixteen kinds of behavior representing the goals sought by the principal as well as the ways in which he achieves that goal and the reactions of subordinates. The complexity of this approach is worth contemplating by anyone who would try to simplify the power motives; therefore the author's own gigantic, intricate, ingenious diagram is reproduced at the end of this chapter as the Interpersonal Figure (note A). Another psychologist has offered a different model or "structural analysis" in which the three main subdivisions are those which are "parent-like'' or involving others (ranging from ''endorse freedom'' to ''manage, control''), those which are ''childlike'' or involving the self (ranging from ''freely come and go'' to ''yield, submit, give in''), and others which include ''introject of other to self'' (ranging from ''happy-go-lucky'' to ''control, manage self.'')[23] Noteworthy is the existence of diverse schemas such as these—and others can be cited[24]—which in effect pay tribute to the multitudinous ways in which power is expressed. Equally important is the fact that the power motive, however designated in these analyses, cannot be isolated from its effect upon other participants and also from the participants' effect upon the person giving expression to that motive. The scholars, moreover, are conscientious probers whose analyses are the products of tremendous labors and are impressive in their own right. But there are no signs whatsoever that any one analysis is more useful or valid than its competitors, as a result of which no standards exist; pleasant, provocative chaos reigns.

Since power motives, like other predispositions, function within personalities, it is to be anticipated that they are almost always related to other motives. On one paper-and-pencil questionnaire the respondent is required to ''choose between happiness and greatness'' if given the choice;[25] that this item apparently appears sensible is a simple indication of the presence of possibly conflicting impulses. In many bargaining sessions the participants may wish to exercise power by winning, but they may also seek to reach an agreement concerning the division of available resources.[26] The angry writer quoted in the previous section of this chapter believes that ''power is exercised through the medium of some other pursuit.''[27] Politicians in the West, it has been asserted, seldom pursue power directly, but seek one or more of the following goals associated with power: adulation (''personal affection and praise''), status (''socially defined 'success' ''), a program (''solution of policy problems''), mission (''identification with a 'cause' ''), obligation (''sense of civic duty''), and game playing (''exercise of skill in political competition'').[28]

On the other hand, the pursuit of power per se is also useful to achieve almost every conceivable goal. Marxian theorists emphasize the economic motives behind the power of the ruling class or classes.[29] Social scientists with a broader perspective call attention to the use of power by individuals to achieve the goals of broadly gauged groups like governments or specialized groups like organizations and associations. A careful investigation of participants in two American communities once revealed that those low in alienation (as measured by a four-item schedule, one of which was ''The old saying, 'You can't fight city hall,' is basically true'') contained a higher proportion of decision-makers (operationally defined as those actually making the decisions or having the reputation for doing so) than those high in alienation similarly measured,[30] probably a Spiral Relation.

A Spiral Relation also often exists between power motives and other motives or behavior. In some psychiatric patients, the power motive may cause their difficulty: to compensate for feelings of inferiority, as previously suggested,[31] they may become overaggressive and require therapy to learn to be less of a nuisance to their peers and themselves. Others may be neurotic because they fear to express the authority that is rightly theirs; they resort to therapy to fortify their self-confidence. Power and authority also are intertwined. On the one hand, a subordinate may recognize the need for lines of authority and the regulation of power if the impulses of others are to be curbed ultimately or immediately for his benefit; and he himself may seek to do the curbing or regulating. On the other hand, he may resent the restrictions he himself must inevitably accept. What seems to be true is that men and women are either "typically role-determined" or "role-determining,"[32] and thus they, respectively, react to a power motive in others or express that motive on their own.

Guide: The goal of a power motive usually but not always includes that of some other motive.

1.A.2 In any situation what is called a power motive may or may not be aroused and, when aroused, its *strength* may be strong or weak; in either case there will be repercussions. Some persons occupying a position of power may be unable or unwilling to exercise that power;[33] then the assumption must be that these principals are pursuing some other goal or that their power motive is weak. In fact, avoidance of power is probably the outcome of past experience. On the basis of not very impressive evidence painstakingly gathered largely from college students whose power motive was tapped through stories composed in response to a Thematic Apperception Test, a psychologist has postulated different forms of what he calls "the fear of power." One he calls "fear of other's power" which he believes results from the presence of "many powerful others," such as older siblings; it may consist of a fear of homosexuality which in turn can lead to paranoia or a fear concerning what others may impose upon the self. When the participant is also punished for his own "power actions," he may develop either a fear of his own power or a fear of losing it. The former is characterized by a "reluctance to engage in power actions" and by "ineffective, 'over-aroused' performance"; the latter by detachment from one's peers.[34] In addition, as indicated in the next section of this chapter, the belief of an individual concerning his inability to control himself and events may result from or induce a sense of powerlessness so that his strivings are minimal. Certainly, common sense suggests, the "internally affirmed dependence" of some persons upon others may become "habitual."[35]

Conceivably the power motive is stronger in some societies than in others. The Dobuans of New Guinea were once noted for their "dangerousness": they put "a premium upon ill-will and treachery" and made these "the recognized virtues of their society." In contrast, the Zuni of New Mexico were said to "value sobriety and inoffensiveness above all other virtues": they centered their interest upon "their rich and complex ceremonial life."[36] The Dobuans, a fair inference must be, have had stronger power motives than the Zuni. Somewhat similar differences were reported in East Africa toward the end of the colonial days.[37] Possibly, differences in the strength of the power drive within a society can be ascertained by analyzing its folk tales.[38]

1.A.3 It is not necessary to assume that participants, whether principals or subordinates, are at all times completely *aware* of the power motive affecting their judgment or behavior. Perhaps brow-beaten subordinates are likely to realize they are laboring under a "psychic restraint" upon their overt behavior,[39] but the powers themselves may not appreciate the power implications of their own actions. A very gentle, devout clergyman of my acquaintance would, I believe, never dream of asserting himself, except in behalf of his religious principles, in order to demonstrate either his power or his authority; but, it seems to me, he takes inordinate pride in being able to name the various peaks on a mountain range in the hearing of others who have never known the names or have forgotten them.

Related to this question of awareness is the problem of the phenomenology of the power motive. That problem has been probed in a book whose appropriate subtitle is "The Inner Experience."[40] The data therein come almost completely from the "imaginative stories" written largely by American college students spontaneously or after witnessing a power-related event; a "social emotional maturity" scale, another version of the Thematic Apperception Test, has been derived from Harvard freshmen. In this study the investigator and his colleagues adduce four types of what they call "power orientations" to which they append sensational labels in the classical Freudian tradition:

1. *Oral* (being supported): the power comes from outside the self, the strength-giving referent for which may be God, mother, spouse, friends, leaders, or food; tends to serve others.
2. *Anal* (autonomy, will): the power comes from the self which appears to strengthen, control, and direct that self; tends to refuse to comply.
3. *Phallic* (assertion, action): the power comes from the self and takes the form of demonstrating strength; tends to be competitive.
4. *Genital* (mutuality, principled assertion, duty): the power comes from outside the self and takes the form of participating in groups; tries to influence and serve others.[41]

The mode of approach is stimulating and often impressive not because it uses Freudian clichés but because it brings together a number of provocative, hitherto unrelated tendencies. The data reveal marked sex differences. In a sample of 115 American women, the power orientation (combined with the score for the genital stage) correlated positively but only very, very modestly with membership in organizations, with the belief that knowledge is less important than action, with a preference to seek help from psychiatrists, with pride in being able to share in general and with husbands, with refraining from betting, with "Oedipal identification," and with a preference for "castration death metaphors"; but for 85 males, selected from the same area, none of these relations or their equivalent ones turned out to be significant.[42] Small amounts of alcohol increased the frequency with which subjects tended to feel a sense of "socialized" power, but larger amounts promoted thoughts of "personalized" power.[43] There was thus a connection between the inner experience of power and action: sometimes it depended on the state of the organism (alcohol), sometimes it gave rise to action (perhaps exemplified by the folk tales which have been systematically analyzed),[44] and sometimes it did both ("presumably the sex differences").

Guide: Power motives, weak or strong, are aroused by many but not all events.

1.B *Beliefs*. The expressions, the strength, and the awareness of power drives are affected by beliefs. A modern philosopher once declared that "Muhammad added nothing to the knowledge or to the material resources of the Arabs, and yet, within a few years of his death they had acquired a large empire by defeating their most powerful neighbors."[45] Without attempting to locate and disentangle the myriad forces accounting for the military and political successes of Islam in Europe from the seventh to the fifteenth centuries, nor for their subsequent history, it is clear that Muhammad gave his followers a powerful credo at a crucial time. He instilled in them beliefs concerning not only himself as a prophet, but also their relation to God, the cosmos, and their own destiny which, together with other factors in the milieu, played a significant role in their development, expansion, and accomplishments. Plato recommended that each of his laws be prefaced with a statement explaining its rationale, and many binding documents, such as the United States Constitution, begin with a preamble setting forth the objective to be achieved.[46] An effective authority is one in whose legitimacy followers and other participants, including leaders, can believe. Self-fulfilling prophecies and psychosomatic diseases are among the impressive consequences of beliefs. In short, beliefs, whether called that or given a fancier name such as stereotype, ideology, or myth and whether valid or not, are important both in their own right and in conjunction with other psychological processes.

The pecking order, a synonym for hierarchy, is said to be "a biological and universal phenomenon," but the capability of justifying it is "a purely human invention."[47] That order must be "known" to animals for genetic or acquired reasons, and hence in this inferential sense it may be asserted that they too are guided by beliefs concerning their own power or authority, so that they guide their behavior accordingly. Sometimes the observer of power and authority in human beings is no better equipped to judge their beliefs than he is those of animals. Although he may never know to what extent animals' beliefs derived from past experience are "consciously" stored within them, nevertheless he can note human beliefs as they are expressed in words, which I suppose is a mixed blessing.

1.B.1 Any human belief is supported by what its possessor considers to be relevant, valid *knowledge*. This is not to say that the knowledge is accurate or that the individual can give a coherent account of why he believes what he does. The knowledge of participants concerning power may be elaborate, though also limited on objective standards. Followers and other participants seldom can comprehend fully or adequately the nature of the power affecting them, such as large business enterprises in the West. Similarly, peasants and farmers in developing countries may not be aware that the price they receive for their cash crops depends on conditions in the world-wide market.[48] The "exceedingly complex systems" of political parties in the United States are not likely to be grasped by most voters,[49] in spite or because of the voluminous, conflicting information they receive from candidates and the mass media. Participants whose knowledge of authority and power is vague or almost nonexistent from the standpoint of the observer, nevertheless, may believe they comprehend both the events affecting their existence and the identification of the principals manipulating those events. They may be convinced that they know how and why government officials possess power and authority, yet their conviction is dependent upon the limited or distorted information transmitted to them and upon their own perceptions and interpretation—and they may be wrong, tragically or trivially.

1.B.1.a Many beliefs, whether buttressed with knowledge or not, cannot be *verbalized* easily. Instead they lurk within the foreconscious and are formulated somewhat coherently after being challenged. When beliefs of many or most persons in a society are similar or dimly present, it can be said that the ideology of the society is not clearly articulated, in fact it may not be formulated until a crisis arises.[50] In addition, sometimes beliefs are held with such tenacity that their possessors do not crave supporting facts, actually they may even defy the challenge to produce evidence: "I don't care what you say, I know this is so because I believe it." Some of the most compelling beliefs, such as those associated with religion and most cosmic questions, are accepted on faith not because they are documentable but because they satisfy human needs or are links in a chain of other beliefs. Or, in the words of a challenging aphorism, "thinkers, like scientists, believe in proof without certainty, while those who put their trust in faith believe in certainty without proof."[51]

Knowledge buttressed by belief in its validity is also an essential component of another predisposition, that of skill. To be effective a participant may have to possess certain technical, verbalizable knowledge, the kind necessary to be an authority with power in a profession or occupation. Successful functioning within a group, whether as principal or subordinate, requires knowledge of how that group functions. The utilization of controlled forces by human beings depends upon prevailing knowledge within the society concerning the animals that may serve as beasts of burden or as sources of food or concerning the sources of energy to be harnessed to heat houses or drive engines. Adaptation to the controlling forces of climate, weather, wild animals, and viruses presupposes similar knowledge that can be expressed and transmitted to other persons.

The common beliefs, the *modal beliefs,* to which most persons
1.B.1.b subscribe reflect prevailing knowledge as well as values in the
society or group. Even when they apparently are invented anew, they have historical antecedents. Thus under a complex but facilitating set of conditions Hitler popularized anti-Semitism which generally had been latent but ever-present within some Germans and Austrians. Often, to be sure, beliefs are grounded solidly in what competent persons consider to be reality. Scientific beliefs are or should be based upon the best available knowledge and, when that knowledge changes, the competent scientists change their beliefs which they properly call hypotheses or theories. In South Africa the dominant Europeans as well as the dominated Africans and other ethnic groups have always known that the former possess the arms and the brute strength to retain their position in the society. In contrast, for centuries the Africans there, vastly superior in numbers, had not believed that eventually they themselves would take over the government, a conviction which in the last quarter of the twentieth century dramatically changed among their leaders. More generally it is usually difficult for persons to imagine a society radically different from the one in which they have been socialized, unless somehow they acquire knowledge concerning alternative arrangements indirectly by hearing of other possibilities, directly by experiencing contrasting milieux through travel, or by convincing themselves that fantasies can be converted into reality. Subordinates who absorb the ideologies of their societies in particular have no knowledge other than that concerning the status quo in which they are embedded; they may lack the knowledge that could indicate the noninevitability of their present status. Perhaps, more often than not there is a discrepancy between reality and attending beliefs. No relation existed, a study once revealed, between the perceived powerlessness of American students and workers as measured on a questionnaire and their position within society or the company employing them, a finding the author asserts runs contrary to Marxian theory.[52]

Beliefs include *expectations and anticipations.* Knowledge de-
1.B.1.c rived from folklore, wishful thinking, and philosophical expecta-
tions intermingle. Will a principal with power take advantage of his position? Can a particular authority be trusted? Is it the function of government to provide unemployment insurance or medical care? Are people responsible for their own actions? Anyone who would answer questions such as these must supply facts and values, but ultimately—as is especially true with reference to most religious tenets—part of the belief system is grounded in unverifiable faith and in unverifiable knowledge. For the same reason so many of the soul-gripping issues associated with power and authority are unresolvable.

Guide: Beliefs stem from knowledge, whether true or false, partially true or false, verifiable or not.

1.B.2 For the first but not the last time, the puzzling, provoking relation between predispositions and *behavior* intrudes. What role do *beliefs* play? Is it sufficient for an observer to note the connection between a participant's motives and his overt behavior and to ignore his beliefs? He is conditioned, it is said, to respond to stimuli in a specified manner. He is hungry and therefore he eats; he itches, and therefore he scratches. For the participant, however, the motivation to act is mediated by intervening processes. He believes, for example, that by eating his hunger will be reduced or by scratching the itch will be relieved; when hungry, he does not scratch or, when itching, he does not eat. Even in these simple instances he anticipates that "the performance of any act" will be "followed by a consequence."[53] Such an expectancy is a belief acquired through experience in the past and performs an instrumental function. But again multidimensionality must be noted. The potential thief may have two beliefs, one concerning the punishment administered by a power if he is caught, the other concerning the probability that he will not be caught. His decision to obey or disobey the authority of the law depends upon the relative strengths of these beliefs as well as upon his needs and the attractiveness of whatever goals he seeks, which is not to assert that his decision is "rational."

The phrase "false consciousness" is used by scholarly and semischolarly observers to refer to a particular relation between beliefs and behavior. That consciousness, of which Marx spoke, refers largely to the assertion that, as capitalist society develops, men believe they have no alternative other than to accept the machine and its accompanying modes of production and distribution, as if those modes were as inevitable and unavoidable as the force of gravity or as if they themselves were completely powerless subordinates. Such a belief leads to passivity, it inhibits action. A reference to the power of machines should suggest the additional beliefs as well as the attitudes and the various forms of human behavior accompanying their utilization. Whether a metaphor is useful or misleading is a somewhat intriguing question, one discussed in note B at the end of this chapter, "Power as a Metaphor." That question is especially challenging in connection with frequent references to nuclear power or weapons in the modern world. Again, not the ingredients but men, fallible human beings, possess the skill and hence the power to construct the power plants and to manufacture the weapons; they believe that either or both can perform useful functions, they themselves are the principals who control the physical and chemical forces. Those forces, however, completely or almost completely control human beings when there is a serious accident in a plant and when the nuclear wastes, as far as is known, remain lethal for thousands of years.

Generally, moreover, some beliefs do not play a significant or discoverable role in affecting behavior. This view is expressed in hundreds of different ways by clergymen. Their congregations, they know, ostensibly subscribe to the beliefs of the church which they learned as children, yet those beliefs infrequently govern their behavior. Witness, they cry, all the evils today which surely could not exist if church-going participants acted in accordance with their religious beliefs or principles. Beliefs, moreover, may be forgotten, or they play no significant role in behavior unless they are reinforced by actual experience or by symbolic communications;[54] thus, by joining clubs and associations, adult American males once reported an increase in the strength of their belief that the world is manageable and that they themselves were not powerless.[55] It may be evident to virtually all persons in the West that the world is round in a loose sense and not flat; but this belief of theirs has no immediately discernible effect on their everyday existence.

More than a word of caution, however, must be added before beliefs are considered to be clichés or of little or no significance. Knowledge concerning the roundness of the world and the tenets of a religious sect may have no direct effect upon those who can glibly and freely utter them, but they exist within the society and hence affect some participants significantly—and those participants may influence institutions and various social practices which in turn affect the very persons for whom the knowledge appears unimportant. A particular person may never give a moment's consideration to his belief about the world's roundness, but that knowledge within the repertoire of navigators enables him to travel safely on a ship or a plane. And surely religious beliefs, though so weak that their possessors seldom if ever enter a church, do guide those who are lawmakers or educators as well as devout subordinates who thus affect others.

Indeed virtually every native living in the north temperate zone believes that snow is unlikely during the summer and virtually every adult American knows he must pay an income tax under specified conditions; hence relevant behavior is guided accordingly. For the fact is that snow almost never falls in specified areas during the summer and tax dodgers may be caught and prosecuted. Obedience probably results from a belief that it more desirable to comply with a power or an authority than to disobey.[56] But why desirable? It is easy to reply in terms of anticipated rewards and punishments,[57] but then it becomes clear that the rewards and the punishments may or may not vary with other predispositions[58] or demographic attributes.[59] An infinite regress is encountered, therefore, when an explanation is sought for the reward and punishment value behind the belief. The act of obedience, moreover, may have only symbolic value: the subordinate would indicate that he respects the principal or that he performs the duty for reasons associated with convention or the situation.

Beliefs, therefore, can sometimes have a significant, instrumental effect upon the expression of power motives. On a simple level, a principal may express himself shyly if he believes that the display of naked power in a social or political situation tends to be disapproved by the relevant participants. Much more complicated may be the belief that it is or is not better to postpone gratification in the present if a larger reward seems probable or certain in the future.[60] The individual, for example, may refuse a position of power or authority at the moment when he believes that by waiting he can attain greater power in the future. In this context another Arbitrary Limitation should be apparent: even though it may be crucially important for an observer to know the reasons why a power or an authority is or is not able or willing to postpone a judgment, the analysis of power and authority cannot embrace every detail, cannot pursue every predisposition back to Adam, Aristotle, or the atom.

It is not surprising, in short, that many but not all participants acquire beliefs enabling them to justify more or less satisfactorily their own status within relevant hierarchies, whether they be leaders or followers, principals or subordinates. For the more powerful, beliefs allay guilt and prevent contradictions from arising between behavior and values; for the less powerful, beliefs serve the function of rationalizing whatever frustrations are being endured.

1.B.2.a In many societies, including those in the West, some of the wisdom of the ages concerning power and authority is stored in *proverbs,* so that it is relatively easy to locate beliefs concerning power and authority. Among the Fanti of Ghana, for example, the following proverbs have been recorded:

> A birds roosts with its own clan.
> If you are getting your hair cut by your mother's child, you do not look into a looking glass.
> We follow the words from the mouth of an elder, not his thoughts.
> The child who provokes his mother and father eats food without salt.
> One cannot make the same tracks as an elephant.
> The child has ears like those of an elephant.
> When the chief has good advisers, he reigns peacefully.
> If you follow a bad dog, you come across a dead rat.
> Do not tell your wife anything that cannot be said in public.[61]

It would be difficult to contend that these proverbs have a direct effect upon the behavior of those who quote them. Indeed to measure their effects as well as those of most beliefs it is essential to try to determine how important the respondents believe them to be or how certain they are that the beliefs are true. Another infinite regress thus emerges: the belief about the belief about the belief, etc. In addition, contradictory proverbs may persist in the same society ("Make hay while the sun shines" vs. "A penny saved is a penny earned"). Such proverbs are somehow embedded, if only subliminally, in the belief system of almost everyone; in American society, since the incompatible proverbs can be blithely quoted at different times or by different persons, they then may determine one set of behaviors rather than another. Among Somalis, proverbs tended to be better known by a sample of tribesmen following the traditional nomadic existence than by those with permanent or semipermanent abodes near a modern city; yet educated Somali students also were well acquainted with them, probably because they wished thereby to preserve the traditions of their society.[62]

A critical belief of participants concerns the *credibility* of leaders,
1.B.2.b other principals, and communicators in general. In addition to
attractiveness and power, this belief is one of the factors significantly influencing the effectiveness of communications.[63] An authority's reputation stems from the way in which subordinates perceive his actions, his truthfulness, his consistency, and his adherence to the values he is supposed to express. Then they believe or do not believe that he really means what he communicates and that he will carry out whatever punishment he threatens or whatever rewards he promises. The credibility of parents as authorities perhaps may be transferred to adults who function as surrogates.[64] In modern society participants must decide whom to trust. Should the less informed and less powerful customer, a cipher from many standpoints, believe a salesman who badgers him for the first or nth time?

Beliefs are held with varying degrees of *confidence*. Pollsters at-
1.B.2.c tempt to assess such confidence when they ask respondents how
certain they are in responding to a closed question or when they offer them alternatives, usually five consisting of "strongly agree," "agree," "don't know," "disagree," and "strongly disagree." Presumably a belief evoking a high degree of confidence is likely to be more influential in determining a decision than one with a lesser degree. Leaders who lack confidence in their power—that is, who fear their own weakness—instead of succumbing to their adversaries, may perhaps seek power and thus overcome their insecurity.[65]

Beliefs, therefore, cannot be dismissed as unimportant, even when they are expressed effortlessly and without firm conviction. Leaders in totalitarian states are prone to punish severely those persons who hold or especially express the "wrong" beliefs. The persistence of inquisitions, Spanish or otherwise, testifies again to the fact that ideas are dangerous and that, as believers in civil liberties stoutly and rightly maintain, they must freely circulate if society is to prosper.

Guide: Beliefs affect behavior but seldom invariably.

Leaders and principals seek to make their hierarchal position ap-
1.B.3 pear *legitimate* not only to appease their own consciences but also
to justify the authority they do or would possess.[66] Elaborate theories ranging from divine will to popular sovereignty have been proclaimed in the West both to explain and justify the way in which power and authority are distributed. Perhaps a theory is most likely to be influential when it reveals "a transcendent principle behind the Power" sought,[67] whether that principle involves God, experts, or the majority.[68] Fortifying beliefs are devised when

conflict between participants becomes obvious and painful;[69] ultimately even violence may have to be justified.[70] Beliefs concerning the nature of human nature appear when principals engage in exploitative, cruel, or ruthless actions.[71] Again and again, whether in the South in the United States, the colonial empires of the European powers, or the programs of the Nazis, principals consider themselves biologically or culturally superior to the participants: obviously, it is felt, the superior must legitimately triumph over and direct the inferior. That these beliefs are false or part of society's mythological equipment is irrelevant: they discharge their function effectively during extended or limited periods of time.

The members of many groups have beliefs concerning the purposes, the structure, and the functioning of their organizations. Participants in traditional societies have a strong tendency to believe that the political and social structures are fixed and stable: overall they can or will conceive of no alternative. When citizens elsewhere are convinced that democracy, socialism, or communism is a desirable form, they then also believe that their present government is or is not a true exemplar. Should the state regulate business? Should the powers of a ruler be curbed? Who should help or rescue the truly needy? These questions are perpetually raised in the West and everywhere when the variable regulations and techniques of governing become known. Subordinates ascribe legitimacy in varying degrees to persons and institutions, and they as well as principals also have beliefs concerning the changeability of legitimacy.[72] Conflicts between persons or groups and changes are more probable when the beliefs in legitimacy are weak and accompanied by another belief that such legitimacy is not immutable.[73]

Western scholarship is swamped with theories concerning when and why a government may be considered legitimate and hence when it should command and receive respect and be obeyed.[74] These theories appear in every generation, beginning formally with the classical ones proposed by Greek philosophers (particularly Plato). They include the Old and New Testaments as well as distinguished philosophers such as Rousseau, Locke, Hume, and Hobbes—and the authors of the American Declaration of Independence. Concepts referring to nature, morality, legality, divinity, tradition, and above all consent appear again and again.[75] Behind such concepts is the assumption that good citizens have an obligation to obey their government, it is their duty to do so.[76]

Therefore, after centuries of debate, sometimes exciting though usually repetitious, there is no definitive way to establish the validity of one theory concerning legitimacy over another. Here is another will-o'-the-wisp that cannot lead to a single goal, for surely nomadic and Western societies differ with respect to the conscious and unconscious beliefs of their peoples regarding the sanctity of authority. It may sound profound to assert that the elite in Western societies require historical justifications and the nonelite are content with myths. Perhaps that proposition contains a micrograin of truth—the more highly educated may demand better documented bases than the less educated do—but clearly university graduates are swayed by some myths concerning their society, and followers must be convinced that many of their beliefs have a historical basis. It is certain only that every growing child and every adult possesses some belief concerning his relation to the authority of government. The belief may be expressed in homespun terms—if you do not obey or comply, the cops will get you—but it affects behavior.

For more than fifty years, however, one schema has tended to dominate the scholarly classification of the bases for submitting to authority and hence the nature of the underlying beliefs. Three "pure types" have been delineated. First, it is said, rational grounds exist for considering an authority legitimate: the basis here is legal, and the authority is thought to operate efficiently and effectively in terms of accepted, acceptable rules. Tradition offers a second foundation: custom is sanctified and hence those leaders and principals who fulfill their followers' expectations merit obedience. Finally, a few principals are said to have charisma: their authority stems from "devotion to the specific and exceptional sanctity, heroism, or exemplary character" which their followers believe they possess.[77] In this schema bureaucratic authority is considered to be rational since it follows "intellectually analyzable rules." Traditional authority, however, might also be considered rational since it too adheres to known rules. Charismatic authority, on the other hand, is irrational: it repudiates the past, it flows from the magic of the leader, and it is not likely to endure since it "becomes either traditionalized or rationalized, or a combination of both."[78] In all probability, however, "pure" charisma seldom occurs and, when it does occur, "it cannot be more than an element in leadership, never the whole";[79] a leader must also have skills associated with the exercise of power. A charismatic principal certain of his authority is likely to disparage tradition and to speak ex cathedra. In that portion of the Sermon on the Mount in which Jesus modified the Ten Commandments, he alluded six times to tradition ("Ye have heard that it was said by them of old time") and then immediately pronounced his own injunction ("But I say unto you").[80]

Modal beliefs exist not only within a society, as previously suggested, but also in its subgroups. Members of social classes, as even non-Marxists agree, tend to share similar beliefs: those atop the hierarchy are convinced that their positions of power are thus justified.[81] In South Africa, for example, Europeans have evolved a set of beliefs epitomized by the doctrine of apartheid enabling them to live comfortably while perpetuating conditions of inequality at odds with some of their other religious, legal, and political beliefs. Such a common set of beliefs or ideologies, if successfully propagated, provides political stability; authority is then considered legitimate by those who possess it.[82]

The opportunistic if obligatory procedure to locate the ways in which behavior and actions are made to appear legitimate within a society is to investigate empirically the actual beliefs of participants. Nationalism is our best and most agonizing illustration, best because so many different justifications have been devised, agonizing because this kind of legitimacy is so intimately linked to war. An inventory of beliefs has been formulated for modern nationalism whose leaders or followers would supply reasons, respectively, for national policies and aspirations. The inventory can be quickly presented by classifying the beliefs into the most prominent categories and by illustrating each with what might be considered a prototypical statement:

I. Absolutistic Justifications
   A. Determinist
      1. Divine sanction: What we seek has received God's blessing
      2. Destiny: We follow in the footsteps of the founding fathers
      3. Nature: What we want is perfectly natural
      4. Humanitarian responsibility: We must do this for the good of mankind
   B. Transcendental
      1. Peace: Only thus can war be averted
      2. Freedom: We must control our own lives
      3. Security: We must protect ourselves
   C. Legal and Semilegal
      1. Sovereignty: Our rights dare not be violated
      2. Justice: Right is on our side, justice must triumph
      3. Contract: You agreed to it, you must do it
      4. Majority: We outnumber them, our way must prevail
      5. Superior: We are inherently better than they
II. Personificative Justifications
   A. Familial
      1. Birthright: We were born here, this is our home
      2. Consanguinity: We all belong to one family, as it were, family ties are precious
      3. Culture: Our own traditions must be preserved
   B. Temporal
      1. Primacy: We were here first—ahead of them
      2. Duration: We have been doing this for a long time
      3. Status quo: So it is, and that is that
      4. Posterity: We must do this for the sake of our children
   C. Human
      1. Need: We must have this if we are to grow and prosper
      2. Achievement: We have developed this area
      3. Public opinion: What will they think of us?
      4. Revenge: They started it[83]

The mere recital of these assertive beliefs is sufficient to indicate that the challenge at hand is to determine which ones are evoked by whom and under what circumstances, in order to justify or explain the authority and power prevailing in one's native land as well as the decisions of its leaders. Nature and Humanitarian responsibility, for example, are employed by imperialists; Peace, Freedom, and Security by leaders favoring increased armaments; Sovereignty and Justice by leaders declaring war on another country; Birthright, Consanguinity, and Culture by racists—the reader doubtless can complete his own categories without further assistance and then live a little less happily ever after.

Guide: Beliefs derived from past experience or momentary pressures are the bases for legitimacy enabling authorities to be obeyed.

What are the participants' *self-beliefs?* In his view what deter-
1.B.4 mines his own behavior? Does he believe that he is master of his fate or that he merely responds to events beyond his control? This existential problem appears in many guises.[84] A belief in any aspect of fatalism, such as predestination or astrology, implies that the self is relatively powerless: the individual is convinced that outside forces are responsible for his own actions, perhaps for his entire existence. The subtlest and most sweeping expressions of the extreme approaches to self-belief so considered are embodied in the doctrines of free will and determinism. In the Judeo-Christian tradition the belief exists that Adam and Eve were evicted from paradise because, by eating the forbidden fruit, they acquired knowledge. Forthwith they were able to distinguish between right and wrong; and hence they and their descendants are responsible for making their own decisions: we must forever choose between good and evil.

In recent years psychologists and others, particularly Americans,
1.B.4.a have contributed to the measurement of self-belief by referring to the *control* the individual believes he exercises over his own behavior. They have been inspired by what the original author has aptly called "locus of control" and by the numerous specific studies to which his own impressive paper-and-pencil scale and modifications thereof have given rise.[85] He himself and his disciples refer to internal and external control, a very fruitful distinction. For convenience I find it useful to stress the belief aspect of these concepts rather than the referent of the beliefs, and hence reference will be made to external and internal self-beliefs.

Commonsense and scholarly research suggest the existence of a continuum between external and internal self-beliefs.[86] Individuals seldom if ever believe that they are controlled completely either internally or externally, rather they think some phases of their existence are determined by outside forces, others by themselves. The staunchest advocate of free will must concede that he is powerless to control the weather or as an adult to learn to speak a foreign language flawlessly. Similarly the most staunch determinist also believes that he himself decides to drink coffee rather than tea or to vote for one candidate over another. Even though he may belittle his own conviction in this respect and attempt to trace his choice to previous events, that same person may also admit that the tracking down of some or many of the factors "causing" his actions is only theoretically feasible. Ultimately, no matter how invulnerable human beings believe themselves to be—whether in battle, in a plane, or in daily life—they appreciate their own mortality over which they have no control: however the fact is symbolized, death is all-powerful.

Even though human beings believe they possess varying degrees of control over their own behavior, their tendency to lean in one direction rather than the other is likely to reflect the modal tendency within the society in which they have been socialized and continued to dwell. Paper-and-pencil research carried out in Nigeria, Zimbabwe, and the United States illustrates possible cultural differences with respect to self-beliefs. Those beliefs were similar among samples of white university students in Zimbabwe and the United States, but both groups inclined significantly more toward internal self-beliefs than did the samples of Zimbabweans and Northeastern Nigerians. The cultural difference, according to the investigator, may reflect greater reliance on the Protestant ethic among the whites and a stronger belief in destiny among the blacks.[87] Differences also appear within multiracial countries; thus among samples of university students and adolescents in South Africa the conservative whites tended to a greater degree to possess internal self-beliefs than the Indians, Africans, Coloreds, and liberal whites.[88]

As can easily be imagined, so significant a predisposition as self-belief has intimate connections with other predispositions, whether as cause or as effect. Possibly,[89] in comparison with those possessing external self-beliefs, individuals with internal self-beliefs tend to be more active, which may include a stronger power motive[90] and a greater tolerance of frustration.[91] Conceivably, too, internal rather than external self-beliefs may be associated with keener skill in judging the power of others.

It might also be anticipated that self-beliefs are related to physical attractiveness as judged by the individual or his contemporaries: persons who are exceedingly attractive or unattractive may be externally oriented since life for them is, respectively, relatively easy or difficult. In contrast, those who are only moderately attractive may have to fight their way ahead and hence they are oriented internally. Possibly[92] such a stereotype exists among American undergraduates concerning not only others but also themselves.[93] And attractiveness is often associated with power.

1.B.4.b The participant believes that he himself possesses or does not possess power or authority: this is *self-attribution*. He asks himself in effect: do I or do I not have power or authority? To answer affirmatively he must believe that events will prove him correct.[94] The belief springs from knowledge derived from past experience and from perceiving the situation at hand. Up to some point success or failure in the past produces the conviction or doubt and hence the anticipation that past performances concerned with power will be repeated; or the knowledge of a participant's position in a hierarchy more or less indicates the authority in which he is or is not clothed. An ongoing experience, however, may intervene and affect self-attribution: the participant may arrive at a judgment concerning another participant's power or authority during the conflict itself, especially if he has had little or no previous experience with that individual and also if he believes that the antagonist is preventing him from achieving the goal he seeks.[95]

Any human being, other than a detached paranoid, at least on occasion attributes less power or authority to himself than someone else. He appreciates the fact that he is not omniscient in all respects and must therefore seek information or assistance in some situations. He may accept the information or assistance either critically or uncritically; or he may accept it because he believes that it is correct or that an authority may be able to punish or reward him. Even the most powerful despot knows he is mortal and therefore admits privately or publicly that he has less power than the force of biological aging or whatever supernatural being, in his view, controls him and the universe. For some persons a weak self-attribution of power is almost all pervasive. Under these circumstances they may or may not adopt measures to repress or express their power motive. Children, for example, may continually strive for "power and dominance" to compensate for the inferiority they experience in "an environment of adults" in which they consider themselves "weak, small, incapable of living alone."[96] According to the psychoanalyst whose name, as previously indicated, is always associated with a concept of power, later on there may be an unfavorable or a favorable development of the power motive: unfavorable when personal power is sought, favorable when power over "general difficulties" is the goal and the individual is "informed by social interest."[97]

The experiences giving rise to a confident or uncertain belief concerning one's own power and authority have also been considered both theoretically and empirically.[98] According to one interpretation of the Marxian view of alienation in capitalist societies, participants feel powerless because they believe or realize that their own actions cannot affect the outcome of social or economic conflicts or that they cannot achieve the goals they treasure.[99] An individual's belief in his own effectiveness in situations of power is said to be momentarily reduced when he perceives that his opponent is deliberately rather than involuntarily offering resistance, when he believes that he himself lacks resources to win, and when he loses self-confidence.[100] Police know they possess both authority and power, to which they add specific beliefs on the basis of experience; for example, the conviction expressed by one policeman that for him "family beefs," which he was supposed to try to settle, are "invariably perilous."[101] A person's own philosophy or religion, either of which embodies a series of more or less interrelated beliefs, affects his attitude toward authority and power. The individual who is convinced that the version of creation given in Genesis is literally true may attribute more power to God and less to all mortal men and to himself.

The individual develops *self-confidence* with reference to some of
1.B.4.c his own motives, beliefs, and skills, unless he remains hopelessly
dependent or neurotic. When long past being dependent as a child,
nevertheless, he may undergo experiences that make him believe he is powerless. Ordinarily, for example, he may have a "sense of invulnerability," which

means he believes he can escape harm, that the plane in which he is a passenger will not crash. But if he chances to be in a situation from which he cannot escape danger—a combat plane or burning house—he may lose that self-confidence and afterwards become generally anxious because of his own judgment of powerlessness.[102] Other experiences may lead to similar judgments or perhaps only to dismay. If the person is convinced he cannot deal with people or enter into a warm relation with them, he may withdraw by and large and try to lead an isolated existence.[103] His judgment concerning his own power may be realistic or not; if it is markedly exaggerated, it may resemble the "megalomaniac's feeling of omnipotence."[104] A sense of powerlessness may be an essential ingredient of alienation, so that the participant is unwilling or unable to make decisions or to execute them. Such a sense, it may be speculated, is more likely to pervade a participant whose self-belief is external rather than internal: he believes he is tossed about by forces beyond his control. And yet self-beliefs, whether internal or external, may function only on a verbal level, their consequences may not be fully appreciated, or they may not be consistent with other beliefs. Someone may believe "in theory" that he is a product of his milieu, but in practice he may convince himself that he nevertheless controls his own destiny. Perhaps he is generally more likely to attribute his own behavior to circumstances and that of other persons to their own personality traits, whether or not such behavior involves success or failure.[105] These tendencies among self-beliefs may not be consistent; but consistency, though allegedly a virtue and an impulse, is more honored in the breach.

In addition, human beings are resilient and hence may be able to overcome an objective state of powerlessness by judging their own values to be superior even to those of persons oppressing them. Botswana men, subject to discriminations and other frustrations while working in South Africa, are reported not to suffer from "the scars of bondage" and hence to retain their sense of self-identity as well as their core values.[106] Indeed, if a reckless leap be permitted, the sweep of history, at least in the West, has been viewed as a change from the view that the "world," by which in large part is meant natural forces, appeared "decisive and controlling," to the belief that "man himself" is dominant, so that these forces as well as "the absolute state" have become devalued "in favor of the claims of the subjective ego."[107] Perhaps such a characterization is true of nature vs. man, but it is not true of human beings vs. human beings when reference is made to wars and other ever-plaguing evils.

Guide: Generally or specifically every participant has a belief, varying in confidence, concerning his own power and authority with respect to (a) his ability to exercise control over what happens to him and (b) his possession of these attributes.

NOTES

A. Interpersonal Figure

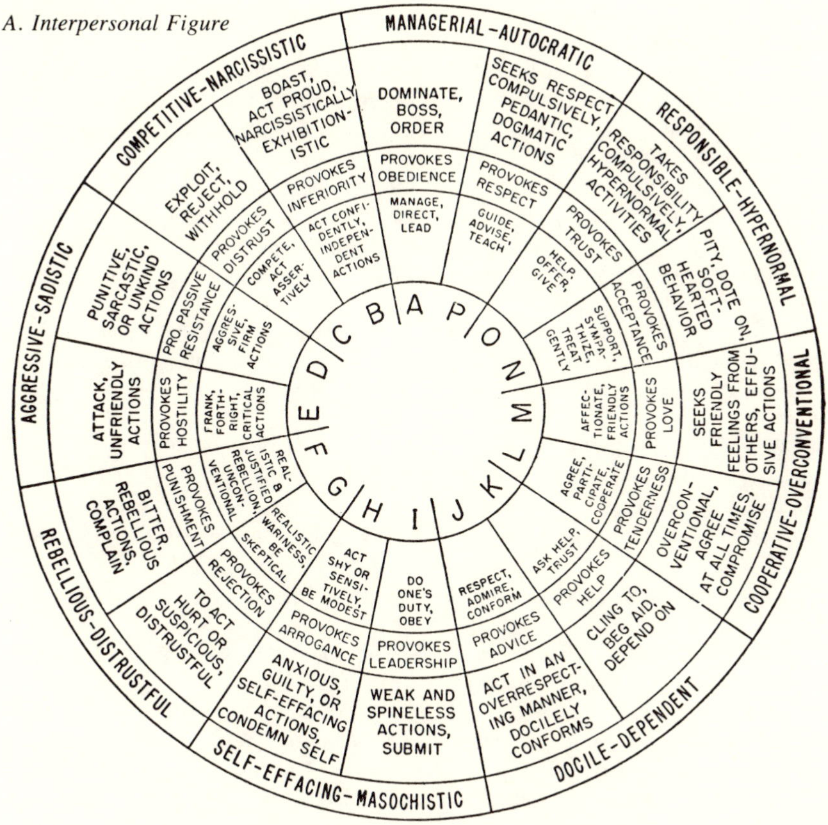

Source: Timothy Leary, *Interpersonal Diagnosis of Personality*. New York: Ronald Press, 1957. P. 65. Reprinted by permission.

B. Power as a Metaphor. The brilliant author of a book entitled *The Pentagon of Power* often uses a phrase such as "the demands of the machine" in describing the history and consequences of technology.[108] Such an expression must be called a metaphor, for obviously the machine as such can make no demands upon persons except when it is considered a principal force. A machine requires fuel if it is to function, but the need for the fuel originates with the human being who wishes to use the machine. Or when the same writer suggests that "machine power was replacing muscle power" during the industrial revolution,[109] again he is referring to persons who replaced the force their bodies could exert with the strong forces they could elicit from machines under their control. But when he writes later on in the same volume that "To enjoy total automation, a significant part of the population is already willing to become automatons" in our modern age,[110] he is effectively if elliptically pointing to a vast system of beliefs and attitudes. For modern technology to prosper, some principals must have adequate knowledge to produce the machines, and many more must share the belief that the machines are desirable. Metaphors are not needed to describe certain kinds of power, such as the three kinds of human ambition derived from Francis Bacon and noted by the same writer: personal power in one's country, power of one's country over other countries, and power over nature.[111] But, I contend, it may be necessary, if regrettable, to refer to the power of the machine when the beliefs and knowledge about the machine, being embedded in different persons over generations, cannot be located in specific persons. One final quotation from the same source: "When through the glasses of science" at the time of the Copernican revolution, "man shrank in size: in terms of astronomical quantities the human race counted for little more than an ephemeral swarm of midges on the planet itself."[112] Once more, as a result of increased knowledge, men's beliefs changed, and these beliefs, it is being asserted—and it is only an assertion because we do not know how widely the beliefs have diffused throughout the population—affected attitudes toward the self.

1. Calvin S. Hall and Gardner Lindzey, The relevance of Freudian psychology and related viewpoints for the social sciences. In Gardner Lindzey and Eliot Aronson (eds.,) *Handbook of Social Psychology*. Reading: Addison-Wesley, 1968. Vol. 1, pp. 245–319.

2. Romano Guardini, *Die Macht*. Würzburg: Werkbund-Verlag, 1951. P. 47. Lewis Thomas, *The Lives of a Cell*. New York: Bantam Books, 1974. P. 151.

3. David G. Winter, *The Power Motive*. New York: Free Press, 1973. P. 5.

4. Leonard W. Doob, *The Plans of Men*. New Haven: Yale University Press, 1940. Pp. 147–49.

5. Eduard Spranger, *Types of Men*. Halle: Max Niemeyer Verlag, 1928. Pp. 109–246.

6. Gordon W. Allport, *Pattern and Growth in Personality*. New York: Holt, 1961. P. 299, italics his.

7. Ibid., p. 455.

8. H. Cantril and G. W. Allport, Recent applications of *The Study of Values*. *Journal of Abnormal and Social Psychology*, 1933, 28, 259–73.

9. Charles E. Osgood, George J. Suci, and Percy H. Tannenbaum, *The Measurement of Meaning*. Urbana: University of Illinois Press, 1957. P. 36.

10. Alexander L. George, Power as a compensatory value for political leaders. *Journal of Social Issues*, 1968, 24, no. 3, 29–50.

11. Andrew Czartoryski, *Education for Power*. London: Davis-Poynter, 1975. P. 25.

12. Edgar Howarth, Major factors of personality. *Journal of Psychology*, 1980, 104, 171–83.

13. Stanley S. Guterman, *The Machiavellians*. Lincoln: University of Nebraska Press, 1970. P. 3.

14. Ibid.

15. Richard Christie, Why Machiavellianism? In Richard Christie and Florence L. Geis (eds.), *Studies in Machiavellianism*. New York: Academic Press, 1970. Pp. 1–9.

16. Robert Presthus, *Men at the Top*. New York: Oxford University Press, 1964. P. 29.

17. Cf. Eleanor Emmons Maccoby and Carol Nagy Jacklin, *The Psychology of Sex Differences*. Stanford: Stanford University Press, 1974. Chap. 17.

18. A. Jones Gregor, *Young Mussolini and the Intellectual Origins of Fascism*. Berkeley: University of California Press, 1979.

19. U.S.A.: Sixty-three young dating American couples, one of whom was an undergraduate in college. *Method:* a measure of fantasy from stories (a verbal form of a

Thematic Apperception Test) composed without knowledge of the study's purpose, producing a measure called "hope for power." *Results:* for the young women, the scores were unrelated to virtually all their feelings concerning their dating partners and to their subsequent behavior. For the young men, there were slight, statistically significant relations between their power motive revealed in the stories and their dissatisfaction with the dating relation, with problems anticipated, and with reported feelings of boredom concerning that relation. Two years later, one-third of the relations between the pairs no longer existed, but again for only the men 50 percent of those high in power and only 15 percent of those low in power no longer were continuing the relation in any form. *Comment:* possibly the different results for the two sexes may be ascribed to real differences between them with respect to the dating relation or to the role of power in their lives: the men and not the women may have valued power more than the prospect of a marriage. Or perhaps there may have been defects in the mode of measurement for the problem at hand. Abigail Stewart and Zick Rubin, The power motive in the dating couple. *Journal of Personality and Social Psychology,* 1976, 34, 305–9.

20. U.S.A.: 160 undergraduates. *Method:* in the laboratory they were led to believe they could contribute more than their peers to the common product in competition with other groups in a very simple task, viz., reaction time. *Result:* they improved their performance. Eugene Burnstein and Robert B. Zajonc, Individual task performance in a changing social structure. *Sociometry,* 1965, 28, 16–29.

21. Rollo May, *Power and Innocence.* New York: Norton, 1972. Pp. 23–27.

22. Leonard W. Doob, *Panorama of Evil.* Westport: Greenwood, 1978. Pp. 91–92.

23. Lorna Smith Benjamin, Structural analysis of social behavior. *Psychological Review,* 1974, 81, 392–425.

24. E.g., Myron Wish, Morton Deutsch, and Susan J. Kaplan, Perceived dimensions of interpersonal relations. *Journal of Social and Personality Psychology,* 1976, 33, 409–20. Hope R. Conte and Robert Plutchik, A circumplex model for interpersonal personality traits. *Journal of Personality and Social Psychology,* 1981, 40, 701–11.

25. Milton Rokeach, *The Open and Closed Mind.* New York: Basic Books, 1960. P. 76.

26. Cf. Charles L. Gruder, Social power in interpersonal negotiation. In Paul Swingle (ed.), *The Structure of Power.* New York: Academic Press, 1970. Pp. 111–54.

27. Czartoryski, op. cit., p. 25.

28. Robert D. Putnam, *The Comparative Study of Political Elites.* Englewood Cliffs: Prentice-Hall, 1976. P. 77.

29. Cf. W. Wesolowski, *Classes, Strata, and Power.* London: Routledge & Kegan Paul, 1979.

30. Presthus, op. cit., p. 365.

31. Alfred Adler, *Understanding Human Nature.* New York: Greenberg, 1927.

32. C. Wright Mills, *The Power Elite.* New York: Oxford University Press, 1956. P. 24.

33. Cf. Dorwin Cartwright, Influence, leadership, control. In James G. March (ed.), *Handbook of Organizations.* Chicago: Rand McNally, 1965. Pp. 1–47.

34. Winter, op. cit., pp. 143–63.

35. Theodor Eschenburg, *Über Autorität.* Frankfurt: Suhrkamp Verlag, 1965. P. 11.

36. Ruth Benedict, *Patterns of Culture.* Boston: Houghton Mifflin, 1934. Pp. 59, 131.

37. Kenya: 47 Luo Males, Uganda: 133 Ganda males. *Method:* a long interview, in

which they were asked whether they agreed or disagreed with a series of statements, including "A person should not become too successful because people will be jealous of him" and "The world is a very dangerous place in which men are very evil and dangerous." Also they were asked, "Who is more important in helping people improve their lives: (a) the people's leaders or (b) the people themselves?" *Results:* the percentages of Luo agreeing with the first two statements were, respectively, 23 and 81 percent, whereas the corresponding figures for the Ganda were 57 and 54 percent. Leaders rather than the people themselves were selected by 62 percent of the Luo, 75 percent of the Ganda. Leonard W. Doob, *Becoming More Civilized.* New Haven: Yale University Press, 1960. Pp. 286, 290, 294.

38. David Lester, National motives and psychogenic death rates. *Science,* 1968, 161, 1260. S. A. Rudin, National motives predict psychogenic death rates 25 years later. *Science,* 1968, 160, 901. Cf. Claus Mueller, *The Politics of Communication.* New York: Oxford, 1973. P. 145.

39. Ronald V. Sampson, *The Psychology of Power.* New York: Random House, 1966. Pp. 233–34.

40. David C. McClelland, *Power: The Inner Experience.* New York: Irvington, 1975.

41. Ibid., pp. 13–21.

42. Ibid., pp. 70–72.

43. Ibid., p. 257.

44. Ibid., pp. 25–29.

45. Bertrand Russell, *Power.* New York: Norton, 1938. P. 145.

46. Carl J. Friedrich, *Tradition and Authority.* New York: Praeger, 1972. P. 53.

47. Benjamin Wolman, On saints, fanatics, and dictators. *International Journal of Group Tensions,* 1974, 4, 359–85.

48. Cf. Kenneth Evan Sharpe, *Peasant Politics.* Baltimore: Johns Hopkins University Press, 1977. P. 29.

49. Cf. Andrew S. McFarland, *Power and Leadership in Pluralist Systems.* Stanford: Stanford University Press, 1969. P. 26.

50. Cf. David V. J. Bell, *Power, Influence, and Authority.* New York: Oxford University Press, 1975. P. 51.

51. Ashley Montagu, *Growing Young.* New York: McGraw-Hill, 1981. P. 142.

52. David E. Payne, Alienation: an organizational-societal comparison. *Social Forces,* 1974, 53, 274–82.

53. Cf. John W. Atkinson, Motivational determinants of risk-taking behavior. *Psychological Review,* 1957, 64, 121–39.

54. Cf. Abner Cohen, *Two-Dimensional Man.* Berkeley: University of California Press, 1974. P. 82.

55. Cf. Arthur G. Neal and Melvin Seeman, Organization and powerlessness. *American Sociological Review,* 1964, 29, 216–25.

56. West Australia: 1,184 children, grades 5–7. *Method:* two paper-and-pencil tests devised to measure "docility," one requiring the subject to signify agreement or disagreement with straight-forward statements, the other with statements based on a simple story. *Results:* the most significant variable was that of age. Older children tended to be less docile than the younger ones. Gender was not significant, but social class was: those from lower-class backgrounds tended to be less docile than those from the middle class. *Comment:* perhaps obedience for children means a reliance on "authority figures for assistance in decision-making, and also for support and approval"; if so, then younger

children may have a greater reliance on them than older ones, and middle-class families may encourage more "self-direction" than those in the lower class. K. F. Punch and Leonie Rennie, Some factors affecting docility in primary school children. *British Journal of Educational Psychology*, 1978, 48, 168–75.

57. Cf. Rokeach, op. cit., pp. 43, 63.

58. U.S.A.: 326 undergraduates. *Method:* a carefully constructed scale measuring dominance and submission, requesting agreement or disagreement with statements such as "I control others more than they control me" and "In working with others, I let someone else take charge of things." *Results:* scores were not related to another scale seeking to measure "social desirability" defined as behavior that is "culturally sanctioned and approved" but "improbable of occurrence" (e.g., "I always try to practice what I preach"). Albert Mehrabian and Melissa Hines, A questionnaire measure of individual differences in dominance-submissiveness. *Education and Psychological Measurement*, 1978, 38, 479–84.

59. U.S.A.: forty-eight four-year-old children. *Method:* a task having "no inherent purpose or value" (carrying marbles one at a time and dropping them into a box) and accompanied or not by a verbal threat ("If you don't keep doing what I told to do while I'm gone, I will be mad when I come back and something bad will happen"). *Results:* obedience increased among the girls but not among the boys. Kenneth L. Higbee, Factors affecting obedience in preschool children. *Journal of Genetic Psychology*, 1979, 134, 241–53.

60. Doob, *Becoming More Civilized*, pp. 84–93. Also Walter Mischel and Bert Moore, The role of ideation in voluntary delay for symbolically presented rewards. *Cognitive Therapy and Research*, 1980, 4, 211–21.

61. James Boyd Christensen, The role of proverbs in Fante culture. *Africa*, 1958, 28, 232–43.

62. Leonard W. Doob and Ismael M. Hurreh, Somali proverbs and poems as acculturation indices. *Public Opinion Quarterly*, 1970–71, 34, 552–59.

63. Cf. William J. McGuire, The nature of attitudes and attitude change. In Lindzey and Aronson (eds.) op. cit., vol. 3, pp. 136–314.

64. U.S.A.: seventy-two middle-class boys, ages five to seven. *Method:* the boys listened to a thirty-second, closed-television tape in which an adult discussed various actions from a moral standpoint; they then had an opportunity immediately afterwards to act more or less in accord with the model's recommendation by touching or not touching toys; and their moral judgments were assessed projectively. *Results:* they were affected somewhat in both respects by the model. *Comment:* the longer-range effects of the microscopic sermon were not investigated. Ignatius J. Toner and Richard Potts, The effect of modeled rationales on moral behavior, moral choice, and level of moral judgment in children. *Journal of Psychology*, 1981, 107, 153–62.

65. Cf. John Rowan, *The Power of the Group*. London: Davis-Poynter, 1976. Pp. 128–29.

66. Cf. Jean-Paul Montminy, Les grands thèmes de l'étude du pouvoir au Québec. In Fernand Dumont and Jean-Paul Montminy (eds.), *Le Pouvoir dans la Société Canadienne-Française*. Québec: Les Presses de l'Université Laval, 1966. Pp. 245–50.

67. Bertrand de Jouvenel, *Power*. London: Hutchinson, 1948. Pp. 34, 45.

68. Cf. William W. Meissner, *The Assault on Authority*. Maryknoll: Orbis Books, 1971. P. 114.

69. Cf. Pierre Ansart, *Idéologies, Conflits, et Pouvoir.* Paris: Presses Universitaires de France, 1977.

70. W. J. M. Mackenzie, *Power, Violence, Decision.* London: Penguin, 1975. Pp. 166–71.

71. Stephan L. Chorover, *From Genesis to Genocide.* Cambridge: MIT Press, 1979. P. 4.

72. Henri Tajfel, Interindividual behaviour and intergroup behaviour. In Henri Tajfel (ed.), *Differentiation between Social Groups.* London: Academic Press, 1978. Pp. 27–60.

73. Henri Tajfel, The achievement of group differentiation. In Tajfel (ed.), op. cit., pp. 77–98.

74. Cf. Terry Hoy, *Politics and Power.* New York: Putnam, 1968. Pp. viii–x. Thomas McPherson, *Political Obligation.* London: Routledge & Kegan Paul, 1967. P. 17.

75. Glenn Negley, *Political Authority and Moral Judgment.* Durham: Duke University Press, 1965. P. 74.

76. McPherson, op. cit., pp. 66–75.

77. Max Weber, *On Charisma and Institution Building* (selected by S. N. Eisenstadt). Chicago: University of Chicago Press, 1968. P. 46.

78. Ibid., pp. 51–54.

79. McPherson, op. cit., p. 32.

80. Matt. 5:21, 27, 31, 33, 38, 43.

81. Burkart Holzner, *Reality Construction in Society.* Cambridge, Mass.: Schenkman, 1968. Pp. 69–70.

82. Claus Mueller, *The Politics of Communication.* New York: Oxford University Press, 1973. Pp. 108, 129.

83. Leonard W. Doob, *Patriotism and Nationalism.* Westport: Greenwood, 1976. Chaps. 10, 11.

84. Cf. Bernard Weiner, A theory of motivation for some classroom experiences. *Journal of Educational Psychology,* 1979, 71, 3–25.

85. Julian B. Rotter, Generalized expectancies of internal versus external control of reinforcement. *Psychological Monograph,* 1966, 80, no. 1.

86. Herbert M. Lefcourt, *Locus of Control.* Hillsdale, N.J.: Erlbaum Associates, 1976.

87. Gunars Reimanis and Clive F. Posen, Locus of control and anomie in Western and African Cultures. *Journal of Social Psychology,* 1980, 112, 181–89.

88. Zoé V. A. Riordan, Locus of Control in South Africa. *Journal of Social Psychology,* 1981, 115, 159–68.

89. Northern Nigeria: seventy children aged twelve to thirteen, mostly Hausas. *Method:* questionnaire was given to the children, a rating scale to their teachers. *Results:* those with external self-beliefs tended to be considered more antisocial by their teachers and to be less proficient in mathematics and English than those with internal self-beliefs. *Comment:* Internal self-beliefs may have been accompanied by an increased sensitivity to the demands of the schools and a stronger motive to achieve; or the power motives of those with internal self-beliefs may have been stronger since they believed they could determine their own success, an interpretation supported by another study about to be described. Muhammad Maqsud, The relationship of sense of powerlessness to antisocial behavior and school achievement. *Journal of Psychology,* 1980, 105, 147–50.

90. Canada: 321 undergraduates. *Method:* in the laboratory, the somewhat puerile task of using scissors to cut out the outlines of eight common objects. *Results:* among

males but not among females, those with internal self-beliefs tended to find the exercise of power in performing the task more satisfactory than not being able to exercise it, and the reverse was true for those with external self-beliefs. Igor Hrycenko and Henry L. Minton, Internal-external control, power position, and satisfaction in task-oriented groups. *Journal of Personality and Social Psychology,* 1974, 30, 871–78.

91. Canada: 235 undergraduates. *Method:* two paper-and-pencil scales. *Results:* a slight tendency for the externally oriented to be more aggressive and hostile than the internally oriented. *Comment:* aggression and hostility frequently result from frustration. Christine Blanton Williams and Florence E. Vantress, Relation between internal-external control and aggression. *Journal of Psychology,* 1969, 71, 59–61.

92. U.S.A.: 744 undergraduates. *Method:* judgments concerning photographs of varying attractiveness. *Results:* external self-beliefs tended to be attributed more frequently to unattractive photographs than to moderately or very attractive ones. Male students considered such external self-beliefs to be more characteristic of females than males, a distinction not made by the female students. Arthur G. Miller, Social-perception of internal-external control, *Perceptual and Motor Skills,* 1970, 30, 103–9.

93. U.S.A.: sixty-three students. *Method:* a paper-and-pencil schedule filled out by the students whose attractiveness was being secretly rated by other students. *Results:* those judged moderately attractive by their contemporaries tended to believe themselves internally oriented to a greater degree than those rated very attractive or unattractive. Rosemary Anderson, Physical attractiveness and locus of control. *Journal of Social Psychology,* 1978, 105, 213–16.

94. Cf. John R. P. French, Jr. and Richard Snyder, Leadership and interpersonal power. In Dorwin Cartwright (ed.), *Studies in Social Power.* Ann Arbor: Research Center for Group Dynamics, 1959. Pp. 118–49.

95. Cf. Joseph S. Himes, *Conflict and Conflict Management.* Athens: University of Georgia Press, 1980. P. 14.

96. Adler, op. cit., pp. 70–75.

97. Henry L. Minton, Contemporary concepts of power and Adler's views. *Journal of Individual Psychology,* 1968, 24, 46–55.

98. A summary of then current investigations, most of which were conducted in laboratories and employed American college students as subjects, has been provided by Albert Bandura, Self-efficacy. *Psychological Review,* 1977, 84, 191–215.

99. Melvin Seeman, On the meaning of alienation. *American Sociological Review,* 1959, 24, 783–91.

100. David Kipnis, *The Powerholders.* Chicago: University of Chicago Press, 1976. P. 127.

101. William Ker Muir, Jr., *Police: Streetcorner Politicians.* Chicago: University of Chicago Press, 1977. P. 84.

102. Irving L. Janis et al., *Personality.* New York: Harcourt, Brace & World, 1969. Pp. 67–71.

103. Ibid., p. 353.

104. Frederick C. Redlich and Daniel X. Freedman, *The Theory and Practice of Psychiatry.* New York: Basic Books, 1966. P. 87.

105. Cf. Leonard W. Doob, *Pathways to People.* New Haven: Yale University Press, 1975. Pp. 169–71.

106. Hoyt Alverson, *Mind in the Heart of Darkness.* New Haven: Yale University Press, 1978.

107. Herbert Rosinski, *Power and Human Destiny*. New York: Praeger, 1965. Pp. 79–88.

108. Lewis Mumford, *The Pentagon of Power*. New York: Harcourt Brace Jovanovich, 1970. Pp. 43–44.

109. Ibid., p. 42.

110. Ibid., p. 332.

111. Ibid., p. 118.

112. Ibid., p. 29.

4

Personality: Attitudes and Skills

Motives and beliefs account for many aspects of behavior associated with power and authority. The insight they afford and their predictive values are increased, moreover, when their interaction with two additional components of personality—attitudes and skills—is also analyzed. To this challenging, semipleasant task we now turn.

1.C *Attitudes*. From beliefs to attitudes is no great leap: knowledge, convictions, and ideologies are seldom neutral or completely objective, but are linked to feelings and emotions. Just as participants have beliefs about persons, objects, and events, so they have attitudes toward the same referents. The attitudes range from positive to negative, from approval to disapproval, with neutral affect or feigned ignorance in between. A pecking order among human beings implies both beliefs about persons above and below in some hierarchy as well as attitudes of acclaim or disdain toward them. Unless an individual has a favorable attitude toward acquiring relevant knowledge, he may never have the skill to control nonhuman forces; and such knowledge is accompanied by a belief in its utility or validity.

1.C.1 The *scope* of attitudes may be specific or general, depending upon the number of persons or situations evoking similar feelings. A follower may like, respect, or feel obedient toward a particular leader and not toward others in the same or similar position: the attitude is specific. Or he may have almost identical feelings toward all persons in that position, belonging to a specific political party or organization, or having such-and-such characteristics: the attitude is general. Outstanding authorities in a society, such as rulers, often evoke general attitudes so that the dicta they communicate, even though outside the area of their competency, are considered valid and credible. The king, as it were, can do no wrong, a phenomenon psychologists were once prone to call a "halo effect." That effect is sometimes noticeable among Nobel Prize winners, a few of whom may not be loath to deliver judgments and to provide advice concerning subjects unrelated to their accomplishments. The competence of some authorities, notably politicians and clergymen, is so ill-defined that their opinions on a variety of themes are likely to have prestige. Young children lack skills and therefore usually have a generally favorable attitude toward their parents. As they mature, the attitude becomes less general and they discriminate among the commands they receive and the advice they are given—or at least we hope they do. General attitudes toward specific persons cloud over specific attributes which conceivably could arouse attitudes different from the general ones: there is a tendency to approve or disapprove generally of other persons—I love him, I hate her—and hence to ignore attributes not conforming to the overall pattern attributed to them.

Attitudes may cluster so that they become tinged with similar affect. Perhaps, maybe, possibly—according to one laudable, courageous attempt to summarize "recent studies" (mostly American of course)—a so-called democratic personality has attitudes toward himself which stress his own worth and dignity; toward others which stress the same attributes in them; toward authority which stress personal autonomy with some distrust for authorities with power; toward the community which stress openness, an acceptance of varying viewpoints, and a willingness to change and compromise; and toward a schema of values which stress many values rather than an exclusive goal as well as a tendency to share rather than to dominate others.[1] Such a democratic saint would have a degree of consistency few mortals ever hope or perhaps should wish to attain. The converse appears in another summary based mostly on paper-and-pencil responses: authoritarian traits in the West are said to include "dominance of subordinates; deference toward superiors; sensitivity to power relationships; [the] need to perceive the world in a highly structured fashion; excessive use of stereotypes; and adherence to whatever values are conventional in one's setting." A person with those predispositions tends to be aggressive toward his inferiors and to be submissive toward his superiors. His attitudes toward superiors are likely to be "highly ambivalent": he praises them and represses the hostility he feels.[2] In any case, most human beings have a tendency to generalize their feelings and, although they may frequently be in error and commit injustice (as with prejudices), they profit from experience. Perhaps one of the reasons why so many investigators have been able to employ so-called projective techniques, especially in their attempt to measure power, is that general attitudes can be tapped when participants compose stories on the basis of fuzzy drawings.

All attitudes, like the general or specific ones regarding foods, have a cultural component. Have you ever tasted gazelle, which is considered a delicacy in parts of Africa? It follows that attitudes must be learned, either as a result of a unique experience or a series of experiences that may be either direct or indirect. A direct experience is one in which contact between the individual and the referent is immediate and compelling. A whipped child develops anxiety, respect, or hostility toward the punishing authority, almost always a parent. Persons convicted of crimes and then fined or imprisoned are supposed to learn that crime does not pay and that they should conform to the authority of the state. An indirect experience is mediated verbally: the child is told, or nagged, again and again that he must obey specified adults and that these adults are authorities with power. Thus the communicators of attitudes are the usual influential authorities: parents, peers, teachers, and—at least in the West, and now virtually everywhere on this planet—the mass media.

The different attitudes toward the power of men and women in Western society provide a favored and valid illustration of a general attitude resulting largely from indirect indoctrination. This "birthright priority whereby males rule females," as a prominent forceful feminist asserts,[3] finds expressions almost wherever one has the temerity to look. American college students in an unstructured situation, being observed as they became acquainted with one another, tended "to fit the sex role demands of the situation"; in mixed groups, the women seldom asserted themselves or assumed positions of leadership.[4] Such a culturally determined attitude, moreover, may interact with other attitudes which in turn vary from person to person.[5]

1.C.2 Just as there is no invariant relation between beliefs and behavior, so a similar indetermination arises in connection with *attitudes and behavior*. An attitude, whether general or specific, must first become salient before it can be influential. Unless the person knows that the principal issuing an order is indeed a leader, his attitude toward authority will not be evoked. Generally, therefore, leaders are literally and figuratively clothed in the symbols of their position so that their authority can be recognized and accompanied by appropriate attitudes. Secondly, attitudes also vary in strength and certainty, and hence may or may not direct behavior. In a democratic society like the United States respondents are usually willing to cooperate with pollsters, or at least they once were before survey organizations began to make nuisances of themselves by conducting their business over the telephone. They have been known to express definite preferences for referents which do not exist or with which they have no acquaintance, such as a fictitious or little known piece of legislation being debated before the American Congress.[6] When suddenly confronted with an observer such as a pollster, therefore, individuals may be reluctant to say "don't know" or "no opinion," for fear they will make a bad impression upon that stranger. In an effort to determine the strength of individuals' convictions, consequently, a commercial organization has ingeniously designed a "mushiness index" to indicate the degree to which respondents actually subscribe to their attitudes. The criteria are largely behavioral in nature: whether or not the respondents feel "deeply involved," whether they believe they "need more information," whether they frequently discuss the issue with friends and family, and whether they believe they could change their minds on that issue.[7]

Guide: Attitudes affect behavior but seldom invariably.

1.C.3 Whereas self-belief refers to whether or not a participant believes he or others possess power, *self-power* suggests the attitude that person has toward possessing it: does he value or avoid power for himself? Another clue is thus provided to the strength of his various power motives. If his self-belief is internal, he may believe he can attain power, but he may or may not wish power for himself; if it is external, he may believe that attaining the power toward which he feels favorably or unfavorably disposed will depend not upon himself but upon circumstances beyond his control. Possibly an internal self-belief is more likely to be associated with a favorable attitude toward self-power than an external self-belief.

Children at an early age in Western society may be proud of the ways in which they obey their parents, but at adolescence they usually seek independence, they no longer wish to be automatically obedient. In our times, many persons have an unfavorable attitude toward being without power: it is shameful to be dependent, one must be free—and this vague abstraction is supposed to be validated by references to morality, occupation, and political participation.[8] Possibly the attitudes of Americans regarding self-power are related to experiences during socialization (or their memories of those experiences) as well as during their adulthood.[9] One writer advances the plausible if undocumented thesis that, when a person has continually and successfully influenced participants with less power, his conception of himself and others changes: he acquires a confident attitude regarding his own ability to hold and wield power.[10] In view of their statuses within the society, it is not surprising to discover that among both children and adults American males may attribute more power to themselves and value this attribute more than do females.[11]

The general attitude toward self-power tends to be strong and persistent because it can be positively or negatively reinforced by many different human contacts. Even in contemporary American utopian communities in which power is supposed to be exercised for the common good, according to one writer who has participated in such communities, some members continue to be possessed by "the envy of power." This envy, though in attenuated form, reflects a desire to be held in high repute, to use power "for its own sake," or to influence the direction in which a community is moving.[12]

Unquestionably some persons fear power for themselves: "the contemporary American style of power is to pretend that one has none."[13] If this is so, it would follow that the power motive may be strong in some Americans but that all, most, or some of them have a negative attitude regarding its possession. Maybe yes, maybe no. This possibility has been fairly widely discussed. An analyst of projective stories scores protocols as indicating a fear of power "if the power goal is for the benefit of some other person or cause, or if the person or story writer reacts to power with doubts, conflict, irony, or feelings of deception."[14] The reasons for such fear may be a lack of self-confidence: the individual believes he does not have the skill to be successful in achieving or retaining power. Religious zealots everywhere, perhaps all Christians at some time, are aware of the danger of power when they seek worldly riches and power over their fellow men, instead of submitting to the one power of significance, that of God. The way to escape from power is through humility,[15] as

Christ himself proclaimed: "he that humbleth himself shall be exalted."[16] Critics of a social system, whether Marxian or liberal, contend that the sense of powerlessness results not from a hostile attitude toward self-power as such but from hard reality: subordinates find themselves in situations they experience as overpowering within their society.

Guide: Favoring or fearing power has deep roots in the personality and the society.

1.C.4 *Obedience* stems from general and specific attitudes the participant feels toward powers and authorities both within and without his society. In the West the very word "authority" probably evokes a general attitude of respect or contempt.[17] Other symbols of authority also facilitate obedience. In this context reference must be made—and not in a footnote—to a deservedly well-known series of experiments. Naive American adults were told that the purpose of the exercise was to advance scientific knowledge by determining whether punishment by electric shock would facilitate learning and memory. They believed that they, rather than another person (the "learner" who was a confederate), had been chosen by lot to be the "teacher" who would administer a real electric shock whenever the "learner" failed to associate pairs of words correctly. In fact, no shock was administered but the bogus apparatus was designed so convincingly that the "teacher" believed he was administering real shocks. These subjects were requested by the experimenting scientist, whose authority was symbolized by his position in a laboratory and by his white coat, to continue to administer the "shocks" to the "learner" who feigned extreme pain especially when he pleaded to have the "experiment" halted so that he would no longer have to endure the "pain." Most of the "teachers" obeyed the experimenter, but about one-third did not.[18] In this fiendish situation, a general attitude toward authority was evoked among the majority by the laboratory, the white coat, and the request of the "scientist." That respect for authority held by the minority who disobeyed the command of the white coat must have been either nonexistent or weaker than a specific or general attitude of compassion for the "learner."

When the same technique was employed in Australia,[19] Germany,[20] Italy,[21] and Jordan,[22] it seems evident that the attitude toward the authority, the bogus scientist, interacted with other predispositions. First, an obscure cultural disposition was operating: although in all four studies over half of the so-called "teachers" obeyed, the percentage was highest of all in the German experiment—which perhaps illustrates the stereotype, true or false, of obedience being a strong trait among Germans. Then obedience fluctuated with the precise role of the "teachers": fewer of the Australian and the German students obeyed when they were to do the actual "shocking" than when they were asked to communicate the order to "shock" to a peer who was to administer the apparent punishment. In both roles fewer females than males in the Australian study were fully obedient. The precise instructions were also important: in the Jordanian experiment, which tested samples of children between the ages of about seven and fourteen, fewer of them administered the "shock" when they were told that shocking was optional than when they had been told to increase the "shock" every time the "learner" made a mistake; here no sex differences appeared, and age was unrelated to obedience. Being "cruel," moreover, required justification. In the Jordanian experiment those who had administered the "shocks" were asked later why they had done so: the predominant response of the boys was that such "punishment" was "beneficial for learning," whereas the girls tended to maintain only that they were obeying orders. It is not surprising that outside observers of this experimental technique have difficulty explaining what occurs. American college freshmen who watched a contrived exhibition of the same experiment tended to attribute the obedience to the situation rather than to the personality of the "teachers" only after they had been given an opportunity to think about what they had witnessed and to write down their impression for half an hour. Those who were questioned immediately afterwards and those who were distracted for a half hour before being questioned tended to point to the personality.[23]

Obedience requires that there be a generally favorable attitude toward whoever occupies the designated position in the hierarchy and, in most cases, that this principal or leader be respected. Such a general attitude may then be learned during socialization, as typified by most members of religious denominations. Or it may be acquired later as often happens with respect to organizations, political parties, and government itself. Probably whenever legitimacy is questioned, this general attitude interacts with another attitude which also may be general or specific.[24] Ordinarily, for example, legitimacy is accorded the police in line of duty, as when they direct traffic or make an arrest. But a particular policeman who is unruly, overbearing, or impolite may appear to be exercising his authority illegitimately: the civilian dislikes such behavior in general or especially in policemen.

Considerable stimulating speculation exists concerning the reasons for differences in attitude toward authority in various groups. Among traditional peoples assessment of authority is said to be "seldom necessary" since relations between principals and subordinates tend to be "so thoroughly regulated" by custom.[25] In addition it has been suggested, a trifle recklessly, that subordinates easily identify with their authorities and respect and obey them without hesitation or challenge. Their conscious expression is in effect, "I love the one I would like to be, and therefore I obey." In modern societies, the same author asserts, authorities are criticized; and the criticism is accompanied by a desire and the ability to select one's authorities—the essence of freedom, perhaps. The conscious component, if there is one, is transformed to "I would like to become like the one I admire and envy." Under these new conditions, the participants' level of aspiration shoots upward at the expense of "a great sense of personality anxiety," even though "their fulfillment" appeals to "the highest level of individual aspiration.''[26] According to a brilliant, opinionated humanist, such anxiety results from the fear that subordinates will be deceived by authorities. Simultaneously, however, while most participants would have their authorities possess legitimacy, some are also attracted to those who are not legitimate. Terrorists and some younger persons, he suggests, are in complete rebellion: they seek the ''freedom to disbelieve in authority.''[27] The sharpest expression of this attitude and its accompanying belief can be found in philosophical anarchism: All ''political authority is unjustifiable because by its very nature it involves some kind of evil—oppression, domestic and international war, and other human misery.''[28]

By means of catchy, easily intelligible labels one writer has designated four ''schools of thought'' concerning desirable attitudes toward authority. ''Authoritarians'' are favorably disposed to have national and international power concentrated in a single leader and to subsume under him a hierarchy of power. ''Moderates'' prefer a balance of power in which no single principal possesses all the power but in which an oligarchy remains in control. ''Radicals'' disparage both a concentration of power as well as an oligarchy and prefer to have power widely dispersed and shared. ''Revolutionaries,'' finally, approve of a concentration of national and international power provided they themselves possess that power.[29] These schools may be viewed as categories which call attention to the probability that attitudes toward authority are often part of a syndrome of other predispositions.

As must be repeatedly emphasized, almost everyone in a society accepts the proposition that legally constituted authorities should evoke favorable attitudes because controlling or prohibiting various actions presumably benefits the commonwealth. Even anarchists find certain criminal behavior, such as murder and burglary, intolerable. But there is a gray area where, a distinguished jurist has suggested, participants' general attitudes exclude from the authority of laws some actions evoking specific attitudes of disapproval. In England adultery is a case in point: most persons consider such behavior ''a grievious wrong,'' yet making it a criminal offense ''would attract little, if any, support.'' Similarly in spite of its association with cancer, ''the vast majority of reasonable people'' would consider it absurd to make cigarette smoking a crime.[30] Of course attitudes change; in the United States smoking in general is not prohibited, but smoking in designated public places has become a misdemeanor backed by the power of legal authorities.

Both within a given generation and over time, principals, together with the hierarchical positions they occupy, gradually acquire authority as a result of their actions. They arouse favorable attitudes because they dispense what is judged to be wisdom as well as rewards and punishment. They stabilize a society so that participants find it convenient and economical to comply rather than to dispute and spend time and effort making their own decisions. Not only Freudians but also other theorists and laymen alike recognize the possibility that in many instances leaders exercise authority when they are able to function as father substitutes for their followers.[31] Such a relation depends upon both participants: the skill of the leader to give the impression or to behave in such a way that he appears to be performing paternal functions; the needs of the followers which require that they find such a surrogate. Some institutions, such as the Roman Catholic Church when it refers to the Pope as the Holy Father, encourage this tendency. When an early Christian theologian wrote that, even as "the Bible has divine authority because God is its author, so also has the law of the state whose author is the Emperor,"[32] he was in effect suggesting that the favorable attitude toward each of these authorities should be transferred to the other.

It is thus clear that an agonizing Spiral Relation exists between the power of authorities enabling them to produce favorable attitudes among their followers and the followers' favorable attitudes bestowing legitimacy upon them. In a democratic society, for example, powers evoke respectful attitudes as a result of the position they occupy. But for various reasons ranging from their conduct of the economy to that of their own personal lives they may eventually evoke unfavorable attitudes. By voting one regime out of office, constituents' attitudes thus create new authorities. A survey of relevant surveys and experiments suggests that an individual's conception of justice, whether based on law, equity, equality, or the need of the other participant, is affected by his attitude toward that individual. In fact, his attitude may help determine whether he initially perceives an injustice and condemns it.[33] An authority who is not automatically obeyed may be that other person.

The means or tactics employed by authorities also evoke attitudes leading to various reactions that range from resistance, whether active or passive, to obedience, whether accompanied or not by ingratiation. These attitudes in turn are related to other predispositions. As suggested in a summary of the relevant research—American research of course, and usually undergraduates—those who approve or claim they employ Machiavellian tactics—as measured by the same paper-and-pencil scale to which frequent references have already been made—are likely to be persons who are "cool" (i.e., "not distracted by irrelevant affects"), who have "self-defined goals," who seek success, who tend to resist social influences, and who attack problems with "the logical ability" they possess. In contrast, those who do not approve of such tactics or who do not claim to use them are likely to be persons who are "open" (i.e., "susceptible to affective involvement"), suggestible, and sensitive to the cues provided by others.[34]

Attitudes toward authority and obedience, in short, have far-reaching implications for the participants and the society. According to a Jesuit priest who is also a psychiatrist: "All authority derives ultimately from God. But it exists only in intellectual beings. It involves man on the level of his distinctively human capacities—his freedom and intellect. . . . Rightfully understood . . . it is operative only where it is given free acceptance and recognition. It becomes something else when it becomes an exercise of power in violation of personal freedom. Authority in its authentic sense is not the exercise of power."[35] Such a conception of authority stresses its beneficial function: it is considered the "matrix within which values are communicated and reinforced"; it aims at "the proper good of the governed," it brings "unity into the action of the (religious) community," and it enables that community to achieve "the common good."[36]

Guide: Obedience, whether believed to be legitimate or not, requires appropriate attitudes.

1.C.5 For the same reason that nationalism has been schematically examined in a previous section, *patriotism,* its nonidentical twin, must be quickly surveyed. We live in an era of actual and threatening wars which perforce entail power: the motive of leaders to assert sovereignty or supremacy, that of subordinates to comply. Patriotism is ever present among human beings: they have a strong tendency to feel attached to their territory, their country. And patriotism consists of an inextricable combination of beliefs and attitudes.

The beliefs center around the conscious conviction that the individual's own welfare and that of the groups he considers significant depend upon the preservation or expansion, or both, of the power and culture of the region in which he lives or once lived.[37] The attitudes revolve around various positive and negative values, accompanying which are also beliefs. They are arbitrarily listed below and, in place of formal definitions, each is accompanied by a quotation, sometimes very slightly modified, from an essay written by South Tyrolean children in response to the question, "What do you like and what do you not like about your country [*Heimat*]?" This Germanic region in Northern Italy is actually Alpine in character.

1. Hedonistic: Old customs and traditions brings us a great deal of joy and love for our native land.
2. Aesthetic: The flowers and the bushes please me greatly because they are beautiful.
3. Moral-religious: What pleases me particularly above everything else is that we hold on to the correct religion.
4. Utilitarian: The forest brings me joy particularly because it protects us from winds and because it provides us with shade; it is also a savings bank in time of need.
5. Meaningful: My native land is so beautiful that I do not know what I should say, I do not know what does not please me about it.
6. Demanding: I also like the winter in my native land. . . . I know how to take full advantage of it; I go tobogganing the entire day.

7. Conventional: Our country is defaced by the advertising posters on many barn doors and barns.
8. Prestigeful: Our country is one of the most fertile regions. We can be very proud of the fact that we produced one of the most famous painters, Michael Pacher.
9. Interpersonal: My neighbors . . . often play with me; we get along very well.
10. Powerful: What does not please me are the malicious people who oppress our native land.[38]

This list, together with that of the beliefs given in the previous chapter represent the orchestra of patriotism and, to a certain extent, nationalism. Some combination is essential if the individual is to have a favorable attitude toward his country. With such attitudes and beliefs the authority of the state is recognized, willingly so, and the power of leaders is cheerfully acknowledged, provided it does not impinge unfavorably upon the individual's personal existence. The greatest impingement, however, occurs in time of war and then the patriot allegedly gives the one life he has to his country, or he exposes or is forced to expose himself to that possibility.

And now the fourth and final personality variable:

Skills. The prerequisites for achieving or retaining power and au-
1.D thority are double-edged: the motives, beliefs, and attitudes of
principals must somehow be complementary so that the principals seek a top position in a hierarchy and the subordinates accept or tolerate a lower one. To mesh these two requires skill. In addition, potential leaders may also depend upon supporters whose loyalty must be skillfully cultivated.[39]

Positions of power may be inherited, as in monarchies or their equivalent according to established principles of descent, or as in families with wealth or property in accordance with customs or legal codes. The heirs become the acknowledged possessors of power and, even before they acquire their inheritance, are trained so that they can eventually discharge their responsibilities with skill. In a broad sense every individual in any society is born into a position of relative power or powerlessness since societies, as stressed in Chapter 2, are always structured and since the status accruing to the members of each stratum affects the skill he eventually learns and the influence he is able to exercise.[40] Whether or not slaves in a highly stratified society with long-standing traditions of servitude will or can remain forever obedient without a display of force by their master is a moot question; yet it is clear that masters must be sufficiently skillful to impress subordinates with their ability to punish and reward. Similarly a participant may be highly motivated to attain power, his potential followers may believe that the time is ripe for a new leader, and he himself may be self-confident. Even so, he may fail to achieve his objective because he lacks the necessary skill; or, as it were, potential subordinates may be deficient in some complementary respect. The search here is for attributes associated with the skills of participants as they interact.

Every principal *toward the top*, and especially every great leader,
1.D.1 is more or less unique which, as previously stated in Chapter 2, adds to the difficulties of promoting leadership. A good policeman, one study reveals, must have an ability that is not necessarily part of the repertoire of other authorities: he must strive to "resolve the contradiction of achieving just ends with coercive means."[41] Leadership has a large number of components, including intelligence, plasticity, experience, and some unknowable traits, all of which contribute to the desirable skill. The importance of each component varies with the individual and the situation. There is no way of knowing whether De Gaulle's above-average height contributed to the authority he exercised because it made him seem impressive and powerful; or whether Napoleon's below-average height spurred him to achieve a position of leadership in a faction-ridden France.

Particular positions require *specialized skills*. To wield power or
1.D.1.a display authority in any kind of enterprise—business, education, government—concrete competencies are necessary such as the knowledge of a foreign language, computers, or administration, all the products of previous experience. For some positions it is extremely risky even to try to outline the skills for prospective candidates or to assess them on the basis of those possessed by successful persons in the past. Possibly, for example, mediators and intervenors in international disputes should be blessed with certain demographic attributes, a high motivation to succeed, a knowledge of available techniques, and self-confidence. Perhaps also other skills are useful, such as patience, flexibility, sympathy or empathy, intelligence, tact, administrative know-how, ability to diagnose difficulties, and a sense of timing.[42] Listing such attributes is relatively easy in comparison with the task of locating persons with a most propitious mix to function effectively in a particular conflict. Engineers are supposed to possess the relevant knowledge and hence presumably the necessary skill to control the power potentially present in natural forces. Sometimes, however, that skill is not quite adequate, as accidents in nuclear power plants suggest. Similar skills are those of farmers and animal trainers or owners who thus directly or indirectly demonstrate their power over nonhuman forces.

Not exactly a skill but often as essential as a skill is the *appear-*
1.D.1.b *ance* of the participant. What is considered attractive or unattractive may be loaded with cultural components, but principals so judged have an advantage: they are admired and may be thought to possess the skill associated with leadership.[43] Related to appearance, realistically or according to popular stereotypes in the West, may be the attributes of energy: strong-looking, healthy persons are thought to be energetic. These characteristics affect overall attractiveness which, as might be expected, may perhaps contribute to the power he is able to exercise.[44]

Certainly *intelligence* is an essential skill of effective leaders. But
1.D.1.c what, it is fair to ask, is intelligence? After decades of research and millions of measurements with standardized tests there is no

easy or unanimous answer to this question, other than to repeat that intelligence is what the intelligence tests test; or it is the ability to learn quickly and effectively; or it refers to the capability to perceive the essential, to throw information into abstract categories, and thereafter appropriately to utilize past experience. Probably there is an innate component which varies from person to person but not very likely from group to group.[45] A word of caution: the ingenuity and creativity exhibited by some principals reflect not only intelligence but also experience or acquired expertise.

1.D.1.d *Age* is an obvious and virtually universal attribute of power and authority. All societies have a method of age grading so that prestige is associated with maturity. Rites de passage occur at a more or less specified age, before which obedience to the authority of parents is the general rule and after which the young assume various responsibilities and come to possess specified privileges. Wisdom is usually believed to increase with age, probably because experience is gained, so that eligibility to occupy significant positions in hierarchies is possible only at designated ages. Prodigies, when permitted to exercise power, evoke admiration and suspicion. Eventually seniority is a handicap: in fact or in the imagination of followers, older persons cannot function with sufficient resilience. In Western societies mandatory retirement from most occupations is the rule, which means that professionals and workers lose whatever prestige they formerly had within those occupations and also from their younger contemporaries. In the United States the problems facing aging minorities are especially acute since they are in "double jeopardy": their status tends to be subordinate because they have grown old and also because they belong to an ethnic group against which prejudices are directed.[46] In addition, attitudes toward power may change with age. As they grow older participants may reach out to seize power because there is little time left, or they may become resigned to the need to disengage themselves from their society. Among predominately white, middle-class students in California, a decrease in the incidence of "authoritarian" attitudes has been found to be associated with increasing age,[47] even within such a narrow age range, presumably as a result of wider experiences in the milieu. After death the name of the deceased may be evoked symbolically in behalf of principals claiming authority or power; in some societies it is believed that the dead continue to be influential not through symbols or memory but through actual intervention.

1.D.1.e Related imperfectly to age may be *education* which signifies a degree of expertise and which may also have symbolic value in its own right.[48] It was once claimed that about one-half of very rich Americans, those therefore with economic power, had attended Ivy-League colleges.[49] If so, then studying at such allegedly glamorous educational institutions may have resulted in effective training for the positions these persons were to occupy. Or they may have been thus assisted to attain their positions as a result not of expertise per se but of the provenance of their diplomas and of the formal and informal contacts they established as undergraduates which subsequently enabled them to gain admittance more easily to the houses of power.

Again and again *expertise* is singled out as the attribute most
1.D.1.f likely to be respected:[50] the utilization of detailed knowledge to solve whatever problems arise in connection with the functioning of a system. A significant component of expertise is insight into the subordinates to be influenced. A skillful principal has a working, practical psychology enabling him to comprehend sufficiently the motives and attitudes of subordinates as well as the way in which groups and associations in the society function. In the West fluency, including the ability to be glib and yet sound convincing, as well as a sense of humor may be impressive symbols of expertise; in one study of twelve finance boards of different Connecticut communities the active chairmen tended to have such fluency and also to be self-confident, both characteristics which "high education, conversational experience, and occupational achievement engender."[51] In some West African societies the ability to cite appropriate proverbs brings acclaim in ordinary conversation and even success in court disputes.

Skill is needed to acquire and allocate *resources*.[52] The success-
1.D.1.g ful exercise of power depends upon the sanctions at the principal's disposal; he must have the capability of "providing or withholding gratification" from subordinates.[53] Officers of a labor union, for example, may seek their objective by threatening a costly strike which in practice will be effective only if they have a war chest sufficiently large to support their members during the walkout. But some leaders use similar threats and war chests more skillfully than others.[54] As ever the unique or surprising circumstance appears. On the basis of interviews obtained from a sample of American wives, for example, it appears that the husband's annual income was significantly related to whether he or his wife wielded power in the family: if the wage was above the mean, he tended to be dominant in making certain decisions concerning the family (such as purchasing life insurance, selecting a house or apartment, allocating the budget, planning vacations); but, if it was below that mean, she tended to dominate.[55]

Often only the skillful are able to command the goods and services which wealth unmiraculously bestows in the Western orbit. An empirical challenge is whether persons in a particular income bracket also affect the ways in which power is allocated within the social and political system in order to preserve or enhance their own power. Do they exert pressure upon political leaders; do they seek special tax privileges for themselves? The possession of wealth is no guarantee that the power will be exercised.

Patronage is the term frequently employed in the American language to refer to the skill or expert utilization of resources to retain power. In government, at least in democratic countries, political plums are the reward of loyal support during an election campaign: the less powerful persons thus secure the promised remunerative positions or contract if they help bring a patron into power and then later, after being sufficiently rewarded, they feel gratefully obliged to keep him there. In turn, the principal's own reputation is thereby increased when it becomes known that he has these rewards at his disposal.[56] Similarly, managers and not the stockholders usually control the jobs to be allocated, and bankers have jurisdiction over credit and mortgages.[57] On a dangerous level, the skill of government leaders in their relations with their counterparts in other countries may depend upon their diplomatic guile, the material resources under their control, and—alas and alack—their armed forces.[58]

1.D.1.h Often it is not the actual skills of the participants but the *ascribed skills* that give them authority or power. The basis for the ascription may be other attributes, personal or demographic. Here beliefs function: persons with red hair may be thought to be short-tempered and hence not qualified to make delicate decisions. Principals in or out of government are considered to possess or lack power or authority only because of the positions they do or do not occupy: he is a leader and therefore he must have the requisite expertise. In multiracial societies it assumed that participants do or do not possess the skills or competences associated with their membership in particular groups. Colonialists and others, such as the European rulers of South Africa, proclaim that members of the subordinated group lack the skills required for them to assume positions of power and therefore it is necessary to keep them subordinated. A twist of a self-fulfilling prophecy may be operating: the subordinates undoubtedly possess the potentiality of being as competent as the principals, but the belief that they are less competent relegates them to their subordinated position so that they are unable to acquire the desired skills. Or they may possess those skills but not be given an opportunity to exercise them.

1.D.1.i A vague but intriguing attribute associated with the skills of participants, perhaps summarizing their attraction in a cliché, is that of *charisma*, an elusive halo around "great" leaders. The concept is seldom objectively defined, but its presence or absence, as indicated previously, provides one of the rationales for submitting to authority. Without being able to isolate this attribute one can guess that some of its components are charm, physical appearance, self-confidence, apparent sincerity, and perhaps an ability to make significant decisions and execute them with maximum speed.[59] Possibly in stable societies leaders possess "solidity and sound judgments" to retain their hierarchical positions, whereas during periods of crises or strain they must exhibit such an unusual flair as charisma.[60] In any case power or authority is enhanced when the principal has the skill enabling him to win the support of his peers and the groups to which he belongs or to which he refers his behavior.

Guide: The combination of necessary or desirable skills of effective leaders is too complex and often too unique to be specified generally.

1.D.2 One bit of wisdom adequately summarizes an answer to the problem of viewing those *from the bottom:* "Want of science, that is, ignorance of causes, disposeth, or rather constraineth a man to rely on the advice, and authority of others."[61] Whenever information is needed, truly needed, the principal and not the subordinate *may* have superior knowledge. The word "may" is underscored since in some situations the subordinate may know more than the principal, yet he skillfully suppresses his superiority in order to ingratiate himself or to avoid punishment resulting from a display of arrogance or from appearing disobedient: Do not contradict a superior even if you know better—or think you do.

Some but not all leaders, therefore, require instant, unquestioning obedience for reasons associated with themselves or the task at hand. An insecure dictator—and has there ever been a dictator who has not endured or suffered some kind of insecurity?—constantly needs reassurance that he is the authority and that he has adequate power: the obedience of subordinates supplies him with fleeting proof. In the face of enemy fire, the commanding officer at hand must make the decision and be obeyed: there is no time to hold a council of war. Leaders in other situations seek not disobedience but counsel from their subordinates. In a free-for-all or somewhat free discussion they hope to obtain guidance or new ideas, although the final decision may be theirs.

Good subordinates from the vantage point of leaders recognize the legitimacy of authorities and are favorably disposed toward them, inwardly if possible, but at least outwardly;[62] and they possess the necessary skills to function in subordinate roles. A somewhat extreme illustration can be given: for a variety of reasons, the early American colonists selected blacks as slaves rather than native Indians or indentured servants. After being brought over from Africa, the Africans had no resources on which they could depend and hence could not resist being enslaved. They could be considered inferior on the basis of skin color and, with an ethnocentric twist, of the African cultures from which they had come. Most important, they had a background of agriculture, the very occupation for which the colonists required labor.[63] They were eminently qualified, in the eyes of the plantation owners, to be slaves.

Those at the top may force skills upon those at the bottom. Competence tests may be required in order to vote: the individual must own a certain amount of property, he must be literate, his skin color must be white. In the United States immigration quotas were once partially established on the basis of the average intelligence thought to be forever associated with ethnic groups. Residence is always a criterion for obtaining citizenship. Some of these attributes, particularly skin color and residence, are not directly a function of skill, rather desirable or undesirable skills are believed to be associated with them. Or at least so the rationalizations state.

Principals, no matter how harsh or gentle their behavior toward subordinates, may unintentionally serve as models. The slave who realizes he may never be free or, if that is possible, who may not wish freedom learns how his master behaves toward him: within his own hierarchy he may adopt similar techniques to command his subordinates, perhaps his wife, children, or neighbors. Sometimes, moreover, principals are "forced by the situation in which they find themselves to pass on some of their skills" to subordinates.[64] The master craftsman deliberately teaches apprentices what they need to know to carry on the craft. Everywhere colonial governors once favored Western-style education for some of the native inhabitants who then could discharge a limited number of the duties associated with government; or they were motivated by a Western or religious tradition favoring "civilization" or "God's word" for all mankind, sometimes even by a desire to prepare their peoples eventually for self-government. The better or the highly educated thus acquired Western skills which they eventually employed to liberate themselves from the ruling European powers and to govern their own peoples after the departure of the "foreigners."

The skills needed to accept or seem to accept a subservient position are diverse. A participant whose self-confidence or self-power is weak may find it easier to give the impression of wishing to cooperate with a principal: at least on a conscious level he genuinely wishes to fulfill the assigned role. The prototype here is not necessarily the individual whose skills spring from masochism but one who, because he genuinely enjoys lack of responsibility, responds sensitively to the commands, wishes, or the very presence of designated authorities. The unwilling subordinate who would throw off his chains but who knows he cannot do so may be able to develop skills which conceal his discontent. Such skills require some kind of communication that somehow conveys satisfaction or at least neutrality and not dissatisfaction. He displays a poker face rather than anger or dismay. He executes orders faithfully and to the letter. He may try to ingratiate himself with the principal. These subservient skills are acquired more easily in societies where statuses are fixed, the most extreme forms of which contain slaves and castes. Probably, too, in any society tyrannical parents produce timid children who learn to survive under such conditions, and who then later on either are loath to change their hierarchical positions or else burst out in rebellion.

> *Guide:* The combination of necessary or desirable skills of subordinates results from an interaction between their predispositions and the actions of leaders.

* * * *

As this analysis of the predispositions of personality ends, it is well once again to consult the Guiding Figure that indicates the parameters of power and authority. Those predispositions may be the starting and the end point as far as the individual is concerned, but they are always predispositions in a social context. Personality by itself does not provide the magic key to unlock institutions and social action; indeed "personality structures," it has been asserted,[65] do not "necessarily predict" political beliefs or individual political actions. Personality, however, can never be dismissed, since persons always play a role in authority and power. And so it is time, perhaps high time, to consider what occurs next as individuals participate in and are affected by events.

NOTES

1. Robert A. Dahl, *Modern Political Analysis*, 3d ed. Englewood Cliffs: Prentice-Hall, 1976. P. 120.

2. Fred I. Greenstein, *Personality and Politics*. New York: Norton, 1975. Pp. 103–10.

3. Kate Millett, *Sexual Politics*. Garden City: Doubleday, 1969. P. 25.

4. Elizabeth Aries, Interaction patterns and themes of males, females, and mixed groups. *Small Group Behavior*, 1976, 7, 7–18.

5. U.S.A.: eighty adults from "all walks of life." *Method:* interviews analyzed on the basis of categories derived from Thematic Apperception Test protocols previously administered to other respondents. *Results* (expressed only qualitatively): those displaying high general prejudice tended to view the opposite sex with a "power orientation" and appeared to favor exploiting and manipulating them; those low in prejudice sought a loving relationship tinged with warmth and affection. Such tendencies appeared, it is reported, in both men and women. Else Frenkel-Brunswick, Dynamic and cognitive categorization of qualitative material. *Journal of Psychology*, 1948, 25, 253–77.

6. Howard Schuman and Stanley Presser, *Questions and Answers in Attitude Surveys*. New York: Academic Press, 1981. Pp. 147–60.

7. Editors, An editors' report on the Yankelovich, Skelly, and White "Mushiness Index." *Public Opinion*, 1981, April/May, 50–51.

8. Richard Sennett, *Authority*. New York: Knopf, 1980. Pp. 47–48.

9. U.S.A.: 483 white-collar and managerial employees in twenty-six hotels located in the northeastern part of the country, about two-thirds male, with an age distribution ranging from eighteen to over fifty. *Method:* various paper-and-pencil questionnaires, including twelve items from the so-called Machiavellian Scale which sought to measure self-power. *Results:* by and large, in comparison with those scoring low on the scale, those scoring high tended to recall or believe that their rapport with their parents and teachers had been less than satisfactory, to report that they were more outwardly aggressive toward others, to claim that they did not value social approval as highly, and to seem to have less of an inclination to develop "close friendships." These scores, moreover, were closely related to scores the respondents believed their parents would obtain or would have obtained; and they were affected, apparently, by the ambience of the hotels in which the individuals worked, especially by management. Stanley S. Guterman, *The Machiavellians*. Lincoln: University of Nebraska Press, 1970.

10. David Kipnis, *The Powerholders*. Chicago: University of Chicago Press, 1976. Pp. 169–79.

11. David C. McClelland and Robert I. Watson, Jr., Power motivation and risk-taking behavior. *Journal of Personality*, 1973, 41, 121–39.

12. Kathleen Kinkade, Power and the utopian assumption. *Journal of Applied Behavioral Science*, 1974, 10, 402–14.

13. Michael Korda, *Power!* New York: Random House, 1975. P. 6.

14. David G. Winter, *The Power Motive*. New York: Free Press, 1973. P. 143.

15. Romano Guardini, *Die Macht*. Würzburg: Werkbund-Verlag, 1951, Pp. 31–42.

16. Luke 18:14.

17. U.S.A.: over 4,000 children, grades 8–12, in three midwestern communities. *Method:* three questionnaires, one of which sought to measure "respect for authority" by having respondents agree or disagree with six statements (e.g., "People should show

more respect for authority," "Obedience and respect for authority should be the very first requirement of a good citizen"). *Results:* the statements received almost unanimous approval; such approval showed a very slight but not a statistically significant tendency to decrease with age and to be slightly lower in a predominately middle-class than in a mixed or lower-class community. *Comment:* even on this purely verbal level, the attitude toward authority was related to other verbal reports by the children: slightly negatively to their reported use of drugs, drinking, smoking, and heterosexual relations; more impressively and positively to their professed beliefs concerning orthodox religion. Karoly Varga, nAchievement, nPower, and effectiveness of research and development. *Human Relations,* 1975, 28, 571–90.

18. Stanley Milgram, *Obedience to Authority.* New York: Harper & Row, 1974. Pp. 2–6.

19. Wesley Kilham and Leon Mann, Level of destructive obedience as a function of transmitter and executant roles in the Milgram obedience paradigm. *Journal of Personality and Social Psychology,* 1974, 29, 696–702.

20. David Mark Mantell, The potential for violence in Germany. *Journal of Social Issues,* 1971, 27, no. 4, 101–12.

21. Cited by Milgram, op. cit., p. 210, note 24.

22. Mitri Shanab and Khawla A. Yahya, A behavioral study of obedience in children. *Journal of Personality and Social Psychology,* 1977, 35, 530–36.

23. Günter Bierbrauer, Why did he do it? *European Journal of Social Psychology,* 1979, 9, 67–84.

24. U.S.A.: 555 children, grades 1, 3, and 6. *Method:* a questionnaire pertaining to what their teacher could do and what they liked about her. *Results:* beliefs concerning what teachers could do were not related to age, but the children's liking for their teachers tended to be less among the older than among the younger pupils; in addition, girls tended to accord more authority to the teachers and to like them more than boys did, and those with an average IQ tended to be more favorably disposed toward their teachers than those with IQs at either extreme. Ann M. Dunbar and Beverly W. Taylor. Children's perception of elementary teachers as authority figures. *Journal of Social Psychology,* 1982, 118, 249–55.

25. William H. Riker, The nature of trust. In James T. Tedeschi (ed.), *Perspectives on Social Power.* Chicago: Aldine, 1974. Pp. 63–81.

26. Fred Weinstein and Gerald M. Platt, *The Wish to Be Free.* Berkeley: University of California Press, 1969. Pp. 197–99.

27. Sennett, op. cit., especially pp. 15, 17, 28, 119, 191.

28. Fred J. Abbate, *A Preface to the Philosophy of State.* Belmont: Wadsworth, 1977. P. 87.

29. Hans F. Petersson, *Power and International Order.* Lund: G. W. K. Gleerup, 1964. Pp. 27–28.

30. Lord Stow Hill, The law. In Clifford Rhodes (ed.), *Authority in a Changing Society.* London: Constable, 1969. Pp. 98–138.

31. Cf. Cecil A. Gibb, Leadership. In Gardner Lindzey (ed.), *Handbook of Social Psychology.* Cambridge: Addison-Wesley, 1954. Pp. 877–920.

32. Theodor Eschenburg, *Über Autorität.* Frankfurt: Suhrkamp Verlag, 1965. P. 35.

33. Melvin Lerner, Social psychology of justice and interpersonal attraction. In Ted L. Huston (ed.), *Foundations of Interpersonal Attraction.* New York: Academic Press, 1974. Pp. 331–51.

34. Richard Christie and Florence L. Geis, Implications and speculations. In Christie and Geis (eds.), *Studies in Machiavellianism.* New York: Academic Press, 1970. Pp. 339–58.

35. William W. Meissner, *The Assault on Authority.* Maryknoll: Orbis Books, 1971. P. 8.

36. Ibid., pp. 21–26, 67.

37. Leonard W. Doob, *Patriotism and Nationalism,* Westport: Greenwood, 1976. P. 6.

38. Ibid., pp. 95–102.

39. Cf. Robbins Burling, *The Passage of Power.* New York: Academic Press, 1974. P. 14.

40. H. Andrew Michener and Martha R. Burt, Legitimacy as a base of social influence. In Tedeschi (ed.), op. cit., pp. 310–48.

41. William Ker Muir, Jr., *Police: Streetcorner Politicians.* Chicago: University of Chicago Press, 1977. Pp. 3–4.

42. Cf. Leonard W. Doob, *The Pursuit of Peace.* Westport: Greenwood, 1981. Pp. 262–67.

43. Cf. Ronald Sampson, *The Psychology of Power.* New York: Random House, 1966. P. 230.

44. Barry E. Collins and Harold Guitzkow, *A Social Psychology of Group Processes for Decision-Making.* New York: Wiley, 1964. Pp. 128–30.

45. Stephen Jay Gould, *The Mismeasure of Man.* New York: Norton, 1981. Pp. 146–320.

46. Ron C. Manuel (ed.), *Minority Aging.* Westport: Greenwood, 1982.

47. U.S.A.: 517 students in grades 9, 11, and 12. *Method:* two ''presumably parallel'' questionnaires consisting of forty-one agree-disagree items pertaining to a wide variety of attitudes. *Results:* significantly but slightly more of the older adolescents than the younger ones tended to be somewhat less ''authoritarian'' in expressing their political and economic attitudes; they also revealed a ''greater understanding of the complexity of human motivation'' and were more favorably inclined toward current political and social changes facilitating greater economic equality in American society. *Comment:* the authors speculate that more of the older students had been able to free themselves from concrete, egocentric modes of thinking, had ''a broader range of social experiences,'' and had had greater access to more information than their slightly younger peers. Paul Mussen, Lawrence B. Sullivan, and Nancy Eisenberg-Berg, Changes in political-economic attitudes during adolescence. *Journal of Genetic Psychology,* 1977, 130, 69–76.

48. Cf. Frank A. Heller et al., A longitudinal study in participative decision-making. *Human Relations,* 1977, 30, 567–87.

49. C. Wright Mills, *The Power Elite.* New York: Oxford University Press, 1956. Pp. 106–7.

50. E.g., Ralph B. Kimbrough, *Political Power and Educational Decision-Making.* Chicago: Rand McNally, 1964. P. 277.

51. James David Barber, *Power in Committees.* Chicago: Rand McNally, 1966. P. 86.

52. Theoretical systems or models have been designed to deal with the problem of who allocates what under which circumstances. Aside from appealing to an Arbitrary Limitation, I am convinced that the variables thereunder are implicit in the present

analysis; therefore I beg off considering them in their own right. See Gerold Mikula, On the role of justice in allocation decisions. In Gerold Mikula (ed.), *Justice and Social Interaction*. New York: Springer-Verlag, 1980. Pp. 127–66.

53. Sanford M. Dornbusch and W. Richard Scott, *Evaluation and the Exercise of Authority*. San Francisco: Jossey-Bass, 1975. P. 34. Cf. Collins and Guitzkow, op. cit., pp. 123–25, 133–35.

54. Cf. Dahl, op. cit., pp. 117–18.

55. George Levinger, The development of perceptions and behavior in newly formed social power relationships. In Dorwin Cartwright (ed.), *Studies in Social Power*. Ann Arbor: Research Center for Group Dynamics, 1959. Pp. 83–98.

56. Cf. Malcolm T. Walker, *Politics and the Power Structure*. New York: Teachers College Press, 1972. P. 65.

57. Cf. Dorwin Cartwright, Influence, leadership, control. In James G. March (ed.), *Handbook of Organizations*. Chicago: Rand McNally, 1965. Pp. 1–47.

58. Cf. Petersson, op. cit., pp. 25–26.

59. Cf. Robert Michels, *Political Parties*. Glencoe: Free Press, 1949. P. 72.

60. Cf. Bertrand Russell, *Power*. New York: Norton, 1938. P. 46.

61. Thomas Hobbes, *Leviathan* (1651). New York: Dutton, 1950. P. 83.

62. Cf. Gene W. Dalton, Louis B. Barnes, and Abraham Zaleznik, *The Distribution of Authority in Formal Organizations*. Boston: Harvard University Press, 1968. P. 148.

63. William J. Wilson, *Power, Racism, and Privilege*. New York: Macmillan, 1973. Pp. 73–76.

64. Philip Mason, *Patterns of Dominance*. London: Oxford University Press, 1970. P. 26.

65. Greenstein, op. cit., pp. 123–27.

5

Events

The preliminaries have been tucked away: both the observer and the individual participants are presumed to have had a variety of experiences in the past which constitute the critical background, respectively, for understanding and judging what may or may not transpire. Then something happens in the objective world: an event is perceived by or communicated to one or more participants. Psychologists refer to an event as a stimulus, some change in the external environment produced by someone or something that is likely to be perceived by an individual. Of course no event connected with power and authority is ever a simple stimulus the way a sudden pressure elicits the reflex of a knee jerk or a beam of light an eye blink. The concept of stimulus, however, suggests an essential feature of events: they are of no real or psychological significance unless or until they are perceived by a human being. The proverbial tree falling in the silent forest is not a stimulus or an event until someone hears the sound, moves away before being hit, or saws the trunk and the branches into firewood.

In actuality and not as a philosopher's puzzle, that tree, whether it has been felled by an ax, struck by lightning, or attacked by age or termites, illustrates one of the three kinds of stimuli or events to be conveniently separated, that of force. As previously indicated, the power of a force, unless it is utterly out of human control like a sudden tidal wave, is likely to be partially guided by human subordinates: with advance warning, inhabitants evacuate the threatened coast and thus the wave's power, as it were, is blunted. Individuals for better or worse exercise power over forces when they fertilize or erode the soil on which their crops are grown. Dogs and cats have been domesticated over the ages so that, unless they are vicious, beaten, or antisocial, they usually obey their masters. Forces affect persons and vice versa.

The second kind of event stems from persons. The problem both for the observer and for the participant is to locate the persons who in fact elicit or constitute the event. The assailant who would assassinate a pope, a president, a policeman, or any potential victim is the conspicuous stimulus, but there may lurk behind him—and hence behind the event itself—others who have some responsibility for his actions. They may have immediately collaborated by supplying ideas or the gun, or as parents, peers, employers, or officials they may have contributed to his antisocial development.

The remaining kind of event is a communication through which the stimulus of the force or the person reaches the participant. The communication may be simple and direct, as when the individual experiences a hurricane through all his five senses. Or it may be indirect: he reads about the storm in a newspaper or sees it via television. The communication may affect and be affected by persons. A force, however, affects only the communication; the reverse occurs when persons interact.

The tripartite division of events is necessarily pitched on a highly abstract level and does not indicate the precise nature of events. A catalogue of concrete events concerning power and authority is utterly impossible since every occurrence conceivably can give rise to the experience of power or authority or the resistance thereto: all that is required is that the stimuli affect one or more participants or forces. Will pedestrians conclude from distant thunder that a storm is approaching? An observer knows they are powerless to affect this event; will they, then, ignore the threat or take cover? How will confident persons express themselves in a situation of love, war, or tennis? And how is an observer to know whether they are really confident or compensating for feelings of insecurity?

II.A *Dissection.* To render events intelligible or somewhat intelligible a dissection of their critical contents, the anticipation of their occurrence, and an estimate of their salience are essential. As historians constantly emphasize and thus demonstrate the need to utilize their craft, it is particularly difficult to dissect past events. Documents may be nonexistent or scanty and forever subject to varying interpretations. Similar problems arise when life histories are employed to try to gain insight into the events of crucial importance to the individual. The recapitulation of a person's background is necessarily "reported within a theoretical framework" of the participant and the observer, and it may be further distorted by the situation in which those events are recalled.[1] In addition to being valid, an acceptable dissection must adhere to the usual methodological criteria of reliability and objectivity previously mentioned.

II.A.1 In the spirit and with the methods of an academic pursuit known as *content analysis,* an observer can analyze events in their own right as though they were detached from human beings.[2] A system of categories is selected whose objectivity is tested by determining whether different analysts similarly categorize the event or sections; the system is applied to those sections especially when they change over time. The simplest illustration of the method is its application to that of a written communication, such as the editorials appearing in a newspaper during a specified period. Objective categories are usually fairly primitive, such as the number of references to the United States or the Soviet Union. The categories become less objective but more meaningful when additional details concerning the content are specified: the references to either country are classified as favorable or unfavorable. Further complications categorizing the nature of the favorable or unfavorable content increase the meaningfulness of the analysis, but are likely to reduce its objectivity.

While it is true that events can be analyzed in their own right, it is always more useful to make a simple assumption in selecting categories: when those events are perceived and affect participants, their effects will be such-and-such. In utilizing affective categories, the presumption is that the potential audience will categorize the event as favorable or unfavorable just as the analyst or the observer does. Undoubtedly, other matters being equal, the account of an event in a newspaper is more likely to be seen by more readers when it is accompanied by a screaming headline and when it appears on a front page than when it is buried inconspicuously on a back page; it may be anticipated, therefore, that the power of the flaming layout will be greater than that of the less attention-getting one. Of Gandhi it was once said: "Surely his method of non-cooperation was a use of power, the only power he and his followers had: the non-payment of taxes, the boycotting of English merchandise, refusal of honours and titles of civil and military posts, refusal to attend schools, etc."[3] Gandhi's tactics are thus listed and categorized as events without indicating whether at the time they effectively influenced the British. Such information is valuable in its own right when power tactics are to be evaluated, yet an analysis beyond content requires insight into the judgment of the British and their consequent decisions and actions.

A typology has been proposed which would classify communications themselves with respect to power. Two main categories have been distinguished: the "message type" (a promise or a threat) and the "explicitness of the message" (with a request that may be specific or nonspecific, and with consequences that likewise can be specific or nonspecific).[4] There are thus eight possible combinations: 2 types × 2 requests × 2 consequences = 8. A communicator or an observer may select one of the eight, but he has no way of being able to forecast with complete certainty how a group of participants will in fact react to the communication. What he believes to be a promise they may interpret as a threat, a request he believes to be specific they may consider nonspecific. His intuition may or may not be correct. A better guide for the communicator is often a pretest: how in fact does a sample of similar participants interpret what he would communicate? And the observer can only try, after the fact and if feasible, to break down the barrier between himself and the participants by establishing some kind of direct or indirect contact with them.

II.A.2 The *anticipation* of events is both intriguing and theoretically challenging. There is a difference between anticipating how most persons in the West will react to a traffic light when they are the drivers and their treatment of strangers at a cocktail party. In the first case, the observer knows in advance how most of them will respond to the light which is a symbol of the state's power, in the second he is much less certain how they will behave until the give-and-take of the social interaction is at hand. A knowledge of the society or of the relationship between the participants provides some basis for anticipating the consequences of power and authority. Obeying traffic lights is structured within the society; conversations are not, or at least not quite as fully structured.

When it is stated that "the exercise of power depends on the consent of the ruled,"[5] attention is called not only to the relation between principals and subordinates but also to a possible personality trait, viz., a tendency to be submissive, to submit to power or authority in a variety of situations. If it is known that a participant possesses such a trait, his reaction to many but not all events is somewhat predictable. Even if he is not always dominant or submissive, but dominant or submissive in certain situations and not in others, his behavior can be objectively anticipated with a high degree of accuracy. Obviously the enlisted man obeys his officer, and his wife obeys him, at least most of the time, if perchance she is very conventional according to modern standards in the West; the events are somewhat predictable.

Unless an event is a complete surprise, the observer has various ways to predict its occurrence. Foremost is experience: he knows that under certain circumstances events have taken place in the past and hence are likely to recur in the future. That experience in turn gives rise to the belief that events will recur in regular or irregular cycles or under specified conditions. Those conditions then require prediction in their own right, so that an infinite regress looms.

It may be anticipated that events resulting from or giving rise to conflicts are most likely to lead to power and authority sequences. The conflict may be between persons or groups of persons: incompatible goals are sought by the contending participants so that interactions of some kind with a consequent display of power and authority are usually inevitable. The observer may assume that conflict both affects and is affected by authority and power. A careful, modest attempt has been made to give substance to such a spiraling hunch. Two periods of stress or "threat"—and hence presumably conflict—in the United States have been compared to two periods when the stress or threat was presumably slight. By and large there is statistical support for the thesis that symptoms of power were more likely to be associated with the former than with the latter periods. There tended to be more powerful comic strip characters, more loyalty oaths demanded of teachers, larger police budgets in two large cities that were examined, longer sentences for rapists in a particular county during the depression years of 1930–1939 than during the "prosperous" years of 1920–1929. Some of these differences reappeared, when a comparison was feasible, and other similar ones appeared during the tense years of 1967–1970 (recession, disorders, escalation of the Vietnam War) in contrast to the relatively stable years of 1959–1964.[6] Obviously thousands of events and millions of participants produced such relationships: the events need not be specified and the persons need not be located to establish the tendency for more powerful symbols to be sought and more power to be exercised during the year with fewer conflicts. The same investigator has illustrated a similar tendency in the laboratory: paper-and-pencil, self-reported authoritarianism showed a very modest tendency to increase when failure rather than success was the outcome in solving anagrams and arithmetical problems. That tendency was more pronounced among the subjects whose self-belief in these situations was internal rather than external.[7]

The observer conceivably could analyze the content of a communication and anticipate the occurrence of an event even if he were incarcerated in Plato's cave and had no influence upon the shadows outside. Usually, however, he shows some concern for a potential or actual audience; therefore:

II.A.3 The observer must know when an event of interest to him is *salient:* are specifiable participants affected? A distant ruler who would demonstrate his power to persons in another country through verbal threats or armaments must possess the means to have them perceive his words or actions. What is salient, however, may not indicate the whole truth or the actual state of affairs, since power and authority may be exerted indirectly,[8] as when a politician is pressured or bribed by a lobbyist to support legislation in which his employer has a vested interest. A follower may be well acquainted with a regulation of his government without knowing who has originated it; or he may read and comprehend a report in a newspaper and not know who has wished to have it circulated. Forces when extreme almost automatically become salient, as when the weather is abnormally cold or warm; otherwise their salience depends upon human knowledge and goals, as when minerals are deliberately sought and discovered.

Events may be salient without provoking conscious awareness. The German word *Zeitgeist* suggests that the spirit of an age, whether cheerful or gloomy, may affect people's judgments and actions even when they themselves cannot or do not appreciate the influence of a complicated series of events. In a study of American couples, when one spouse perceived that his or her power over the other had increased, he or she then tended to increase that power still further.[9] The perception of the increase must have been the culmination of another series of events which, slowly or quickly, consciously or unconsciously, led to the tendency to increase the power even more. In bargaining sessions, participants provide one another with reasonably clear-cut demands that are expressed verbally and hesitations that are conveyed unwittingly through grimaces and other nonverbal behavior.

Potentially salient groups are likely to be numerous, particularly in modern society. A participant assumes many roles which depend, an observer must assume, not only upon the groups to which he belongs and in which he participates but also upon those to which he refers his behavior constantly or at a given moment. These latter groups range from out-groups like foreign governments or the social classes from which he is excluded to in-groups to which he belongs either remotely (his central or local government) or more intimately (his trade association, church, clubs, etc.). The peer group may affect his reactions to persons of higher status within the society: if he is supported by that group, he may be less obedient and more self-assertive in their presence.[10] According to a popular stereotype, the executive in business or government may play a less powerful role in his own family; but conceivably, a participant with a strong need to exert power is less likely to be dominant in some situations and meek in others. Within each association or organization are rules determining how the more and less powerful are supposed to interact, how indeed power may be acquired and lost, for whom membership is intended, and the kinds of symbols and ceremonies associated with membership.

Some attitudes may become salient only as a result of momentary circumstances and hence their significance is to be belittled by an astute observer. When asked whether communist journalists from abroad should be permitted to work freely in the United States, 37 percent of a sample of Americans replied *yes* in 1948 and 55 percent in 1980. Commonsense immediately suggests that the increase must have stemmed from the differences in the hysterical and the more tolerant later era. The percentages, however, were obtained *before* a similar question relating to American journalists in the Soviet Union was given the same informants on the same ballot by the same interviewers. When the order of the two questions was reversed for different but comparable samples, the figures changed dramatically: that of 37 percent for 1948 became 73 percent, that of 55 percent for 1980 became 75 percent; thus the previous differences of 18 percent was reduced to an insignificant 2 percent. The conclusion to be drawn is that possibly during thirty-two years there may have been a significant change in attitude, but that the change did not occur when the belief in reciprocity (treat their journalists the way we want ours treated) had not become salient.[11] Many but not all surveys require a large dose of critical skepticism before their implications can be evaluated by an observer.

> *Guide:* The elephant, which is the event variously analyzed, whether salient or not, and anticipated by observers, who are perforce blinded by their own purposes and biases, can never be fully grasped.

II.B *Communication*. Like the high priest of American political science mentioned at the very beginning of this book, the author of a searching analysis of power and authority has redefined the entire study of politics "in terms of language and communication." For him, therefore, "politics is talk" which he admits is an "oversimplification."[12] Oversimplification or not, communication plays a significant role in connection with all authority and power and hence requires treatment in its own right. The observer's conception of an event can emerge from his cave and become salient only when it is communicated to participants, the intended audience. The treatment of communication here is in two phases: the present section concentrates upon some aspects from the standpoint of the observer, the next chapter from that of the participants.

To analyze authority and power, the communication of event must be considered very broadly. Even force—brute, physical force—is an event that is communicated: a cuff on the ears or a musket pointed toward the body communicates authority and perhaps also prescribed behavior. A complete analysis of communication, it has been suggested elsewhere, requires a breakdown into a dozen steps or variables. The process is portrayed in note A, the Communication Figure, at the end of this chapter. To be noted by an observer are the contents of the communication, the restrictions, and the networks (that is, the basic and extending media). The content analysis of communications has been considered in the previous section; here it is necessary only to indicate that nonverbal communications are also events that can be analyzed less systematically than verbal communications and that the analysis can also transpire without reference to the participants.

Principals strive to communicate events in language likely to be comprehended by participants in what they consider to be a correct manner. Dangers lurk. Even in face-to-face situations, when participants perceive one another directly, words can be misunderstood and grimaces and gestures misinterpreted. Indeed a single word may have different connotations from person to person or over time. Prior to Hitler, for example, the German word for "hard" (*hart*) was used by communicators in a negative sense, but during his regime the same vocal vibration acquired a positive affect in keeping with the Nazi philosophy.[13]

Events can easily be repeated through the use of symbols. Governments in particular frequently remind citizens of their power and authority through what one political scientist once called "the miranda of power," the symbols to be noticed and to be admired. His catalogue of these symbols is as good as any and better than most: "memorial days and periods; public places and monumental apparatus; music and songs; artistic designs, in flags, decorations, statuary, uniforms; story and history; ceremonials of an elaborate nature; mass demonstrations, with parades, oratory, music."[14] Symbols are unavoidable; they will be considered again in Chapter 9.

The communications transmitting events are usually affected by various restrictions, some of which are self-imposed by the communicator, others stem from the milieu. The self-imposed ones include the communicator's political and ethical principles, his resources, and his status within the society. The external restrictions refer to custom, censorship, and the electronic limitations of radio and television.

Basic media reach participants directly through speech, print, gestures, and actions. Extending media serve to increase the size of an audience at a given moment (radio, television) or over time (press, books, art forms). Some observers of the mass media in contemporary Western society are themselves convinced and would convince their readers that the language and content of these media supplement government and industry in perpetuating the status quo: they induce participants to acquire "the needs and satisfactions that serve the preservation of the Establishment."[15] *If* such a view is correct, then the media are one of the resources through which power is exercised.

An observer can sometimes employ as an accurate prototype of the communication process a simple or linear schema which begins with a principal or subordinate who employs basic or extended media or both to transmit his communication, and ends with its reception by an audience, whoever the other participants are. An authority is honored and many persons, hearing about the event through some medium, feel even more friendly toward him; and he himself is pleased. Often, however, chains of communication must exist or be constructed if power is to be exercised: events are immediately or ultimately communicated in more complicated ways. The participant hears of an event through a mass medium perhaps and then later he discusses it with friends or his family; or the original source may actually have been those friends. Communication rarely occurs in isolation: participants are in contact with one another, they share beliefs and attitudes, they try to achieve some kind of understanding; they may never believe a communication, or carry out its intent until they receive support from a group they consider significant. Within a community, club, clique, or primary group such as the family some persons are more influential than others, and it is through them that many powers must first filter their communications. The authority to improve a road may come from the voting preferences of the members of a town meeting, from a committee, or from a single official; then the work is actually done by paid contractors and employees. Any large organization, such as an army, a dictatorship, or a corporation, requires a series of commands from a leader or leaders to followers; there must be messages or messengers from those in authority at the top to followers lower down.[16] Recently this approach to communication has been appropriately if breathlessly called "network analysis"; its adherents gather extremely detailed data concerning the participants who communicate with one another through socially established channels of communication. Breathlessness aside, it is necessary to indicate that the label may sound new but the mode of communication has been known to and exploited by every successful political leader whose lieutenants or ward healers convey information to voters and commands from the top. Lenin must have been acquainted with networks when he made the distinction between propaganda and agitation: "Propaganda uses 'the *printed* word' and deals abstractly with 'many ideas' to be understood by few persons (presumably members of the Party), whereas agitation uses 'the spoken word' to convey 'a *simple* idea to the "masses" . . . to rouse discontent and indignation.' "[17]

Guide: Many are the traversible routes between participants who communicate and their audience.

NOTES

A. Communication Figure

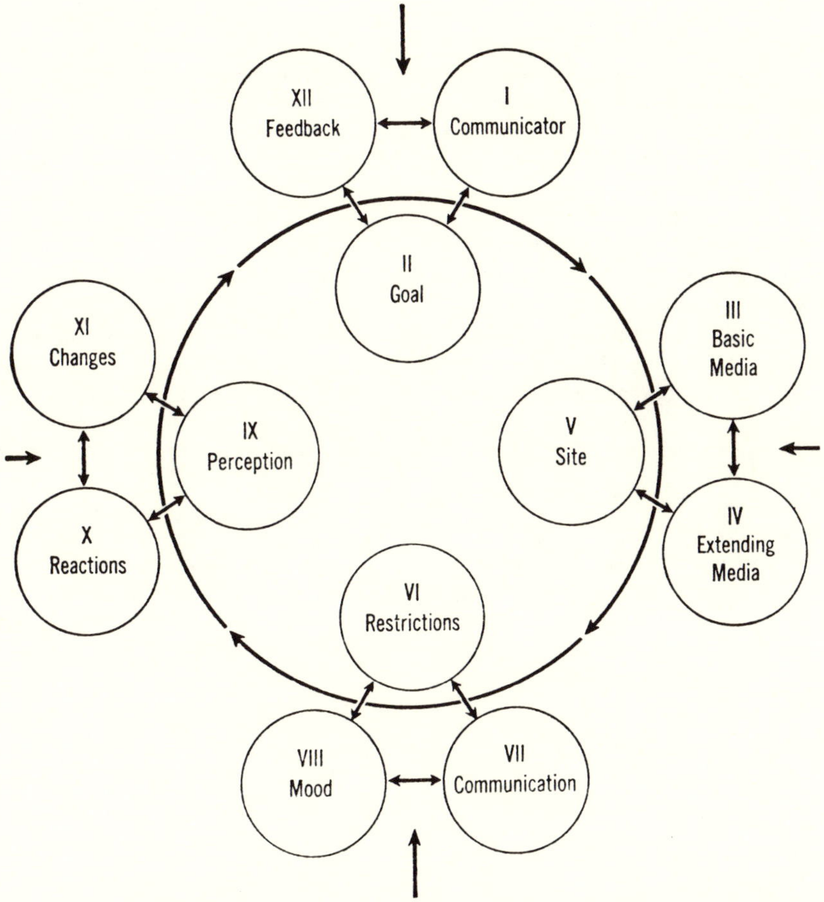

Source: Leonard W. Doob, *Communication in Africa*. 1961. Reprint ed. Westport, Conn.: Greenwood Press, 1979. P. 11. Copyright © 1961 by Yale University. Reprinted by permission.

1. Cf. E. H. Rosenberg and G. Medini, Describing the third person. *Journal of Psychology*, 1982, 112, 245–50.

2. Cf. George Gerbner et al., *The Analysis of Communication Content*. New York: Wiley, 1969.

3. Mary Parker Follett, *Dynamic Administration*. New York: Harpers, 1942. P. 103.

4. James T. Tedeschi, Barry R. Schlenker, and Thomas V. Bonoma. *Conflict, Power, and Games*. Chicago: Aldine, 1973. P. 37.

5. Gene Sharp, *The Politics of Nonviolent Action*. Boston: Porter Sargent, 1973. P. 4.

6. Stephen M. Sales, Threat as a factor in authoritarianism. *Journal of Personality and Social Psychology,* 1973, 28, 44–57.

7. Ibid.

8. Cf. Robert D. Putnam, *The Comparative Study of Political Elites.* Englewood Cliffs: Prentice-Hall, 1976.

9. Boyd C. Rollins and Stephen J. Bahr, A theory of power relationships in marriage. *Journal of Marriage and the Family,* 1976, 38, 619–27.

10. Cf. Ezra Stotland, Peer groups and reactions to power figures. In Dorwin Cartwright (ed.), *Studies in Social Power.* Ann Arbor: Research Center for Group Dynamics, 1959. Pp. 53–68.

11. Howard Schuman and Stanley Presser, *Questions and Answers in Attitude Surveys.* New York: Academic Press, 1981. P. 29.

12. David V. J. Bell, *Power, Influence, and Authority.* New York: Oxford University Press, 1975. Pp. ix, 10.

13. Claus Mueller, *The Politics of Communication.* New York: Oxford University Press, 1973. Pp. 18, 27.

14. Charles Edward Merriam, *Political Power.* New York: McGraw-Hill, 1934. P. 105.

15. Herbert Marcuse, *One-Dimensional Man.* Boston: Beacon Press, 1964. P. 8; cf. pp. 65, 103.

16. Bertrand de Jouvenel, *The Pure Theory of Politics.* New Haven: Yale University Press, 1963. Pp. 14345.

17. V. I. Lenin, *What Is to Be Done?* In *Collected Works.* Moscow: Progress Publishers, 1975. Vol. 1, pp. 142–43; italics his.

6

Perception

The observer notes events and the ways in which they are communicated; the participants who perhaps receive the communication react to and judge what in fact they do or do not perceive. Galileo, a follower of Aristotle, is said to have reported that while witnessing a post-mortem of a human body he noted nerves emanating not from the heart, as Aristotle had believed, but from the brain. He then exclaimed, "You have made me see this business so plainly and sensibly that, did not the text of Aristotle assert the contrary . . . I should be constrained to confess your opinion to be true."[1] By and large, however, the astronomical observations of Galileo himself eventually prevailed even when they contradicted the authority of the Church;[2] but often, too often, prejudices either prevent persons from perceiving the facts and lead to conscious or unconscious distortions. The problem of perception in general terms is to determine the outcome of what is out there (the corpse) and the predispositions inside the perceiver (a belief resulting from having been indoctrinated with the Aristotelian view).

With a broad sweep it may be said that perception in general and specifically with reference to power and authority depends upon the interaction of the stimulus configuration, the intensity of the individual's own predispositions, and various temporal factors. Controlling forces with great power are themselves perceptually unavoidable stimuli, such as a blizzard or a wild beast; but some, such as viruses and bacteria, can be perceived only microscopically or submicroscopically or inferred from their effects. The stimulus configuration refers to the arrangements in the external world which participants have the opportunity to perceive if and when they are inclined or able to do so. Nonevents may be perceived in the sense that the participants respond to the absence of whatever they have anticipated: the speaker does not appear, the military weapons are not displayed, no reply is given to an ultimatum. The absence may then be judged as a symbol of power or powerlessness. Similarly the so-called power behind the throne who does not reveal himself obviously cannot be perceived, but his power may be transmitted through another person or a medium. In contrast, the display of status usually can or must be perceived: the insignia on an officer's uniform indicating his rank, the seal of office ostentatiously and conspicuously displayed by political leaders, the headline rather than the small print, the amount of time devoted to an item on radio or television. Heavy emphasis may be placed on repetition: the more frequently a stimulus event occurs or is exposed, the more likely it is to be initially perceived; and also, when perceived, the more likely it is to be learned and recalled, other things being equal. Those things are not equal when repetition produces boredom and hence avoidance, at which point varying the communication's content becomes propitious.[3]

The outside event is overriden or almost so when the participant's predisposition is intense, even as the belief of Aristotle's disciple dominated his judgment. Perhaps a scientist is someone "who acknowledges no authority"[4] and therefore is guided by his own observations; yet even what he observes may be affected by this theoretical preconception, particularly when he attaches great importance to his favorite hypothesis for reasons of personal prestige. An economist maintains that many of his colleagues continue to perceive the American system as embodying free competition in which therefore consumers have both power and authority concerning supply and prices, whereas the reality, he maintains, is a sharp dichotomy between large corporations and small enterprises.[5] Perhaps what the participant, as it were, chooses to perceive depends to some degree upon one of his own predispositions such as a particular personality trait.[6] If he is anxious, because as a monopolist he seeks power or as a confirmed follower he would avoid it,[7] he may be prone to concentrate upon those aspects of communication that justify or alleviate his feelings. If he is seeking to please an authority, even though success in the venture is not very prominent in his hierarchy of values, he will orient himself toward achieving that temporary goal. There is no guarantee, however, that even intense predispositions will be salient and affect perception: aspects of the communication must be taken into account.

2.A *Discrepancies*. The most fruitful assumption is to anticipate discrepancies between events as perceived by omnipotent observers and by normal participants. Exceptions occur: when an exceptionally loud noise or bright light, the laceration of the skin, or the howling of a gale is the stimulus, the critical aspects of the external event may be perceived with no significant distortion. But events concerned with power and authority are seldom that prepotent: the participant himself supplies part of the resultant perception. The most skillful propagandist or advertiser, therefore, can never be certain that his message will reach the intended audience or that, when they do perceive it, they will do as he wishes them to. In the domain of authority and power, the basic question ever appears: What cues in the stimulus event does the principal employ so that the subordinates are more likely to perceive what he believes is or should be his higher status or his authority?

Since a communication substantially determines the aspect of an event that is perceived, usually principals and leaders communicate more information than followers and subordinates.[8] Members of the audience, however, may be unable or unwilling to grasp all the details in front of them, especially when they hear about an event or see it secondhand by means of an extending medium. Events reach them through a series of filters imposed either by those exercising power over the media or by themselves. Some distortion is inevitable. The mass media are one of the very significant resources in modern society through which principals secure and perpetuate their power and authority.

The distortion, whether interposed by communicators or the audience, resembles rumors and may be of three kinds.[9] First, simplification is likely: many events are too complicated to be described or perceived completely, details are omitted, accuracy is sacrificed in behalf of brevity and intelligibility. Those controlling the media in any society cannot provide all the details even when they wish to: they are confronted with a shortage of space and time, or they supply only those items which are not to their disadvantage. Then exaggeration may be employed to retain, for example, a seat of power: some details are reported or perceived out of context, or their significance is so overstressed that the communication is conveyed dramatically or impressively. Finally, assimilation may occur: details are added, subtracted, or altered so that the communication appears straightforward with virtually no qualifications.

> *Guide:* A participant's predispositions and the event variously determine his perception of that event.

2.B *Site and Timing*. The site at which communications are received and their timing are two factors affecting perception that are closely interwoven and therefore operate simultaneously. How does a candidate for public office seek to communicate with voters who ultimately determine whether he will occupy a powerful position in government? The media he selects, whether electronic or face-to-face, reach participants at different sites—in public halls, in homes—and at different periods of the campaign or at different times of day.

The site affects or determines the size and composition of the group who are the audience for a communication and hence the participants. Obviously the larger the audience, the greater the number of subordinates who potentially can be affected. The interaction among participants is likely to be more intimate in a small group (the psychiatrist and his patient) than in a large one (a public meeting), although in both situations the range of possible behaviors is considerable. Societal or conventional rules play a role: whereas a street-corner meeting may be open to everyone, only specified persons may gain admittance to closed meetings. The power associated with financial resources or status in modern cities enables some but not other persons to use parking lots or to participate at particular sites. At the site itself rules prevail, ranging from the somewhat chaotic, unpredictable ones operating when a leaderless crowd assembles to the strict parliamentary procedure followed by a recognized chairman.

The group to which participants refer their judgments and some of their values is determined not only by that group's importance to them and its power over them but also by the site at which the communication is received and at which the interaction occurs. Participants in face-to-face situations immediately recognize or do not recognize their own group affiliations and behave accordingly. The principal at the site, moreover, may deliberately affect their perceptions: ". . . as good citizens of this Republic it is your duty to. . . ."

The kind of interaction among participants usually is largely a function of the site's attributes. Nonhuman factors, for example, may include the acoustics, the seating capacity, the illumination, in fact the entire design of a hall so that many of the participants' reactions are thus determined: can they hear the speaker, do they see one another, is the general ambiance cheerful or depressing? The site reminds the participants of the rules current there: one does not tell jokes during a church service. Such rules may be relatively flexible or inflexible. The type and quantity of communications may also be affected: a parliament assembles to debate legislation, hunters in a party seek animals to kill and communicate with one another only incidentally.

The mood of the participants who arrive and interact at a site may or may not be typical of their normal or usual state.[10] Indeed strong predispositions regarding power and authority may function regardless of the mood, but their expression may be affected by recurring or unique circumstances. The hour of the day, the day of the week, the season of the year inevitably are variables that can have impact upon receptivity and evaluations. Persons living in the temperate zone claim they feel lethargic or depressed when the weather is hot and muggy; whether the weather actually is responsible for their mood is less compelling than their own conviction concerning its effects.[11] Age may affect an individual's temporal orientation and hence his immediate response to power or authority. Illness, whether a simple head cold or terminal cancer, may disturb even the most angelic of human beings, and the disturbance may spill over into behavior. Food, drink, and drugs can steer an individual in diverse directions. The preexisting esprit within a group undoubtedly affects the mood of recruits or latecomers who find the atmosphere stimulating or depressing.

Moods may be engendered by communications and by the interactions of the participants at the site. In general terms it is known that the effect of a communication may be affected by prior communications, by the order in which themes are presented, by repetition and variation. The effect of the order, for example, raises the issue of primacy and recency: if a communication contains a series of statements, will the first or the last one be learned and retained and consequently influence behavior? The reply is uncertain, but it is reasonable to assume that, other factors being equal, either the first or the last will be more effective than those parts transmitted between the two extremes. The mood may also be affected by the length of a communication; the evoked excitement or boredom are themselves moods which in turn can be reinforced or extinguished by what occurs during the interaction of the participants. Indeed the content of the communication itself may affect its effectiveness. Thus both sides of a proposition may or may not be presented in a communication, and the conclusion to be drawn or the action to be followed, according to the communicator's intention, may be implicitly or explicitly suggested. A one-sided communication, especially among the well informed and perhaps among the well educated, may possibly produce resentment or suspicion, both of which become part of the relevant mood. An implicit conclusion demands that the participant actively understand the implications; whether or not he draws the correct ones from the communicator's standpoint, the mental activity itself may facilitate learning. In face-to-face situations aberrant behavior by one participant may suddenly produce bizarre reactions among those witnessing it.

> *Guide:* Clues to a participant's perception are provided by his location in space and time.

It is frustrating, I know, to maintain again that the outcome of the interaction of the stimulus configuration, the predispositions, and temporal factors cannot be subsumed under general principles: the weight given each factor depends upon the situation at hand. True, an intense stimulus will be perceived, but not by a blind, a deaf, or a preoccupied person. Although the participant may have great confidence in his self-belief that he almost alone controls his own destiny, he perceives that his country's prime minister is, at least momentarily, more powerful than himself. The appropriate time for displaying authority or exercising power may be overlooked when a more compelling goal presents itself. In no other way can the diversity of human behavior be comprehended: no participant is always pursuing power or displaying authority; it all depends, yes, it all depends.

NOTES

1. Cited by Lewis Mumford, *The Pentagon of Power.* New York: Harcourt Brace Jovanovich, 1970. P. 52.
2. Cf. Sir Bernard Lovell, Science. In Clifford Rhodes (ed.), *Authority in a Changing Society.* London: Constable, 1969. Pp. 42–61.
3. Leonard W. Doob, *Public Opinion and Propaganda.* Hamden: Archon Books, 1966. Pp. 347–51.
4. Richard Peters, *Authority, Responsibility, and Education.* New York: Eriksson-Taplinger, 1960. P. 27.
5. John Kenneth Galbraith, The bimodal images of the modern economy. *Journal of Economic Issues,* 1977, 11, 189–99.
6. U.S.A.: eighty undergraduate ROTC cadets. *Method:* information on manipulated tape records was communicated concerning one of four types of persons (as named by the investigators: "tycoon," "go-getter," "decadent aristocrat," and "shiftless trash"), then the subjects commented on the person they thought they had heard and answered questions about him. *Results:* those cadets high in authoritarianism (as mea-

sured on a popular, conventional paper-and-pencil questionnaire) tended to use "external power cues" such as the socioeconomic status of the voice they had heard and his possession of socially valued material objects. In contrast, those low in the same respect tended to use more "internal power cues" such as his forcefulness and decisiveness in discussions, personality traits; in short, the power he displayed as a result of his own initiative rather than his alleged status. Edward J. Wilkins and Richard de Charms, Authoritarianism and response to power cues. *Journal of Personality,* 1962, 30, 439–57.

7. Cf. Peter Schneider, *Recht und Macht.* Mainz: v. Hase & Koehler, 1970. P. 22.

8. Cf. Barry E. Collins and Harold Guitzkow, *A Social Psychology of Group Processes for Decision-Making.* New York: Wiley, 1964. Pp. 155–57.

9. Cf. Gordon W. Allport and Leo Postman, *The Psychology of Rumor.* New York: Holt, 1947. Pp. 134–37.

10. Leonard W. Doob, *Communication in Africa.* Westport: Greenwood, 1979. Pp. 214–41, 289–90.

11. Cf. Leonard W. Doob, Tropical weather and attitude surveys. *Public Opinion Quarterly,* 1968, 32, 423–30.

7

Ascription and Description

In a fugue-like dissection of power and authority, attention in this chapter is again turned away from the reactions of the participants themselves and is focused upon problems confronting the observer as he describes and analyzes those participants in order to account for their actions which have occurred or are about to occur. He may be acquainted with their background, their culture and society, modal socialization processes, temporal potentials, and resources. He also may note the events that have presumably affected or are affecting them. At this point his understanding of power and authority undoubtedly will be improved if he can make inferences concerning their predispositions and if he can chart their interactions. He is faced with the same problems as those confronting a participant who observes his fellow participants.

III.A *Attribution*. Relatively recently legions of psychologists have concerned themselves with what they call attribution theory: the reasons why individuals assign attributes to other persons on the basis of whatever information is available to them. Some of their findings can be subsumed under the better established concept of projection, viz., the tendency to ascribe to someone else one's own feelings or attributes: I hate him and therefore he must hate me. More than projection, however, is involved when the observer seeks not only to characterize another person but also to account for an ascribed or attributed characteristic. Research, principally among American undergraduates, suggests that another person's actions may be attributed either to external or environmental factors or to internal or personality factors.[1] Perhaps the individual is thought to be responsible for his behavior when it is assumed he intended to act as he has, when that behavior has serious consequences for himself or others, or when his attributed predispositions or his reactions fluctuate over time as environmental conditions remain unchanged rather than vice versa.[2]

Attribution also occurs as forces are appraised. The dog growls and, either on the basis of experience or through anthropomorphic projection, the observer concludes that the animal is dangerous or harmless. The sky darkens and the observer judges that a storm is or is not about to break. Whenever symptoms or only partial knowledge is available, in short, attribution enables a prediction to be made.

When we return again to fundamentals, we must recall that no one, even the most gifted or well financed observer, can get inside another person. Each individual, I repeat, is solipsistically encased and therefore is not accessible to an outsider. On the basis of available information and as a result of his own preconceptions, the observer can only ascribe predispositions to the participants interacting as part of the event. Sometimes attributions are made by persons who may be considered observers, participants, or both.[3]

III.A.1 Attributions are either *direct or indirect*. A simple problem is as good an illustration as any: one observer calls one or more participants an authority.[4] Direct attribution would be one of the following:

1. Single: this participant is an authority.
2. Multiple: this participant is an authority, that one is not an authority, the third one is of uncertain status, etc.
3. Group: this group has authority.
4. Intergroup: the authority of this group is greater than that of another group or other groups.

Indirect attribution refers to the alleged belief of the participant himself or of the participants themselves:

1. Single: this participant believes himself to be an authority.
2. Multiple: this participant believes himself to be an authority, that one does not, the third one is uncertain concerning his authority, etc.
3. Group: within the group, this participant or these participants believe they have authority, those do not.
4. Intergroup: the participants in this group believe their group has more authority than some other group or groups.

Whether the ascription is direct or indirect and whether it occurs instantly or laboriously, the process is complex and includes a number of discrete steps, the details of which are portrayed in the Person-Perception Figure, note A at the end of this chapter. Like the analysis of the participant's reaction to power and authority, the tale begins with a stimulus or event transmitted through a channel of communication and continues as the event is perceived for various reasons. An interaction occurs between the observer's predispositions and whatever is perceived, as a result of which a judgment is passed; that judgment in turn after reflection may be followed by a secondary judgment and finally by an appraisal or evaluation.

When the attribution is direct, as illustrated above, the observer utilizes information provided by some source or event which he perceives, judges, and evaluates. The process may be simple, as when he asks a participant for his credentials in a given situation or when in fact he knows that the individual occupies a specified position on some hierarchy. The same questions concerning the participant may be posed to a knowledgeable informant or respondent. In any case the observer must decide whether the characterization thus secured is valid or not; to pass that judgment all the steps portrayed in the Person-Perception Figure and sketched in the last paragraph, however fleeting or belabored, must be taken. Is the participant himself or the informant telling the truth? Trust, as ever, is not as "simple" as it might seem at first glance.

Ascriptions, whether direct or indirect, are partially an elaboration of perception. The observer must provide his own interpretation, just as any other perception is a combination of the impact of the stimulus and the perceiver's predispositions. Objective description, therefore, is virtually impossible, if objective means complete. Some details about power and authority are likely to be omitted or to be noted by another observer who has other interests or who lives in another age.

Indirect ascription is usually more complicated than direct. For then the observer seeks to pass judgment concerning what is forever concealed from him, the subjective predispositions and the inner responses of one or more informants. In terms of the Guiding Figure he may perceive the outer circles and make inferences and generalizations about them; but he cannot perceive the inner circles, he can only infer their functioning. He is faced with all the methodological problems of validity, objectivity, and reliability outlined in Chapter 1. The problems theoretically may be easier, however, when the ascriptions concern power or authority as such. For by definition power and authority imply a position of privilege (or the lack of it) within a hierarchy; and a hierarchy suggests the interaction of several persons who may also be investigated and judged, in order to determine whether the participant of interest has or does not have power, or is or is not considered an authority. In contrast, the determination of a participant's power motive, his self-belief, his attitudes toward authority, and his skills in exercising or reacting to power or authority can be appraised ultimately only by hazarding the best possible hypothesis or guess concerning what transpires within him. In order to decide who are the real authorities in a community and what power they possess, the whodunnit brand of political science must have more patience and be given more time than the psychologists who quickly administer and score a Machiavellian scale or a Thematic Apperception Test. Then the outcome of the former method of investigation is likely and deservedly to be accepted with greater confidence than a ranking provided by the latter's testing procedure. Probably no one will agree with this opinion, other than those in disciplines who find the comparison complimentary. A parting dart to the dissenters: let them consider the time required by most psychoanalyses and the uncertainty as to whether or not the outcomes are satisfactory and whether or not a real understanding has been secured.

III.A.2 The slippery nature of attribution is increased by the frequent appearance of an *infinite regression,* a summary of which is the following:

1. The observer ascribes attributes to the personality of the participant in order to comprehend his reactions to power and authority.
2. The validity, reliability, and objectivity of that observer's ascription must then be appraised by a second observer.
3. A second observer ascribes attributes to the personality of the first observer in order to comprehend why that first observer has ascribed attributes to the personality of the participant while striving to comprehend that participant's reaction to power and authority.

Obviously there can be a third and fourth observer when attributions are checked as they are made either at the moment or, from the historian's standpoint, over generations. This is the house that Jack built, this is the mouse that lives in the house that Jack built, this is the cat. . . .

III.A.3 The participant may be observed at *first or second hand.* He says or reports something about himself. His phrases or sentences can be variously analyzed before attributing status or a predisposition to him. Attention may be concentrated on the content of what he has said as well as upon his way of saying it. When he knows more than one language and is living in an area where two or more languages are spoken, the language in which he expresses himself may be significant. In face-to-face situations his nonverbal communications, such as his gestures, grimaces, posture, or appearance, may provide the basis for the ascription.

The observer may also utilize whatever experience he has had with the participants as the basis for his ascription. In the past their reactions to authority, their use of power, their characteristic way of behaving may have been noted and then have served as a guide to the present ascription. Equally important generally is the observer's own conception of human behavior or society. His psychological assumptions may range from a tendency to provide a genetic to an environmental explanation or some combination thereof. He may or may not subscribe, consciously or unconsciously, to what some investigators believe to be a modal tendency of observers: perhaps they tend to ascribe their own behavior to situational requirements and the behavior of other persons to personality traits.[5] Or possibly they claim to use both ascriptions to explain themselves and others.[6] In any case information concerning the behavior of others may be considered a better basis for predicting their attitudes than vice versa.[7]

The observer may know nothing about the participant as a person, or he may ignore his more personal or distinctive attributes and base his ascription on a cultural or demographic fact.[8] He is an American or a German, and therefore. . . . They are males (or females) and therefore. . . . She is an adolescent (or an adult) and therefore. . . . He is well (or poorly) educated, and therefore.

. . . Such ascriptions are secondhand as far as the participant is concerned but may stem from alleged firsthand experiences of the observer either with persons possessing the indicated demographic attributes or with others transmitting prejudices or stereotypes concerning those attributes.

> *Guide:* Attributions concerning one participant by another are fraught with possible errors and are seldom, if ever, complete.

III.B *Interaction.* The observer, ideal or otherwise, seeks to know everything about the reaction of the participants to the event and to one another. He would describe and identify those participants, possess prior information about them, attribute internal processes to them, observe them in action, and note the decisions they make and the outcome. Here attention is directed to all these challenges other than the decisions and the outcome.

III.B.1 On the basis of prior *knowledge* the observer may be able to indicate beforehand who the leader is or who has the authority; he may also be aware of the subordinates or followers who are affected. His interest, however, may be in the emergence of leaders and followers and hence he must have information concerning their reactions to one another over time. Obviously leadership changes as a result of competition, as when politicians seek power for themselves or when a social or political revolution occurs. The whodunnit school of political scientists and alert journalists must often expend tremendous efforts to find the participants, especially those who are behind the scenes if there be such. In fact, the search may be the only problem they seek to solve and hence, when they have located the relevant participants and determined their roles, they are content and are ready to write their article, book, or news story.

Varying amounts of information concerning the participants may be available in advance of the interaction. At the very least the observer tries to identify the event—a conversation, an election, a conference, a war—that has provoked a power conflict and initiated the interaction. He may know something about the society in which the participants have been reared; he may even have detailed background information concerning a particular participant, on the basis of which he may attribute fairly specific predispositions to him or her. The attributions may be derived from concrete data, such as school records which reveal whether the individual has been an over- or underachiever or a deviant among his peers. Above all, it may be useful or desirable to specify the resources the participants have at their disposal, the modes of communication they usually employ during the interaction, and consequently their customary techniques to preserve or to advance their positions in the situation at hand or within the hierarchy in which they find themselves. How detailed the information is or should be largely depends upon its availability as well as upon the interests of the observer. What A said to B who said to C who said nothing to D but plenty to E—such factual data, even when procurable by the truckload, may concern only a scandalmonger or a conscientious historian unless the sequence provides additional insight into the techniques.

III.B.2 Elaborate scoring methods have been devised to facilitate direct *observation,*[9] but they can be utilized only when all participants are visible and interacting within relatively small groups. Ordinarily, however, observation of this sort is not possible. Proceedings are seldom recorded completely and often crucial decisions, such as a declaration of war, are made in secret. A participant may function simultaneously as an observer but in medias res he is not likely to be a conscientious observer if he wishes also to be an effective participant. Afterwards he may note down what he has observed in the equivalent of a diary or report. When published memoirs emerge, however, they rarely are not tainted by the ego strivings of their authors.

III.B.3 On the surface it would appear that the ideal solution to the problem of observing interaction is the *experiment* under laboratory conditions. In fact, a staggeringly large number of experiments have been and are being performed in the West for that very reason. The experimenter selects the participants and hence knows who they are demographically; through a questionnaire or interview he may be able to assess them quite subtly beforehand. Then he sets the goal and, alone or with colleagues, observes members of a small group through a one-way vision screen; he may record the entire event on videotape. He can manipulate the resources and statuses he assigns to the participants, he can determine their incentives, and he can inject a confederate into the group and instruct him to act in a specified manner. Later he is able to analyze the proceedings blow-by-blow.

The disadvantages of the laboratory experiment, already outlined in Chapter 1, are particularly pronounced in the present context: they range from the artificiality of the controlled situation to the limited kinds of power and authority that can be simulated. The experimenter brings subjects together through some ruse with or without payment, whereas in everyday life the critical factor may be the very reasons some individuals participate in a situation and others do not. Those subjects, moreover, may respond to the experimenter as a power or authority and hence they behave in such a way as to please or displease him or, for that matter, to present themselves to him in what they consider to be the most or least favorable light.[10] Experiments are almost always completed within a matter of minutes, but real-life interactions may linger for months or even years. Such negotiations, furthermore, are not conducted completely in a cozy room (the usual laboratory situation) but literally or figuratively in corridors, by means of intervening media such as telephones and written communications, and sometimes also with the aid of intermediaries. What the observer is able to observe under these circumstances is limited by his own endurance and by whatever access to the participants he is able to wangle. Observers of "real" settings usually make their observations long after the interactions have ended: they interview as many of the participants as possible, and they consult whatever written or taped records are available.

What, then, is the usually helpless observer able to do in order to improve the data he collects? Simulation of power or authority relations is promising: instead of attempting to foresee the effects of interaction, the investigator finds subjects willing to role-play games whose outlines he prescribes for them. The utility of the emerging generalization is increased because the conditions under which they have been obtained more closely resemble the oncoming real-life situation. Even when they become emotionally involved in the exercise, as so often happens after the first few minutes of playing the game, they remind themselves of the make-believe character of their own behavior and hence their performance is not quite true to life.

A good *theory* suggests the actions to observe and aspects of the
III.B.4 outcome to be anticipated. One theory might be, for example, that coalitions are formed against that participant who seems to be enjoying too much success;[11] if the theory is correct, then the observer must take special note of whoever seems to be emerging as the victor. A helpful theory may possibly emerge from what an author or an analyst believes to be a survey of knowledge on interaction. According to one writer, an individual's impact on any given situation may possibly depend upon three factors: the degree to which that situation can be restructured, his "location" or status therein, and his skills.[12] The first and second of these "quite abstract" factors can be assessed by the observer when he knows the background of the participants, specifically the structure of the society, and when he can observe the interaction directly; and the third is obviously dependent on the kind of attribution he is willing or able to make. In real-life situations he may try to guess when powerful, charismatic principals and leaders will arise, but he is probably kilometers away from being able to predict under what social and personal circumstances a Hitler rather than a Brüning, an F. D. Roosevelt rather than a Coolidge, will exert tremendous influence upon decisions. It is to be doubted whether greatness (i.e., power and prestige) is ever thrust upon anyone, and it is usually uncertain when a thrust or no thrust occurs.

Another suggestive guide stems from an anthropologist's observation of the mode of settling disputes among the Arusha of Tanzania as well as his own insightful surveys of others' schemas. After assuming that information has been exchanged among the participants, he indicates various phases that negotiations traverse: at the outset are a "search for arena" and "agenda definition"; then, as the "field" is explored, the emphasis is upon differences and later a narrowing of these differences; after additional preliminaries, the final bargaining takes place leading, lovers of peace must hope, to the "execution of outcome."[13] Such a schema or indeed any theory can be implemented by an observer only with great difficulty and patience, but it is useful to be sensitive to the possibilities. There is, nevertheless, no escape from multivariance.

Finally, the observer must challenge his own theory: does he assume that the decision-makers are determined by rationality? One careful critique of three major books concerned with foreign policy decision-making and based on experiments, clinical interviews, and above all public documents, reports, and "naturalistic investigations" of officials reaches the conclusion that national leaders are likely to be constrained by the "situational forces" within their immediate milieu and their society. In processing the complex materials at their disposal, consequently, they are prone to cater to their own biased preconceptions: they view their opponents as more rational and orderly than in fact they are.[14] Much depends on the definition of rationality of course, yet there is a vast difference between an attribution which assumes on the one hand that a participant weights each factor carefully and then assembles the pieces into the equivalent of a regression equation or a computer printout, and one which assumes on the other hand that a participant does not weight the various factors but decides on the basis of prejudice or impulse.

> *Guide:* The attribution of predispositions to participants and the charting and description of their interactions cannot be delineated with dispatch, but they are improved by the observer's knowledge, observations, and theories.

NOTES

1. Cf. J. Richard Eiser, *Cognitive Social Psychology*. London: McGraw-Hill 1980. Pp. 106–8.

2. Fritz Heider, *The Psychology of Interpersonal Relations*. New York: Wiley, 1958. Pp. 151–56.

3. Argentina, Brazil, and Chile: 327 university students; Canada: 38 individuals, age fifteen to sixty-one. *Method:* the Latin Americans ranked 122 nations with respect to their "prestige or importance," the Canadians 122 nations with respect to their "power"; neither group provided reasons for their rankings. *Results:* of no interest in this context. *Comment:* should these students and laymen be called observers or participants? As citizens of one of the countries being ranked, they included their own country as well as potential allies or enemies in their judgments; to some degree, therefore, they were attributing "prestige or importance" and "power" to themselves and to other nations. The analysis reveals that their rankings were related both to the gross national product and the military expenditures if the countries had not recently been at war, but were related only to military expenditures among the countries that had been at war. There is thus suggested one or two sources for the attributions, yet there is no evidence that either source was deliberately utilized. This statistically sophisticated investigation, therefore, may be of interest in its own right without providing additional insight into how or why the judgments were passed. Norman Z. Alcock and Alan G. Newcombe, The perception of national power. *Journal of Conflict Resolution*, 1970, 14, 335–43.

4. Leonard W. Doob, *Pathways to People*. New Haven: Yale University Press, 1975. Pp. 35–71.

5. Edward E. Jones and Richard E. Nisbett, The actor and the observer. In Edward

A. Person-Perception Figure

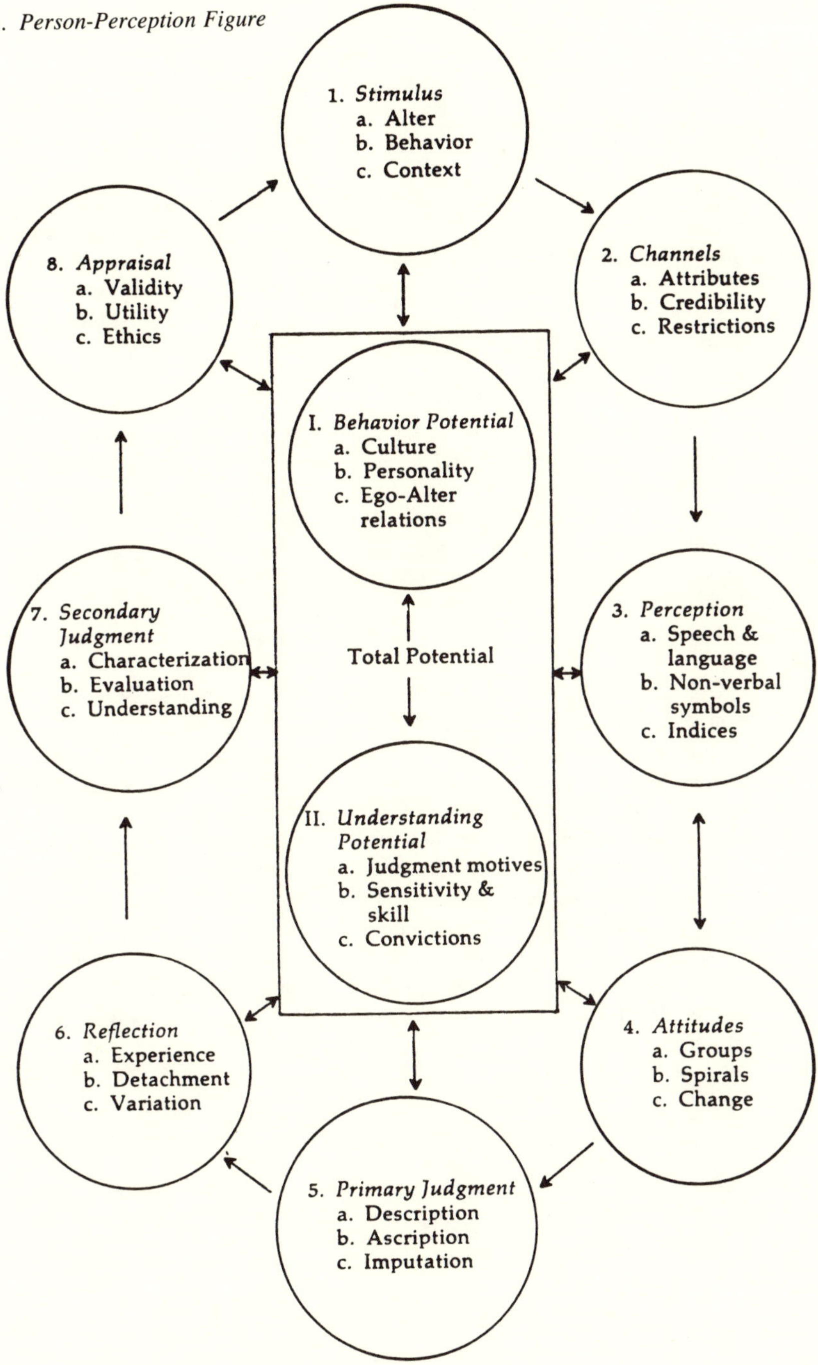

Source: Leonard W. Doob, *Pathways to People*. New Haven: Yale University Press, 1975. P. 8. Copyright © 1975 by Yale University. Reprinted by permission.

E. Jones et al. (eds.), *Attribution.* Morristown, N.J.: General Learning Corporation, 1971. Pp. 79–94.

6. U.S.A.: twenty-five college students. *Method:* the subjects read seven statements concerning the causes of behavior and rated their validity. *Results:* the highest mean rating was given to the "Interaction" explanation ("Different situations determine different behavior in different people. . . ."); there were no significant differences among explanations based upon traits, situations, and relevance of traits to situations, but all four of these explanations were rated significantly higher than explanations based on the sex of the individual or his level of education. Bem P. Allen and Gene F. Smith, Traits, situations, and their interaction as alternative "causes" of behavior. *Journal of Social Psychology,* 1980, 111, 99–104.

7. U.S.A.: 120 college students. *Method:* on a written questionnaire they read statements concerning attitudinal or behavioral expressions and rated the probability that one could be predicted from the other. *Results:* predictions from behavior to attitude were trusted more than vice versa. Bem P. Allen, Perceived trustworthiness of attitudinal and behavioral expressions. *Journal of Social Psychology,* 1973, 89, 211–18.

8. Cf. Shelley E. Taylor et al., Categorical and contextual bases of person memory and stereotyping. *Journal of Personality and Social Psychology,* 1978, 36, 778–93.

9. Cf. Robert F. Bales and Stephen P. Cohen, *Symlog.* New York: Free Press, 1979.

10. Irwin Silverman, *The Human Subject in the Psychological Laboratory.* New York: Pergamon Press, 1977. Pp. 20–36.

11. Cf. U.S.A.: 240 and 160 male undergraduates. *Method:* two experiments in the laboratory in which the subjects played a complicated game and could select their own two- or three-person coalitions in order to win money under conditions manipulated by the experimenter. *Results:* the one principle which explained most but not all coalitions was that of the "Exclusion of the Top-Dog," viz., the subjects tended to enter into coalitions with other players in order to dethrone the player in the lead. *Comment:* according to the experimenter, the explanation for this effect may have included "a norm of rooting against top-dogs, misperceptions of strength, the tendency of weak players to view each other as symbolic equals, and the motivation to form simple 'solutions' in the highly complex and confusing coalition situation." The "norm" of course was for American undergraduates. Jonathan Segal, Coalition formation in triads; Coalition formation and players' incentives. *Journal of Psychology,* 1979, 103, 209–19; 1981, 107, 261–66.

12. Fred I. Greenstein, *Personality and Politics.* New York: Norton, 1975, Pp. 42–46.

13. P. H. Gulliver, *Disputes and Negotiations.* New York: Academic Press, 1979. P. 122.

14. Donald R. Kinder and Janet A. Weiss, In lieu of rationality. *Journal of Conflict Resolution,* 1978, 22, 707–35.

8

Judgment and Decision

The third inner circle occupies the present chapter. The participant, it is assumed, has interacted with other participants either symbolically, as when he perceives them through a medium of communication, or actually face-to-face as in conversation or a crowd. He has, in brief, perceived the event, and relevant predispositions have become salient within him. He makes decisions concerning himself with reference to power and authority, concerning the tactics he will employ, and concerning the actions he will take. What decisions does he reach, and why?

Self in the Situation. Even before perceiving the event and inter-
3.A acting with other participants, the individual has two preconcep-
tions concerning himself: his self-belief and his self-power belief. As already indicated, he believes he possesses some degree of power or authority, or both, and he values or does not value the possession of power or authority for himself. These previously established tendencies may not change: he continues to make similar judgments about himself during the interaction. The dictator and the tramp appreciate their positions on various hierarchies and hence their judgments provoked by an event are effortless; each knows, respectively, that he has and does not have power or authority. But changes of course are possible. The dictator may reach the conclusion that the equipment of his army is inadequate to invade enemy territory, the tramp that it is possible to employ passive resistance effectively to prevent authorities from forcing him out of the quarters on which he has been squatting. In either case the self-belief has been modified by perceived events.

In addition, for most persons and in some situations the self-concepts acquired in the past do not function on an all-or-none basis. Every cultivator knows that he has the power to grow crops, but also that he is powerless in the face of natural forces like floods and droughts. Marksmen, whether soldiers or bandits, are acquainted with their own shooting skill, but they may be shy in front of strangers. Consumers in complex societies are aware that they can avoid or boycott certain products, yet that by themselves they generally have little effect upon overall prices. Principals know they can exploit or control their physical environment only within specified limits. Everywhere women cannot fail to exercise authority over their own young children, still on some matters—especially in male-dominated societies—they acknowledge the authority of their husbands whom they allow to make some decisions.

A coveted attribute associated with judgments concerning the self is insight: does the participant accurately appreciate his own strengths and weaknesses? Can he truly estimate the outcome for himself of whatever conflict occurs as he passes judgment? A participant with an external self-belief, who believes he is buffeted about by external forces over which he can exercise little or no control, may fail to recognize the strength of his own unconscious, favorable attitude toward power for himself. A leader may or may not be correct when he believes that his communications to followers are effective or that he can command enough votes or support to obtain the decision he seeks. A participant who "pursues power as a means of compensation against deprivation" and thus would "overcome low estimates of the self"—a blanket, inadequately documented "key hypothesis" about all power seekers[1]—may be blind to his own shortcomings. What emerges in the situation, then, is a striving self that has been derived from the components of that self in the past and from current perceptions.

3.B *Others*. Since power and authority by definition are exercised and affect more than one person, inevitably each participant judges one or more participants, whether he himself is or aspires to be a principal or a subordinate. He judges them in certain respects and he employs various bases for passing these judgments which in turn affect his own self-judgment in the situation. When a military staff believes that the armed strength of an unfriendly country is superior or inferior to its own, its members may then appraise their resources with confidence or anxiety.

A participant's judgment concerning other participants is similar to the attribution of the detached observer, as explained in the previous chapter; the reader is referred again to the Person-Perception Figure at the end of the last chapter. The judgments of a subordinate or follower are either direct or indirect, with all the advantages and disadvantages each procedure possesses. He judges a single participant or a number of participants as in a group; with respect to each, he produces his own attribution directly ("that man is an authority") or indirectly ("this woman believes herself to be an authority"). During the preliminary stages of a negotiation, he is likely to exchange information, as a result of which he has certain expectations concerning his opponents and hence is able to make tactical decisions on how to proceed.[2]

How competent is a participant to judge other participants? Systematic investigation of the judgments of "intuitive" psychologists or scientists regarding their ability to attribute predispositions and causal sequences to others, to describe relevant events and situations accurately, or to predict outcomes and actions lead by and large to the conclusion that errors are both frequent and inevitable.[3] Such judgments, nevertheless, are essential if each participant is to arrive at his own decision.

When the others in the situation are forces rather than, or in addition to, human beings, knowledge not of their legitimacy but of their power may be essential. Here objective standards exist for many of the inanimate forces and some of the animate ones. An estimate in advance that is high on the Richter scale produces or should produce appropriate judgments and actions for those living in the vicinity of an incipient volcano.

Since from birth onwards every human being is dependent upon
3.B.1 his parents and then upon others in his milieu for survival, growth,
and satisfaction, knowing the *beliefs* of those others almost inevitably is considered valuable information. The very expression "bandwagon effect" suggests that knowledge of the viewpoint or tendency of the majority is likely to induce some participants, as it were, to join the crowd. That knowledge may be accurate or it may result, as has been suggested, from an "impression of universality" and "social projections".[4] Why does knowledge of majority opinion tend to affect many participants? The reply must mention banalities ranging from the fear of disapproval to a feeling of impotence. Consciously or unconsciously many, maybe most subordinates believe that the majority may be correct and hence that dissent upsets the apple cart.[5] Most probably majority opinion can be ignored when so-called experts disagree with that majority,[6] but just as certainly experts do not necessarily produce conformity.[7] Those others may be more likely to affect a submissive rather than an ascendant participant when they present a united or almost united front than when they appear to be in disarray.[8] Above all, the importance of the group to which the others belong influences a participant's reactions; in fact, he may believe that he himself conforms more closely to a desirable norm of a group than its other members.[9] Perhaps principals more than subordinates are affected by their appraisal of others,[10] since they require such knowledge to retain and strengthen authority and to exercise power.

To dissent, to ignore the beliefs of others, it is usually necessary to possess self-confidence, a belief in self-control, and a strong power motive. In addition, probably some individuals may privately disagree with an authority who has power but, particularly under conditions of salience and surveillance, they may verbally or outwardly assent so as not to appear deviant or disagreeable.[11]

Judgments are likely to be affected by the belief as to whether
3.B.2 the other participant's behavior is *intentional* or not. In the sphere
of moral judgments, a noted investigator once contended that taking "intention into account" tends to develop later in children than "judging actions according to consequences," although both criteria may be employed at a given age;[12] and experiments among American children have demonstrated that the type of judgment can be altered through training by adults.[13] Possibly, injustices that are thought to have been intentionally perpetrated and hence preventable are believed to be more "distressing" than those that are unintentionally wrought.[14] A participant also may judge the other's intention as he attributes to him an orientation toward authority and power. Does that other

individual really seek power deliberately or does he believe he is pursuing some other goal although in fact he will achieve or increase his own power thereby? Is his obedience intentional or unintentional? This distinction is of significance in the legal process when juries or judges must decide whether a crime has been premeditated. The consequences of passing a judgment concerning intentions are difficult to discern. On the one hand, it can be argued that a person with conscious intentions is likely to be less susceptible to outside influence because he knows what he seeks; on the other hand, it is equally plausible that in the absence of conscious intentions he may stubbornly follow unconscious dictates. The issue cannot be decided for all persons or all contingencies, nor need it be, since the participant's own belief concerning alternatives affects his judgment about the other person and plays a role in his decision.

3.B.3 The beliefs and intentions attributed to participants contribute to *recognizing* them as principals or subordinates. No problem arises in conventional situations that are highly structured, as in any army or government where the chain of command is usually clear. A detective in plain clothes will not immediately be recognized or identified as a representative of orderly government; the suspected criminal will not judge him in terms of his authority until he produces his badge. The authority of a policeman, on the other hand, will immediately be perceived because of his uniform; whether this knowledge induces obedience is another matter. Status may also be conveyed by behaving in a dominating or submissive manner.

Demographic information of various kinds is almost always available and may assist the participants in identifying the status of other participants. Such information gives rise to judgments which may not be directly or immediately related to the position of another person in a hierarchy, such as aspects of his physical appearance or his birthplace. Others may be related: appearance, as suggested previously, may determine the impression of attractiveness which in turn may affect judgments concerning that person's intelligence or leadership qualifications, validly or not. Still other aspects on occasion may be relevant, such as age and education. And some are always relevant: is the principal an expert with respect to the problem at hand or will his expertise be rewarding?[15] Beliefs may supplement the judgment: if a principal comes from a powerful group or one believed to be powerful, power will be attributed to him, rightly or wrongly. If it is presumed that he comes from a distinctive ethnic group and if the behavioral attributes of that group are presumed to be biologically determined, what he does will be called racially determined and perhaps unalterable.[16] In any case, these demographic judgments lead the participant to categorize the other person and within that category specific characteristics are attributed.

Status is frequently employed to identify hierarchical relations. Victorian wives allegedly judged the authority of their husbands to be legitimate and indeed rewarding, at least most of the time. A writer in "a Lesbian-feminist newspaper'' asserts that ''relationships between men and women are essentially political, they involve power and dominance,'' hence Lesbianism ''is not a matter of sexual preference, but rather one of political choice which every woman must make if she is to become woman-identified and thereby end male supremacy.''[17] In some Latin American countries it is considered legitimate for boys and men to demonstrate the power associated with machismo, hence power is presumably associated with their behavior.[18] Kidnap victims know that the power of terrorists is illegitimate but impossible to challenge.

After the power or authority has been identified, the participant
3.B.4 *evaluates* that person partially or completely in terms of his specific or general attitude regarding power or authority and also in terms of his general or specific attitude toward other persons who possess or do not possess that attribute. He may feel respectful or disapproving. He may have confidence in a principal's ability to carry out a given action or to assume leadership, or he may reach a contrary decision and distrust him.[19] He may be overwhelmed with awe, respect, or anxiety. Possibly he may use him as a model rather than as a fellow participant or rival.[20] He may try to explain the compliance of a follower, perhaps attributing it to a deliberate decision when he believes the person's power or authority to be high, and to external pressure when he believes his power or authority to be low;[21] also conceivably he is more likely to assist the latter, when assistance is needed, than the former because he may view him as a ''victim of circumstances.''[22] Probably the perception and attribution of power or authority to a principal follows similar principles and with more or less the same degree of accuracy as that of any expression of approval or disapproval concerning another individual.[23] The perception and ascription are mired in uniqueness: they may result from a belief based upon past or current experience or communicated by someone else, or they may originate in a wish to seek and possess power. A participant who feels the need for a leader may attribute legitimacy to another person, whereas a participant without such a need withholds the judgment. Since legitimacy is associated with greater value, even perceptual judgments concerning the figurative size of authorities and powers may be magnified.[24] Not the least bit unexpectedly, American college students—when reacting to a hypothetical or experimental situation involving their peers—tended to evaluate more highly the competency and the responsiveness of a leader they themselves had elected or selected than one thrust upon them by appointment.[25]

Persons evaluated as deviants in American society, according to one analysis, are placed in a subservient position as a result of various tactics employed by principals, deliberately or otherwise. They may be considered ''different'' kinds of persons; they are thought to be drug addicts or criminals because of a flaw in their makeup. They may be deprived economically; former convicts have difficulty finding employment. They may be segregated in a physical sense; for example, prostitutes are often allowed to solicit only in red-light districts, convicted criminals usually serve time in prisons. They may be injected with drugs or, like radicals believed to be dangerous, they may be spied upon by police. Usually, therefore, it is almost impossible for them not to become aware of the label being plastered upon them and, as a consequence, they may adopt a deviant role and rebel against authority. They may also believe that others thus judge and brand them. On the other hand, being evaluated as a subordinate in authority may produce no trauma; a law-abiding citizen experiences few if any pangs when he submits to what he considers legitimate regulation, such as driving on the right or correct side of the road or not throwing garbage out of the window of his home.

The significance of one participant's attitude toward another person is dramatically illustrated in psychotherapy. A successful therapist acquires authority and becomes a legitimate authority during the course of his sessions with the patient or client. At first he is likely to be viewed by the struggling patient as a source of anxiety: what will he think of me, what will he do to me, can I trust him, will he really help me? Gradually, as the sessions go by, this anxiety diminishes. Some therapists do not punish or censure what the patient would say or do, they may seldom if ever use an opportunity to suggest their own superiority or power. Throughout the therapy they remain the authority but a benign one who does not exercise his power selfishly; a low degree of self-power, in short, is ascribed to them. In contrast, those therapists utilizing "multimodal therapy" adapt themselves more actively to the patient: they select the therapy best suited to the patient and his difficulties (and thus to a certain extent relinquish some of their power) and they often take a firm stand during the therapy itself.[26]

A miscellaneous, heterogeneous bag of reasons for judging an authority to be legitimate has been assembled by a political scientist from prestigious sources such as Plato, Rousseau, Marx, Max Weber, and others. These include consent of the governed; the will of God and religion in general; an election; blood descent; success; tradition, custom, or existence over time; charisma; an interpretation of history; secular political beliefs; legality, the capacity to issue "convincing" communications; ideologies; and nationalism.[27] The beliefs and attitudes legitimating the authority of those governing a society also shift over time. A detailed survey of governance in England, France, Germany, Japan, and Russia reveals a gradual but pronounced change away from hereditary monarchs whose legitimacy had depended on religious sanctions as well as on "international and external struggles for power"; instead authority "in the name of the people" now ostensibly reigns. The French Revolution is said to have "established the new principle that all sovereign authority" is derived from the nation as a whole and the central government becomes "the only legitimate executor of that authority."[28]

Guide: Participants seek to know themselves as well as others; they also evaluate those others.

3.C *Decisions*. After judging himself and others, the participant reaches a decision which itself is a judgment: precisely how does he appraise the entire situation with special reference to the action he should take? It is not being assumed that, in the manner of a learned judge, he assembles all the evidence, weights each piece carefully, and then decides. More probably his various predispositions, perceptions, and tentative judgments about himself and others interact and somehow a decision emerges. A facile dichotomy is evident, which is the conscious or unconscious rationale for the decision and its contents.

3.C.1 The *rationale* for decisions concerning power and authority are as diverse as the impulses behind any other aspect of human behavior. Rather than pursue that will-o'-the-wisp, emphasis here is placed upon a limited number of broad categories, subsumed under each of which may be so many specific processes that the uniqueness of the individual personality is not neglected.

3.C.1.a The participant is faced with a number of *alternatives* which he may or may not deliberately contemplate. Certainly his response to authority may be almost automatic or habitual: literally or figuratively he receives a summons to appear in a court and does not raise the question as to whether or not he must or should object. Similarly behavior is often prescribed more or less completely: the well-trained dog obeys his master, the enlisted man an officer, the secretary an employer. Unless some extenuating circumstance arises, the decision is made quickly and easily, if not without pain.

Often the prescribed role is less clear and the outcome, as in an athletic contest—or possibly in a marriage[29]—depends upon the interactions of the participants which are likely to be determined by cultural factors and the context of the situation itself. The participant is then confronted with alternative choices. He may have to decide whether he should be a principal or a subordinate and, in either role, what the course of action should be. If he occupies a position of authority, he decides not whether he possesses the authority but whether and how he will exercise it. If he is a subordinate, he notes the possibility or probability of tangible rewards or punishments: after obeying, will he be given a better job by an employer, will his health improve by following the physician's advice? Somehow he tries to select an alternative, yet he may not be successful—the cold war within him continues. Perhaps an immediate impulsive decision concerning a course of action will be less extreme than a thoughtful one after a brief delay, but additional thought and a greater delay may conceivably lead to less extreme judgments.[30]

3.C.1.b During the event and especially as he interacts with others, the participant may consciously recall a *precedent,* some aspect of the past he believes to be relevant to the present situation; or an aspect is unconsciously activated. A previous experience may be his point of reference, his so-called anchoring point from which he judges the possibilities confronting him. On that scale are also his self-belief and the authority or power he attributes to others with whom he has had contact as well as a norm or standard provided by a prestigious person or group in his society.[31]

The communication of an authority who has been proven to be correct or helpful in the past or who ex officio is believed to be the source of wisdom may be judged acceptable without hesitation. Presumably the priest who hears a supplicant confess and then prescribes a course of action is obeyed because his authority comes from the Church. And the surgeon who advises a serious operation? Nowadays in some Western countries he himself may advise the patient to seek the judgment of another physician. In general if indecision remains over a period of time, new events occur, additional stimuli appear, and other predispositions from the past may become both salient and efficacious. In a very long-term interaction a sleeper effect may intrude: the tendency for a participant at first to reject the communication of a principal but then to forget its source more rapidly than its content, so that eventually he may approve of the contents.[32]

3.C.1.c When predispositions are organized into a somewhat consistent core that consciously determines action in a variety of situations, the participant may be said to have a *principle* or a set of principles—a "general rule"—that he may employ in reaching decisions under most circumstances.[33] The principle may be ethically, pragmatically, or personally oriented: should you be guided by what you believe to be the welfare of others or by your own interests? One useful schema suggests that the participant's decision in effect is based upon varying combinations of idealism and realism. A "situationist," high in both idealism and relativism, rejects moral rules and tries to analyze each situation as it arises in terms of its contents and implications. An "exceptionalist," low in both, finds value in moral absolutes but for utilitarian reasons admits the possibility of exceptions. The "absolutist," who is high in idealism but low in relativism, seeks to follow moral principles which he believes to be universal, regardless of consequences. The "subjectivist," who is low in idealism and high in relativism, tends to guide his decisions by personal values and "perspective" rather than universal moral principles.[34] Possibly some participants also utilize as bases for their decisions and behavior principles and criteria that are similar to those they employ—or can be induced to employ—in judging the potentialities of modern technologies, whether they are driving a car or deriving energy from nuclear power plants, viz., the perceived risks and benefits from exercising or accepting power and authority are weighed.[35]

Whether phrased formally or not, participants frequently judge a potential outcome in terms of whether it is just or not for themselves and for others. Conceptions of justice, however, are not uniform and are said to include principles referring to equality, equity, needs, ability, effort, accomplishments (or performance), the common good, a specified minimum, and even "the supply and demand of the market place." The guiding principle for making a decision may depend upon the nature of the relation among the participants: equity for relations concerned with "economic productivity," equality for those fostering or maintaining "enjoyable social relations," and need for those promoting personal development and personal welfare."[36] From a rational standpoint, it has been assumed that an individual suspects inequity when the ratio of his own contributions (inputs) and the conceivable consequences (i.e., the outcome) is less than the corresponding ratio of other participants or of one particular participant.[37] In this exchange he may inflict or accept an equitable outcome by considering the power or authority relation he has with his antagonists—unless of course he judges other factors to be more pressing. Sometimes a principal reaches a decision that will make him appear impartial, and a subordinate may accept a principal's decision to appear polite.[38]

Principles concerned with legitimacy may be salient. The decision to obey or accept someone as an authority may stem from three subprinciples. First, there is personal choice: this in effect is what I wish to do, what I really want. Next may be the criterion: I accept the decision of the surgeon because clearly I lack his diagnostic and operating skill. And finally, economy: I delegate responsibility to someone else because I cannot afford the time to participate in meetings or to perform the tasks associated with public office.[39]

Each of these three principles for accepting an authority reflects culturally induced beliefs concerning the legitimacy of the authority prescribing obedience; each may be phrased differently for a given participant who ascribes a different meaning to them. Personal choice includes a sense of inferiority inducing the individual to be obedient under most circumstances. Or he may decide that the leader or principal is someone he likes or would like to resemble.[40] Expertise can be somewhat diffuse and stems not only from the principal's skill but also from his reputation, appearance, and status. Delegating responsibility reflects the general tendency to recognize the need for order in social life: most citizens wish to be—and are—law-abiding, whether or not the required action is to their liking. There is no magic formula, in short, to decide all the reasons subordinates and followers advance for deciding to conform, whether that conformity is inwardly genuine or, as suggested in the next chapter, only outwardly feigned. After very patiently reading a conscientious summary of existing investigations concerning acceptance of authority,[41] one impression is virtually inevitable: no listing is superior to its academic, political, or philosophical rivals.

The requirements of the situation contribute to the selection of the principle guiding the decision. In terms of the trichotomy of the last two paragraphs, participants may use personal choice regarding the qualifications of a particular candidate, expertise when they willingly allow the plane's pilot to be in charge of the flight, and economy when voting for one budget rather than another. Which beliefs and attitudes are salient at a given moment depends on their strength, the requirements of the situation, and numerous background factors. An anarchist may use personal choice in a larger number of situations than an insecure cipher who prefers to be led. At a time of unrest, as during the 1960s in the United States and elsewhere in the Western world, many rebels wished to be able to make their own decisions regarding political matters and not be guided or governed by experts, without perhaps appreciating the sacrifice of time they would have to make if they were to become the principals in decision-making.[42]

Ultimately and in the broadest possible sense the invoked princi-
3.C.1.d ple reflects the participant's expected *rewards and punishments;*
the satisfaction or dissatisfaction to be anticipated for himself, for other participants, and for principals and followers.[43] Through rationalization or rational thought he may have to reconcile that decision or a contemplated action with other values to which he subscribes or, to use a meaningful if old-fashioned word, with his own conscience. Loose generalizations sometimes appear concerning decision-making in an entire society. Evidence is asserted to be "plentiful"—presumably in the United States—that "avoidance of power is perhaps the most prevalent of the responses to power"; people are said to prefer to mind their own business, to keep out of trouble, not to rock the boat, not to be too conspicuous.[44] Obviously the kinds of Americans ought to be specified to justify such an assertion, for there is overwhelmingly contrary evidence too easy to assemble. Thus those controlling the American motion-picture industry are said to have a driving ambition to demonstrate their power not by running risks or by being creative but by making millions of dollars on mediocre films through the sale of television and overseas rights.[45] A principal's judgment, therefore, may be a function of innumerable factors as weighed by him on the basis of his own personality and what he perceives in the event: the costs, the frustrations, the truth, the value of power to him, and his principles.[46] In addition, cognitive processes are operating as information is perceived, processed, and judged, and they may affect various principles which, though variously defined, include internal rewards and punishments of an existential nature. The fancy labels given to these processes are reviewed in a brief note at the end of this chapter.[47]

Both the predispositions of the participant and the requirements
3.C.2 of the situation at hand determine the *contents* of the decision that
is reached. In the first place, he selects a role: will he be a principal or leader rather than a subordinate or follower? He considers the nature of his goal and his probability of attaining it.[48] For the principal the goal includes the rewards he will receive from exercising or not exercising power, for the subordinate the rewards or punishments that will be his from complying or not. He may decide that he is unable to discharge a particular role because he lacks the resources, such as money, or the skill. Ordinarily, a government assumes that citizens are able to obey its edicts, but their failure to comply may signify neither their unwillingness to do so nor the belief that the regulation is unjust. They may be unable to pay the taxes that are imposed, even as a starving prisoner in a concentration camp cannot perform the hard work demanded by the guards.

When a participant concludes that he cannot or will not be a principal, he must decide whether or not and for what reasons he will obey another participant or the next principal in line. He places himself, as it were, along a continuum ranging from complete obedience, including internal agreement or satisfaction, through outward but not inward compliance and eventually disobedience and resistance. At one end may be the so-called milky-toast who obeys uncritically and more or less automatically; at the other end is the convinced anarchist who rejects all authority, at least that originating from the state, and hence seeks to sabotage or hinder its power. According to a political scientist, the participant is faced with five alternatives as he passes judgment concerning an authority's communication:

> I will obey this law because I think it is right.
>
> I don't agree with this law, but I'll obey it.
>
> I don't agree with this law, and I'll obey it only under protest.
>
> I don't think this law is right, and I won't obey it unless I'm forced to.
>
> This law is wrong, and I won't obey it under any circumstances.[49]

Behavior is planned within a time frame which may be set by external or internal conditions. Voting occurs at specified periods in democratic societies. Participants decide to carry out their decisions immediately or later. Some evidence indicates that in traditional societies participants prefer authorities who compel instant obedience or who administer punishments for infractions without waiting for the due process demanded by formal courts; in addition, the gratification from complying at the spur of the moment may be more tempting than the greater gratification provided by delays.[50]

It is not easy, in fact it is often impossible to reconstruct the bases for significant decisions which have implications for the power the participant will seek or avoid, for the authority he will or will not possess. The individual may be able to report that he has chosen a particular occupation, whether it be the practice of medicine or the role of a housewife, as a result of early models and influences, but methodologically there is no certain way to determine the validity of his report. This is what he says, this is perhaps what he thinks, but has he mentioned the crucial factors? We would need a control person exactly equivalent to him except for the alleged causative factors—an impossibility. Historical research has not uncovered *precisely* how and why the decision was made by President Truman to drop an atomic bomb on Hiroshima. Yes, he made the final decision after receiving advice and data from a host of persons; but how and why did he evaluate what he heard and read? Undiscoverable are all the details concerning the confrontation between him and his advisers, the topic for the next chapter.

> *Guide:* To be or not to be a power or an authority, to plan or not to plan accordingly—or somewhere in between—these are the challenges to each participant.

NOTES

1. Harold D. Lasswell, *Power and Personality*. New York: Viking, 1962. P. 39, italics omitted.

2. Cf. P. H. Gulliver, *Disputes and Negotiations*. New York: Academic Press, 1979. Pp. 83–88.

3. Cf. Lee Ross, The intuitive psychologist and his shortcomings. In Leonard Berkowitz (ed.), *Advances in Experimental Social Psychology*. New York: Academic Press, 1977. Vol. 10, pp. 173–220.

4. Floyd Henry Allport, *Social Psychology*. Boston: Houghton Mifflin, 1924. Pp. 305–8.

5. Cf. Edwin P. Hollander, Independence, conformity, and civil liberties. *Journal of Social Issues*, 1975, 31, no. 2, 56–67.

6. U.S.A.: Sixty-five male undergraduates. *Method:* urban problems were discussed in groups of five, with the subject being in the minority vis-à-vis the four confederates of the experimenters. *Results:* the subjects tended to remain independent when the instruction had not been to reach a majority opinion *and* when they had been privately told that they were performing well according to expert opinion. William A. Carpenter and Edwin P. Hollander, Overcoming hurdles to independence in groups. *Journal of Social Psychology*, 1982, 117, 237–41.

7. U.S.A.: Forty-four female undergraduates. *Method:* the subject judged an ambiguous situation (to determine which of three lights went off first) as three confederates allegedly responded correctly or incorrectly and as a fourth confederate (to whom experience was or was not attributed) deviated from the majority of three. *Results:* the presence of an "experienced" deviant increased nonconformity with the majority, but the example of that deviant also increased nonconformity with both the majority and with her. Richard Kimball and Edwin P. Hollander, Independence in the presence of an experienced but deviate group member. *Journal of Social Psychology*, 1974, 93, 281–92.

8. Cf. James S. Mouton, Robert R. Blake, and Joseph Olmstead, The relationship between frequency and yielding and the disclosure of personal identity. *Journal of Personality*, 1956, 24, 339–47.

9. Cf. Jean-Paul Codol. On the so-called "superior conformity of the self" behavior. *European Journal of Social Psychology*, 1975, 5, 457–501.

10. John W. Thibaut and Harold H. Kelley, *The Social Psychology of Groups*. New York: Wiley, 1959. Pp. 102–4.

11. U.S.A.: 197 black freshmen. *Method:* they listened to one of four tapes in which the speaker, with varying power and prestige, advocated a position at variance with their own; afterwards they replied to a questionnaire requiring or not requiring them to sign their names either immediately after hearing the tape or one to two weeks later. *Results:* more subjects complied when they had heard an authority with power, when they were required to sign their names and believed he would see their opinions, and when they filled out the questionnaire immediately afterwards. Herbert C. Kelman, Compliance, identification, and internalization. *Journal of Conflict Resolution*, 1958, 2, 51–60.

12. Jean Piaget, *The Moral Judgment of the Child*. London: Kegan Paul, Trench, Trubner, 1932. P. 129.

13. E.g., Donald C. McCann and Norman M. Prentice, Promoting moral judgment

of elementary school children. *Journal of Genetic Psychology,* 1981, 139, 27–34.

14. Mary Kristine Utne and Robert F. Kidd, Equity and attribution. In Gerold Mikula (ed.), *Justice and Social Interaction.* New York: Springer-Verlag, 1980. Pp. 63–90.

15. Thibaut and Kelley, op. cit., pp. 109–10.

16. Cf. J. Rex, Race as a social category. *Journal of Biosocial Science,* 1969, Suppl. no. 1, 145–52.

17. Cited by Deborah Goleman Wolf, *The Lesbian Community.* Berkeley: University of California, 1979. Pp. 68–69.

18. Malcolm T. Walker, *Politics and the Power Structure.* New York: Teachers College Press, 1972. P. 107.

19. Cf. Morton Deutsch, *The Resolution of Conflict.* New Haven: Yale University Press, 1973. P. 164.

20. U.S.A.: Seventy-two children, ages thirty-three to sixty-five months. *Method:* one adult provided a meaningful reward to the child, another appeared as a rival for the same attractive play materials. *Results:* more of the children imitated the model with rewarding power than the rival. Albert Bandura, Dorothea Ross, and Sheila A. Ross, A comparative test of the status envy, social power, and secondary reinforcement theories of identificatory learning. *Journal of Abnormal and Social Psychology,* 1963, 67, 527–34.

21. U.S.A.: Forty-one undergraduates. *Method:* in two separate experiments confederates complied, in one they claimed to have been persuaded by the subject's use of arguments to donate blood, in the other to share a dictionary in solving crossword puzzles; the confederates had low or high prestige and they were later rated by the subjects. *Results:* in both experiments, the subjects tended to attribute the compliance of the high-prestige confederate to an internal decision, that of the low-prestige confederate to external pressure. John W. Thibault and Henry W. Riecken, Some determinants and consequences of the perception of social causality. *Journal of Personality,* 1955, 24, 113–33.

22. U.S.A.: Forty-eight male undergraduates. *Method:* the subject and a confederate worked together solving crossword puzzles; help given to the confederate reduced the money obtained by the subject; one confederate was said to have little power and an external orientation, the other more power and an internal orientation. *Results:* more help tended to be given the confederate with little power than to the one with more power, in spite of the monetary sacrifice. John Schopler and Marjorie Wall Matthews, The influence of the perceived causal locus of partner's dependence on the use of interpersonal power. *Journal of Personality and Social Psychology,* 1965, 2, 609–12.

23. U.S.A.: Eighty-eight male high-school sophomores. *Method:* each boy was interviewed by a three-man board who exhibited varying degrees of friendliness and power in questioning him; the alleged purpose of the interview was to decide whether he would be given a ticket to a basketball game. *Result:* interviews afterwards revealed no significant differences in the boys' opinions of the board members. Albert Pepitone, Motivational effects in social perception. *Human Relations,* 1950, 3, 57–76.

24. Cf. J. Richard Eiser, *Cognitive Social Psychology.* London: McGraw-Hill, 1980. Pp. 61–64.

25. Edwin P. Hollander and James W. Julian, Studies in leader legitimacy, influence, and innovation. In Leonard Berkowitz (ed.), *Group Processes.* New York: Academic Press, 1978. Pp. 115–51.

26. Arnold A. Lazarus, *The Practice of Multimodal Therapy*. New York: McGraw-Hill, 1981.

27. Carl J. Friedrich, *Tradition and Authority*. New York: Praeger, 1972. Pp. 89–98.

28. Reinhard Bendix, *Kings or People*. Berkeley: University of California Press, 1978. Pp. 4, 596.

29. U.S.A.: Eighty married couples, half black, half white. *Method:* each spouse separately filled out a schedule of eighteen items indicating who makes the decisions "in the areas of recreation, family purchases, and household tasks"; then the pair was asked to reconcile whatever differences appeared on the separate schedules by debating the issues with each other; subsequently they discussed two timely topics in the presence of the investigator—child training and Richard Nixon—and they also simulated a bargaining session. *Results:* no difference with respect to power appeared between men and women in these situations, a finding contrary to historical studies which had indicated that among American blacks women tended to be more powerful in the home. The only difference of note involved reconciling the two schedules: in this respect working-class husbands tended to be "more powerful" than middle-class men. In each of these three interactions different skills were crucial, so that power appeared to be "context-determined." Delores E. Mack, The power relationships in black and white families. *Journal of Personality and Social Psychology,* 1974, 30, 409–13.

30. Cf. Martin F. Davis, The effects of thought on behavioral prediction. *Journal of Psychology,* 1981, 109, 239–44.

31. Cf. Muzafer Sherif and Carl I. Hovland, *Social Judgment*. New Haven: Yale University Press, 1961.

32. Carl I. Hovland, Irving L. Janis, and Harold H. Kelley, *Communication and Persuasion*. New Haven: Yale University Press, 1953. Pp. 254–59.

33. Cf. Herbert Simon, *Models of Thought*. New Haven: Yale University Press, 1979. Pp. 329–46.

34. Derived with slight modification from Donelson R. Forsyth, A taxonomy of ethical ideologies. *Journal of Personality and Social Psychology*, 1980, 39, 175–84.

35. Cf. Gerald T. Gardner et al., Risk and benefit perceptions, acceptability judgments, and self-reported actions toward nuclear power. *Journal of Social Psychology,* 1982, 116, 179–97.

36. Morton Deutsch, Equity, equality, and need. *Journal of Social Issues*, 1975, 31, no. 3, 137–49. Cf. Dennis A. Bagarozzi, The effects of cohesiveness on distributive justice. *Journal of Psychology,* 1982, 110, 267–73.

37. J. Stacy Adams, Inequity in social exchange. In Leonard Berkowitz (ed.), *Advances in Experimental Social Psychology*, op. cit., vol. 2, pp. 267–99.

38. Cf. Thomas Schwinger, Just allocations of goods. In Mikula (ed.), op. cit., pp. 95–125.

39. Robert A. Dahl, *After the Revolution?* New Haven: Yale University Press, 1970. Pp. 8–58.

40. Cf. John R. P. French, Jr. and Bertram Raven, The bases of social power. In Dorwin Cartwright (ed.), *Studies in Social Power*. Ann Arbor: Research Center for Group Dynamics, 1959. Pp. 15–67.

41. Barry E. Collins and Bertram H. Raven, Group structure. In Gardner Lindzey and Elliot Aronson (eds.), *Handbook of Social Psychology*. Reading: Addison-Wesley, 1969. Vol. 4, pp. 102–204.

42. Dahl, op. cit., pp. 42–46.

43. Cf. Jack H. Nagel, *The Descriptive Analysis of Power*. New Haven: Yale University Press, 1975. Pp. 28–29.

44. William Ker Muir, Jr., *Police: Streetcorner Politicians*. Chicago: University of Chicago Press, 1977. Pp. 275–76.

45. Pauline Kael, The current cinema. *New Yorker,* June 23, 1980, pp. 82, 85, 86–93.

46. Cf. Bertram H. Raven and Arie W. Kruglanski, Conflict and power. In Paul Swingle (ed.), *The Structure of Power*. New York: Academic Press, 1970. Pp. 83–86.

47. Perhaps the participant seeks to avoid "dissonance" and therefore arrives at a decision enabling him to achieve a feeling of "consistency" or "balance." He wishes his various predispositions to be in "harmony." He would reduce "complexity." Each of these concepts at the moment has staunch proponents among social scientists, particularly social psychologists. In my banal opinion, all of the theories behind the concepts, in spite of more than a touch of ethnocentrism, contain a touch of truth backed by somewhat impressive research, with the result that a neutral cannot recommend that one descriptive theory has greater commonsense validity or utility than its rivals. Details, readily available elsewhere, are not offered here; yet another Arbitrary Limitation is invoked. See J. Richard Eiser, op. cit., pp. 30–45.

48. Cf. Henry L. Minton, Power as a personality construct. In Brendan A. Maher (ed.), *Progress in Experimental Personality Research*. New York: Academic Press, 1967. Vol. 4, pp. 229–69.

49. Glenn Negley, *Political Authority and Moral Judgment*. Durham: Duke University Press, 1965, P. 110.

50. Leonard W. Doob, *Becoming More Civilized*. Westport: Greenwood, 1973. Pp. 84–93.

9

Actions and Behavior

Finally, the participant and the observer converge: the predispositions and decisions of the participant result in some form of behavior that can be perceived by an observer. The solipsistic encasement is partially cracked: the individual emerges from his subjective privacy and his behavior is a public, objective action. For the first time, therefore, the two approaches to power and authority—the series of outer and inner circles in the Guiding Figure—can and must be considered simultaneously within the confines of a single chapter.

After the participant has reacted to the event and after he has reached a decision concerning his own role therein, what will he do? Will he continue to remain inactive or will he engage in behavior that implements his decision? The varying relation between predispositions and behavior has already been discussed in two contexts: beliefs and attitudes may have an effect upon behavior, although that effect is seldom direct or invariant. Similarly there may be many discrepancies between the judgment or decision of a participant and his overt behavior. He may have an impulse to slit the throat of another person, but instead he administers a mild rebuff. As political leaders in democracies struggle for power, it is clear that followers with favorable attitudes toward a particular candidate do not always turn out and vote for him: they may not be qualified to vote, they may be too lazy to go to the polls, they may cast their ballot for his opponent on impulse or for reasons of expedience.

The observer, nevertheless, may rescue himself from such complete indeterminacy in two ways. Occasionally, in the first place, one variable affecting behavior can be weighted so heavily that the others may be disregarded or almost always so. If the power motive, for example, is exceptionally intense or weak, it may be safe to anticipate that the participant in almost any situation will be, respectively, a principal or a subordinate. A word of caution must immediately be added concerning the precision of such a prediction. An extremely prejudiced person may almost always feel hostility within himself when he is confronted with someone belonging to the group he judges harshly; on occasion he may seek to assert a feeling of dominance or superiority, but on other occasions—out of politeness, convention, or fear—he may hold that feeling in check. Similarly a recognized authority elicits behavior which almost without exception can be anticipated: a traffic policeman blows a whistle or gives a hand signal, and without reflection all drivers, except criminals in their getaway cars, perceive and judge him to be an authority with power and hence they obey.

Then, in the second place, the observer must recognize the multivariant nature of human behavior under most circumstances. Of late, there have been theories attempting to employ combinations of variables to link verbally expressed predispositions and actual behavior; two of the most promising are quickly summarized in a note at the end of this chapter.[1] From these theories one useful generalization can be salvaged: the greater the number of variables, particularly specific ones, included in the equation that would predict a participant's behavior, the more accurate that prediction is likely to be. The moral, consequently, is that almost never—except for personality traits and similar situations mentioned in the last paragraph above—is there a simple way to forecast how a participant will react to authority and power. It is fruitful to assume that authority- or power-related behavior is associated not with a single judgment but with a series of judgments. Those students in various Western countries, for example, who had engaged in political demonstrations during the 1970s, largely against established authorities, tended to oppose war, private property, the traditional family structure, inequality, and hereditary theories explaining war and aggression.[2]

Guide: The best laid decisions gang aft agley, but not always.

IV,4.A *Confrontation*. The participant enters the arena, as it were, with other participants, and perhaps in the presence of one or more forces; or he decides to withdraw. His reaction is overt and so are the reactions of other participants, if not for him then possibly for an observer. If he enters, his reactions may relate to power and authority; or they may be neutral in one or both respects. In either case he is part of the confrontation with other participants, he employs various tactics, and he may affect the eventual outcome. Thus in a political campaign a principal reaches a decision to run for public office. His action is an announcement to that effect. During the campaign he employs various tactics. Eventually he wins or loses. Or at the outset he may decide not to run for office and hence he does not face opponents and does not communicate to voters. As a citizen, a subordinate decides, formally or carelessly, to vote or not. If he decides to vote or does not immediately make that decision, he is part of the confrontation: candidates appeal to him for his vote. Whether or not he eventually votes, he permits one candidate and not the others to assume power and possess authority.

The analysis in this section, if I may cry wolf again, is especially complicated for two reasons. During the confrontation, as emphasized below, the participant may be affected by the interaction and change his original decision: at first he dislikes, then he comes to like another participant. The change results from the confrontation which has reduced him to reconsider; there has been, as it were, another event perceived by him in terms of his own predispositions which leads to a reconsideration. Then, secondly, similar processes occur simultaneously among all the participants to which an observer may or may not be able to pay attention. It is unlikely, however, that an observer will have an opportunity to concentrate on every participant unless those confronting one another are few in number. In a political campaign he probably observes the contenders very closely and notes only aspects of the electorate's actions, such as attendance at political rallies or fluctuations in voting preferences, that have been recorded in formal or informal public opinion surveys.

The perceived power and authority of the participants at the moment of confrontation and thereafter is likely to have a profound effect upon the roles they assume and the tactics they employ. The guess has been advanced that in international relations negotiation is encouraged "when power relations shift toward equality."[3] Either in the face-to-face situation or outside the negotiations one set of participants may therefore strive either to equalize that relation or else to make it appear to tip in their favor.

IV,4.A.1 During confrontations the norms governing the participants may be *open* or *closed:* many or virtually all of the participants are active or only the leader or principal makes the decisions. Whatever jockeying for power and authority occurs, therefore, may ultimately affect the participants' reactions and can be noted by an observer. A Jesuit priest, in describing how he himself functioned as a psychiatrist in an open ward of a mental hospital, has illustrated the open confrontation:

> The decision-making process was irrevocably mine. But in such a relationship the decision-making that I had to do was carried out in a context of collaboration. Decisions were never made arbitrarily or one-sidedly. They were, whenever and wherever possible, discussed, explored, considered together. The patient was never left out; he was always listened to, consulted with. There were, of course, times when decisions had to be made quickly and consultation was impossible.
>
> Patients could tolerate such exceptions because they were exceptions. They knew and understood that circumstances prevented the usual dialogue, but they also knew that any decision affecting them or the ward community was always open to discussion and reconsideration at any time. They also knew from the context of all other discussions and decisions that the decision was in the hands of someone they trusted, someone who was committed to their welfare and well-being.[4]

Collaboration thus enabled the inmates to be active and to allocate responsibilities and privileges to themselves: the leader limited his own authority and power.

Contrasting confrontations occur in closed systems such as armies or prisons. Authorities are clearly designated: with few exceptions, participants know who those authorities are and they know also whom they must obey since the authorities are powerful. It is platitudinous to be reminded that there can be no participatory democracy on a ship when decisions are made concerning navigation during the crisis of a severe storm. In such situations the confrontations are brief and almost perfunctory. Sometimes, however, even authorities in closed systems may be disobeyed, though the peril to the participants may be great: soldiers and sailors mutiny, prisoners riot or stage hunger strikes. Some followers, nevertheless, may prefer to avoid confrontations and to leave decisions to authorities to whom they submit. One horrifying but understandable example was the tendency, as reported by one observer, for some inmates inside Nazi concentration camps to identify with the authorities and even praise or emulate them.[5]

IV,4.A.2 In many confrontations, especially those with open norms, *bargaining* takes place among the contesting participants. According to one summary of relevant "social psychological laboratory studies," those participants less responsive to the needs of others tended to be motivated by a need to achieve, whereas those more responsive tended to be motivated by a need for affection or power.[6] Other predispositions of bargainers have been probed by social scientists, even though they are elusive. Perhaps, for example, those participants with strong self-beliefs are less likely to comply with the demands of a leader;[7] perhaps, too, they may bargain more vigorously.[8] Contrast the bargaining between a dealer and his customer with the give-and-take between two lovers. Forget the dealer and consider more pleasurably the lovers who are likely to have a more intense relationship, to exchange more information, to be in contact for a longer period of time, to have at their disposal strong rewards and punishments, to exchange not one but more than one of the interpersonal resources available to participants, to be able to substitute one resource for another, and to have a more complete sense of identification with each other.[9] For them a temporal factor plays a crucial role: their confrontation extends over a longer period of time.

Any large organization requires some confrontation, however meager, if it is to function efficiently. The most ruthless dictator confronts his followers and satisfies at least some of their needs if he is not to be overthrown. A large industrial company operates on various levels of authority beginning with the owners (whether private persons, stockholders, or the state), managers, foremen, and numerous strata of workers. The upper echelons are primarily interested almost always in increasing productivity and hence, in capitalist countries, profits. Their problem is how to exercise the authority of their positions to achieve that end. According to one facile but adequate summary, three critical factors leading to an increase in productivity have been identified by different "schools of thought": the work must be made "intrinsically satisfying," the rewards in the form of wages must be adequate, and workers must be permitted or encouraged to play a role in making decisions affecting production and other aspects of the organization.[10] During the depression of the Reagan 1980s in the United States, Japanese practices have been reported to be satisfying those criteria, in contrast with most American practices.

Guide: Precedents and principles guide decision-makers up to an indefinite point.

Some decisions may be made in the quiet of the participant's
IV,4.A.3 mind, dreams, or home, but many occur during the *give-and-take*
of the confrontation with other participants, or with others and one or more forces. The leader seeks counsel from his advisers or they deluge him with his own ideas; a decision eventually emerges. President Truman's decision to bomb Hiroshima, the complicated character of which has been previously suggested, appears simpler than the one we hope must never be made regarding whether nuclear weapons should be unleashed on short notice against an actual or potential enemy. More generally, unless a situation is rigidly structured, principals and subordinates are not likely to respond with uniformity or unanimity.[11]

Sometimes it is possible but difficult to chart the confrontation of participants who are in direct contact with one another. Very elaborate and reasonably thorough coding systems have been devised to plot in detail the reactions of persons in small, but not in large groups. When only the relations of American undergraduates to their instructor during simple discussions within a classroom are considered, the main categories must include the impulse of the members (whether demonstrating hostility or affection), their ego state (whether expressing or denying anxiety or depression or expressing self-esteem), and their relations to authorities (whether showing dependency, independence, or counterdependence).[12] The scoring quite obviously cannot remain static; even during a single academic hour the relations among the members and between them and the instructor keep fluctuating. Outside the classroom or the committee room, relations between leaders and followers become stabilized so that the outcomes of confrontations may be less uncertain. The reader, if extremely conscientious, is referred to perhaps the most complicated schema of all time for analyzing the interactions of small groups: it is based upon six directions or locations which give rise to twenty-six ratings (each of which has five steps ranging from "never" to "always"); yet Chapter 12 of the exposition (there are 38 chapters and 24 appendices) is titled "Each Individual Field Is Unique."[13]

For present purposes it is impossible to codify the numerous factors that may or must be noted during the confrontation because they are likely to affect the outcome. Certainly the composition of the group and the opportunities for communication or feedback may be critical. In larger groups the emergence of coalitions among participants may occur, and members of the groups may become polarized.[14] Little wonder that any confrontation may be coded so variously.

Guide: Action and behavior may be markedly affected by the nature of the confrontation between or among the participants and by existing situational and cultural restraints.

IV,4.B *Principals' Tactics.* "If ye love me, keep my commandments," it has been said.[15] The authority is urging his followers to express their love not only by deciding to follow his commandments but also by acting in accordance with them. Urging is one tactic, but surely in this instance it was and ever should be effective as a result of the inspiration offered by the model. Principals have additional tactics from which to choose when the model is less compelling.

Unless the situation provoked by the event is thoroughly structured and closed—and then a command is obeyed without opposition—a principal or leader must employ some method or device to achieve his goal of exerting power or authority. That goal is relevant here, for it may determine how much effort he expends and possibly also whether he attempts to influence participants openly or slyly.[16] This latter distinction, like most distinctions based upon a communicator's intentions, cannot ignore the reactions of the audience. A sophisticated participant in modern society, for example, may recognize a sly communication reaching him in an ostensibly unbiased form; for him the attempt is open or transparent.

In general, then, the choice of tactics, whether by the principal or the subordinate, stems from a host of factors, including the interaction between them, which vary from situation to situation. The rules within a situation may be clear, as when a written or unwritten constitution specifies that an executive may exercise his authority only through specified channels. In less structured cases the principal may engage in trial and error behavior in response to the ongoing reactions of the participants. A predisposition of the principal himself may be influential. If he has a weak belief in his own self-control, he may hesitate to be decisive or, quite the contrary, he may be even more decisive in order to compensate for his own insecurity. The action of a principal or a subordinate and its link to his internal, private decision may be related to unconscious impulses. Or it may result from experiences he has had in childhood or thereafter.

Principals who believe that an injustice has been committed by themselves and by others while power has been asserted may adopt various means to try to attain some semblance of equity when they are disturbed by the role they have played. According to one analysis, they may seek to restore actual equity by compensating the subordinate. Or they may try to achieve what is called psychological equity: they derogate the subordinate, they minimize the suffering or loss he has experienced, or they deny that they themselves have responsibility for what has transpired.[17] The motive for both kinds of equity may be to appease the conscience of the principal since often, but not always, it is painful to live with the belief that one is responsible for the misery of another person. Perhaps subordinates are more likely to be persuaded that they have not been treated unjustly when the principal is powerful.[18]

IV,4.B.1 Whether determined by the principal or the forms existing in the society, *symbols* by themselves have tactical significance. In Chinese different forms of address are customarily employed when two persons speak, and thus the pair conveys the reciprocity, the solidarity (or intimacy), and the equality characterizing them and their culturally or biologically determined relation.[19] Material objects serve the same function: an African chief demonstrates his authority by a leopard skin at his feet and by shells in his headdress,[20] a business executive by his private office or by the number of telephones on his desk,[21] and public officials by the size and design of the buildings they occupy.[22]

IV,4.B.2 The most frequently suggested dichotomy of tactics is that of *persuasion* and *coercion*. Presumably the distinction is quantitative: with coercion one or only a few alternatives are offered participants, with persuasion many are offered, or at least so it can be made to appear. The persuader gives the impression, which may or may not be true, that the participant does not have to obey but may select alternative modes of action, including disobedience; in logical terms, he is offered the premises by the principal, then draws his own conclusions.

Coercion occurs when in fact a principal possesses a resource or a controlled force he can employ to achieve his goal: either you pay attention to the mass media in modern society or you remain socially ignorant or bored. Face-to-face contacts may be either coercive or persuasive, depending on how they are presented and how participants react to them. When there are apparently insoluble problems, as in zero-sum situations, the solution may require "mutual coercion, mutually agreed upon by the majority of the people affected."[23] The agreement is achieved through persuasion; again coercion and persuasion merge.

Truly legion are the forms of coercion. Obviously they vary from situation to situation. For Americans one writer has outlined measures available in three settings:

Marriage

1. I act cold and say very little to him/her.
2. I make the other person miserable by doing things he or she does not like.
3. I get angry and demand that he/she give in.
4. I threaten to use physical force.
5. I threaten to separate or seek a divorce.

Work

1. I chewed him out.
2. I gave him a verbal warning.
3. I threatened to give him a written warning.
4. I ignored him while being friendly with everyone else.
5. I kept riding him.
6. I scheduled him to work hours he didn't like.
7. I gave him work he didn't like.
8. I put him in a work area he didn't like.

9. I put him in an area of lower premium pay.
10. I gave him a written warning.
11. I took steps to suspend him.
12. I recommended that he be brought before the disciplinary committee.
13. He was suspended from work.
14. He was fired.

Custodial Mental Hospital

1. Warn the patient of loss of privileges (passes, cigarettes).
2. Put the patient in isolation.
3. Scold the patient.
4. Physically control the patient (restraints, etc.).
5. Give medicine to the patient (to sedate).
6. Discipline the patient by removing things or privileges that the patient wants.[24]

Possibly a clue to the reasons for selecting coercion rather than persuasion can be located in the principal's predispositions. One bold writer has "attempted to describe the powerholder's thoughts prior to the use of coercive power and after the coercion has been successfully used." He admits he has "little direct evidence" to support his sketches, and so he cites arbitrary illustrations to indicate "the range of questions one should ask about coercive power." Before the use of power the principal experiences "anger and rage," afterwards "satisfaction"; before "fear," afterwards "relief"; before "envy" and "greed," afterwards "satisfaction."[25] The same writer does not even speculate concerning the effects of coercive power upon the follower or subordinate since he considers this task "beyond the ability of social science, except in very limited contrived situations."[26] Probably he is quite correct.

IV,4.B.3 An exhaustive list of persuasive-coercive tactics would have to mention virtually all aspects of *interpersonal relations*. Included would be the young child who coerces his parents to pay attention to him by refusing to eat,[27] the lawyer for the defense who persuades a jury that his client is not guilty. A baker's half-dozen must suffice.

IV,4.B.3.a The most extreme form of coercion appears when the leaders of modern nations resort to *war*. Although it is possible on a very abstract level to distinguish between the predisposing and precipitating causes of war,[28] and although the violence of modern nations can be classified by means of sophisticated measures and statistics, no simple or complicated generalizations emerge; too many illustrations are at hand. Here are two typical ones of high quality. According to an elaborate analysis of the seven foreign policies (including those toward the cold war, intervention in Africa, alignment with the U.S.A. or the U.S.S.R. in U.N. voting) of 109 nations in a single year, 1963, "accountability" (defined in terms of the electoral system, the freedom of the press, the representative character of the regime, and similar factors) was the factor most closely related to foreign policy measures, more so in the case of the "developed" than the "undeveloped" countries.[29] A study of political violence in ten modern nations for the period of 1948 to 1968 reveals that demonstrations against the government, attempts to overthrow the government, and civil wars tended to occur when changes in the conditions of the population in the direction of modernization outran changes in the political institutions and when population changes occurred more rapidly than economic developments, although the latter factor seems less important when other factors are taken into account.[30] Statistics aside, nobody should be surprised by the fact that the "causes" of the American Civil War, this country's entrance into World Wars I and II, and its muddled intervention in Vietnam do not have a simple, common denominator, unless one invokes a highly abstract principle such as economic determinism or the madness of men.

Violence without war is another form of coercion. Through assas-
IV,4.B.3.b sinations and bombings men coercively seek to achieve social or psychological objectives. In Western Europe the perpetrators express hostility toward political institutions. In the Middle East they often call attention to a group's existence or goals, such as those of the Palestine Liberation Organization, and demonstrate their power against specific authorities. In the United States the political motive may be lacking, and the terrorist may simply be giving vent to twisted tendencies within himself. Indeed an American psychiatrist suggests that violence conceivably may serve a useful function, however distasteful or destructive it may be for the targets: it may have, he writes, therapeutic value for an "endless" number of persons such as "the overly shy" or "the coward who insulates himself from experiences that would enrich him."[31] Here is no valid reason to promote or tolerate violence as a form of egocentric therapy. Anywhere, it must be immediately added, authority is weakened by acts of terror. Probably the increasing incidents of terrorism nowadays result in part from publicity: would-be terrorists thus learn new techniques (e.g., hijacking planes) and receive assurance that they can coerce the media to publicize their deeds.

A power may gain or retain authority by manipulating the allo-
IV,4.B.3.c cation of *resources* to subordinates. According to one investigator, he or she may proclaim the rules under which resources may be utilized: parents indicate the kinds of expenditures children may not make with their allowances. Access to resources may be limited: cookies are stored where young children cannot find them. Resources may be increased under specified conditions: the well-behaved child probably knows he will be given certain privileges. Or authority may be delegated: again the young saint may be trusted to spend his allowance as he pleases or to have access to the cookie jar when the parent is convinced that the child's superego will prevent him from violating parental rules.[32] Good or efficient administrators of large enterprises like governments and corporations delegate authority and responsibility

to those whom they trust and consider competent and who then have authority and power over those still lower in the hierarchy.

A form of persuasion-coercion is to offer actual or potential subordinates some kind of reward in *exchange* for their obedience or cooperation. From one standpoint the tactics of a principal always involve an exchange relation between himself and a subordinate: the principal has a resource to distribute or to bestow upon a participant who is or thinks he is experiencing a need that can be satisfied—and here the element of coercion may enter—by receiving that resource, even when it is negative, viz., avoiding punishment. According to one adherent to such a theory, six dimensions of resources ultimately should be distinguished, all of which, save one, are self-explanatory: money, goods, services, love, information, and—the slightly subtle one—status (a compliment indicating esteem or respect).[33] Noteworthy is that each of these interpersonal resources can be given or taken away by the principal; for example, respect can be displayed or withdrawn. From an economic and social standpoint, institutions and customs function to facilitate exchanges. What does someone in the West do when he has had a very enjoyable meal? In a private home he compliments and thanks the hostess profusely; in a restaurant he says a kind word to the proprietor or the waiter, pays the bill, and leaves a generous tip behind.

Gently or not the human *body* can be used as a tactical weapon.
IV,4.B.3.d In face-to-face situations one participant may dominate another
by moving closer to him, by a threatening gesture, or by facial grimaces. He may invade the other person's space, perhaps only when he believes himself to be more powerful than the subordinate he would thus coerce or when such a maneuver does not violate one of his own beliefs or attitudes. Probably the relative heights of the participants,[34] and possibly too their number, sex, and attractiveness,[35] may affect the outcome of such a primitive encounter.

The most intrusive form of personal space invasion is actual contact. Since virtually every participant to some extent seeks to protect the "inviolability" of his own body, a more powerful principal such as a policeman can assert his authority by touching, even manhandling the body of the civilian he would dominate.[36] Involuntary victims of rape are outraged. Privacy may also be invaded when the authority secretly collects information concerning participants: storing what they have done or bugging what they have said in private may constitute a powerful weapon to employ in court or as blackmail.

Eye-gazing can serve a number of functions for the gazer, such as signifying the end of his contribution to a conversation, trying to reduce an anticipated punishment, or obtaining praise. For the recipient, the gaze of another participant may affect his own evaluation of that individual.[37] In addition, it is possible that, when two persons interact, the less powerful person will look at the more powerful one more frequently than the more powerful one will turn his gaze upon the less powerful one.[38] The individual lower on the hierarchy may thus be seeking to acquire information about the superior one, or he may be wishing to show him respect. A speaker may spend less time gazing than a listener not in order to demonstrate his status but to inhibit the listener from interrupting him.

Verbalisms play a major role as principals express their authority
IV,4.B.3.e or exert power. Verbal threats frequently are employed to induce
obedience. The punishment thus specified may be immediate or far-flung, specific or general. The type of threat, possibly even when a parent tells a "bad" child that God will punish him if he does not behave in accordance with the adult's wishes,[39] reflects an aspect of the principal's status or personality. The grammatical form of language or speech can signify the authority of the speaker and the role he expects his listener to assume. The mode of the verb can convey whether the principal is giving a command, providing authorization, expressing a wish, or simply offering instruction.[40]

Another powerful weapon is silence which can symbolize so much, whether it be that of the psychoanalyst who can demonstrate his authority by listening silently to what a suffering patient is afraid to say or that of the politician who would demonstrate contempt for his opponent by ignoring him or refusing to debate with him. The opposite of silence is another verbal weapon: one person exerts his power or authority by interrupting the speaker or especially, during a moment of hesitation, by completing his or her sentence.[41] In American society there is a tendency for women, consciously or unconsciously, to acknowledge their subservient positions by using more polite language, by avoiding obscenities, and perhaps even by allowing men to dominate conversations.[42]

Laws and regulations are expressed in words and therefore offer verbal threats to the disobedient. The threats consist of actions in the form of punishments. The problem for principals as well as for subordinates is whether such threats are effective. Various forms of crime are prohibited and the punishments range from fines to capital punishment. To our sorrow we know that these verbal threats are not always effective; I shall not add a footnote on the efficacy of the death penalty because, it is evident, the evidence pertaining to the success of this supreme punishment for committing murder or treason is equivocal. Similarly, the efficacy of most threats is doubtful. The leaders of a country who believe that a mighty arsenal of weapons and their supporting troops will keep the peace must publicize their military strength in communications and through both the mass media and diplomatic channels; but it is very uncertain as to whether deterrence has ultimately succeeded over the centuries in preventing or even mitigating wars.[43]

Everyday conversations may contain elements of coercion and persuasion, particularly when the participants are unaware of their own tactics. The very title of the best seller two decades ago, *The Games People Play*, suggests with copious, juicy anecdotes that those games may not be as innocent as they seem and that they can be conducted simultaneously on more than one level. A simple illustration might be that which takes place between a salesman who seeks the victory of a sale and the housewife who would protect her ego. The salesman cleverly says that "This one is better, but you can't afford it," which may or may not be true. The housewife replies, "That's the one I'll take" which is both a statement of fact regarding what she will purchase and an assertion, according to the author, that "regardless of the financial consequences, I'll show that arrogant fellow I'm as good as any of his customers."[44] Here the salesman wins, the housewife's ego also triumphs but perhaps with damage to her budget.

No other examples need be supplied by a psychiatrist or any other writer to suggest that apparently innocent bickerings between two persons, particularly between married couples or between parents and children in Western society, reflect or produce serious conflicts. When person A declines to carry out what person B considers to be a reasonable request and uses the civilized excuse of illness, fatigue, or inability, questions about the game or the encounter can be raised: Is A telling the truth or simply fabricating in order to hurt B or to show his or her independence from B? Or is the request of B really reasonable or necessary, does it represent an effort to dominate A? In this instance the victor or the loser is not immediately apparent: characterization depends upon the motives of the two and of course the outcome. Also B may truly believe the request to be reasonable and A may actually feel ill, even though unconsciously either one or both of them may be trying to crush the other.

The use of one language rather than another can be employed as a device to demonstrate or bolster power among peoples who have or could have access to more than one language. Colonial powers have sometimes attempted to prevent their subjects from learning linguae francae so that they would remain isolated from other ethnic groups and hence would be less likely to unite in throwing out the foreign regime. Or the leaders of the local societies have sought to increase their own distinctiveness by fostering their language or its particular nuances.[45] Sociolinguists are able to cite illustrations of individuals who assert their own power and authority over others by switching to a prestigious language in the course of a conversation.[46]

> *Guide:* Principals select—deliberately or not and on the basis of their predispositions and of the subordinates in the situation at hand—from a cornucopia of tactics at their disposal and hence may utilize virtually the whole gamut of human actions to exert power or assert authority.

IV,4.C *Subordinates' Tactics.* Like the principal, the subordinate is not passive; he also selects from among the tactics at his disposal. His choice, however, is more likely to be influenced by the principal's actions than the reverse. His arsenal is less abundant.

IV,4.C.1 At one end of a continuum the subordinate may *resist* the principal. He refuses to comply, and undoubtedly thus expresses some form of aggression.[47] That aggression, however, can be turned inward: the individual blames himself for his predicament, for occupying a low position on a hierarchy. Possibly, suicides result from feelings of powerlessness.[48] When aggression is directed against principals, there is struggle, rebellion, or revolution. Here the confrontation is direct and the outcome less certain. Resistance may be organized or unorganized, violent or nonviolent, and directed toward general or specific goals.[49] By general goals is meant the overall political system as during a revolution; by specific goals, an objective of limited nature, such as picketing in order to win a strike. On an individual level the relatively powerless wife in Western society may nag or berate her blue-collar spouse not only to achieve a goal beyond her ken but also to be aggressive and troublesome.

Other tactics are available to resist principals. A subordinate, especially if he is repressed by a more powerful principal, may express hostility, withdraw from the situation, or seek some form of compensatory activity.[50] He may try to turn the situation completely around by seeking power for himself. With power he may be able to acquire a degree of self-confidence that he has previously lacked, as well as other benefits.[51] According to one investigator, some of the women in the San Francisco area who sought to be accepted as Lesbians in Lesbian circles played the role of "butch" (i.e., "an approximation" of the domineering masculine role) rather than that of "femme."[52] Resistance may also consist of detaching oneself from the seat of authority: the adolescent weans himself from his parents, the worker changes his job, the member resigns from the club. Psychoanalysis and other forms of psychotherapy frequently set themselves the task of freeing patients from the bondage of authority, whether it be parents or some self-defeating approach to existence.

The impulse of many participants is to *comply* when the principal
IV,4.C.2 has superior authority or power. In fact, the acme of authority is the ability to secure immediate and automatic obedience: the follower does what the leader commands because he has been taught to do so. If there is hesitation, then "a crisis in authority" may be at hand.[53] Inward rebellion but outward conformity may result from a desire to conform to the demands of a reference group which in the long run is considered to be beneficial.[54] Immediate pressure, however, is likely to be more efficacious than long-term consequences. The evidence suggesting that present gratifications are usually more compelling than those in the future is almost overwhelming. Participants tend to be trapped: for a smoker the immediate gratification from a cigarette may seem more compelling than the disastrous consequences for his lungs; his response to the force of tobacco is stronger than his belief. The dictator is obeyed by those who know that the future consequences for themselves will be even more evil: they avoid present punishment or obtain immediate privileges. Leaders in the contemporary world are caught in the social trap of having to stockpile the very deadly weapons they do not wish to employ against their enemies: not to stockpile, they believe, would render their country vulnerable. The authority offering psychological reinforcements in the present may be more likely to be obeyed than if he offers them in the future.[55]

Countless impulses may motivate compliance. A somewhat bizarre but intelligible example: American women whose egos had been harmlessly impugned by the confederate of an investigator were more likely to comply with a subsequent request by another confederate than those who had been previously praised; it was as if those who had been criticized wished "to maintain a positive self-regard" by demonstrating to themselves that the negative labels were unjustified.[56] It is not unfair to say that in this incident the women were manipulated, indeed manipulated even as modern advertisers with their resources profit from linking their products and services to the predispositions of potential customers.

Whether compliance is feigned or genuine, the followers of a leader may overtly comply with his slightest whim and, consciously or unconsciously, imitate his very mannerisms in order thus to curry favor with him and eventually be rewarded.[57] Such an attempt to affect a leader by exaggerating his personal qualities is of course "illicit" when those qualities are unrelated to his competence or authority.[58] Similarly ingratiation may be employed by principals to achieve compliance; yet such actions are more likely to belong within the arsenal of participants who would hereby diminish the likelihood of punishment resulting from not obeying or not conforming and increase the likelihood of rewards from obeying or conforming. Perhaps, then, the leader's own belief that he has the skill to lead may be strengthened by the obedience or compliance of his followers, and hence perhaps his self-confidence increases.[59] And his beliefs concerning those followers, whether accurate or not, affect the ways in which he exerts his authority which in turn influences them and their behavior. A spiral whirls.

Whether or not the subordinate recognizes his lower status, he
IV,4.C.3 may seek *compensation* and thus relieve some of the discomfort
he experiences: he rationalizes his status or finds substitute gratifications.[60] Masochistically or not, he may believe that he deserves to be in a lower status or that he is powerless to behave otherwise. He may take counteraggressive measures in fantasy or symbolically in his dreams. He may believe that in the long run or in another generation the state of affairs will change and that the principals will be punished or overthrown. He may seek to detach himself from reality by finding solace in his personal relations or in religion.

Some subordinates may strive to change their hierarchical position and hence to achieve the status of principals. Immigrants to a country work hard and flock to educational institutions in order to acquire the resources and skills associated with power. Perhaps in international relations the leaders of weaker states connive with one another in order to increase their own strength as they confront the great powers; and their authority may grow when they are able to convey the conviction that in a confrontation both sides may have something to gain through negotiation.[61]

* * * *

This section ends on another pessimistic note. In spite of the availability of communication channels between followers and leaders, there is plentiful evidence from surveys indicating that in the United States significant numbers of plain citizens do not believe either that their voices are heard or that they affect policy. In the summer of 1980, for example, one survey reported that 39 percent of a sample agreed that "public officials don't care much what people like me think"; later the same year, 66 percent felt that "the people in Washington, D.C., are out of touch with the rest of the country."[62] Doubts can be cast on the salience, stability, or even the validity of these findings, but they suggest the presence of beliefs among Americans that their own political tactics are ineffective.

NOTES

1. One theory proposes that behavior depends upon the individual's expressed intention to engage in the behavior in question which in turn depends upon his attitude toward the behavior. The attitude in its turn depends upon a belief concerning the consequences of the behavior and the attitude toward those consequences. Also involved are his subjective norms concerning the behavior which in turn depend upon his belief as to whether other persons important to him in their turn believe he should or should not engage in the behavior. Finally, the last-named belief is affected by the normative beliefs within the society and the individual's own motivation to comply with the norm and the wishes of others. Icek Ajzen and Martin Fishbein, Attitude-behavior relations. *Psychological Bulletin,* 1977, 84, 888–918. A second theory can be stated more briefly: behavior depends upon the individual's beliefs concerning himself; concerning people, situations, and objects; concerning norms and rules in his society; and personal goals—*but* in each case the beliefs must pertain to the specific, anticipated behavior or the person's relation to it. Hans and Shulamith Kreitler, *Cognitive Orientation and Behavior*. New York: Springer-Verlag, 1976.

2. D. Finlay, C. Iversen, and J. Raser, Handbook for multi-national student survey. Cited by William Eckhart and Christopher Young, *Governments under Fire*. New Haven: HRAF Press, 1977. Pp. 15–18.

3. I. William Zartman and Maureen R. Berman, *The Practical Negotiator*. New Haven: Yale University Press, 1982. P. 54.

4. William W. Meissner, *The Assault on Authority*. Maryknoll: Orbis Books, 1971. P. 170.

5. Bruno Bettleheim, Individual and mass behavior in extreme situations. *Journal of Abnormal and Social Psychology,* 1943, 38, 417–52.

6. Jeffrey Z. Rubin and Bert R. Brown, *The Social Psychology of Bargaining and Negotiation*. New York: Academic Press, 1975. Pp. 158–60.

7. U.S.A.: Ninety-six male undergraduates. *Method:* subjects performed an innocuous task (folding paper airplanes) in groups of six. Three had strong beliefs concerning self-control and three weak beliefs as measured on a paper-and-pencil schedule; also in the group was a confederate functioning as a leader who (a) either rewarded or coerced them and (b) either provided or did not provide feedback concerning their success or failure. *Results:* in comparison with those having weak beliefs in self-control, those with

strong beliefs tended to comply less frequently with the "leader's" demands regardless of his tactics. They also complied less frequently under condition of coercion when feedback was provided. In general, therefore, they tended to be less "responsive." Richard W. Cravens and Philip Worchel, The differential effects of reward and coercive leaders on group members differing in locus of control. *Journal of Personality,* 1977, 45, 150–68.

8. U.S.A.: Forty-four undergraduates. *Method:* in a laboratory-simulated setting each subject bargained with another student, a confederate, regarding the price to be paid for a landscape painting. *Results:* those scoring high in self-control or seeking approval, deference, or dominance bargained with greater toughness than those scoring low with respect to those attributes. Avi Assor and Kaern O'Quin, The intangibles of bargaining. *Journal of Social Psychology,* 1982, 116, 119–26.

9. Calvin S. Hall and Gardner Lindzey, The relevance of Freudian psychology and related viewpoints for the social sciences. In Gardner Lindzey and Elliot Aronson (eds.), *Handbook of Social Psychology.* Reading: Addison-Wesley, 1968. Vol. 1, pp. 245–319.

10. Richard Sennett, *Authority.* New York: Knopf, 1980. Pp. 110–12.

11. U.S.A.: 435 councilmen in eighty-two of the eighty-nine cities in the San Francisco Bay area. *Method:* interviews. *Results:* when subjected to pressure groups within their own communities, most of these officials did not consider such groups important, they tended not to turn to them for assistance in influencing the council. About one-fourth, however, held the groups in high esteem, the remainder felt neutral toward them or rejected them. No completely clear-cut differences about the three reactions appeared, although there was a slight tendency for the attitude of the officials toward the groups to be related to their own demographic characteristics (age, education, occupation, length of residence in the community) as well as to the ways in which they themselves participated in the affairs of the council. Those with a favorable attitude tended to be more aware of a larger number of the local organizations and to seek to accommodate themselves to them, especially to those representing economic and other special interests. They were also more likely to align themselves with the organization and become their "legislative allies." Betty H. Zisk, *Local Interest Politics.* Indianapolis: Bobbs-Merrill, 1973. Especially pp. 3, 35, 38, 63–66, 77, 91, 93, 104, 142–43.

12. Richard D. Mann, Graham S. Gibbard, and John J. Hartman, *Interpersonal Styles and Group Development.* New York: Wiley, 1967. P. 42.

13. Robert F. Bales and Stephen P. Cohen, *Symlog.* New York: Free Press, 1979.

14. James H. Davis, Patrick R. Laughlin, and Samuel S. Komorita, The social psychology of small groups. In Mark R. Rosenzweig and Lyman W. Porter (eds.), *Annual Review of Psychology,* 1976, 27, 501–41.

15. John 14:15.

16. David Kipnis, *The Powerholders.* Chicago: University of Chicago Press, 1976. P. 31.

17. Elaine Walster and Jane Allyn Piliavin, Equity and the innocent bystander. *Journal of Social Issues,* 1972, 28, no. 3, 165–89.

18. Cf. William Austin and Elaine Hatfield, Equity theory, power, and social justice. In Gerold Mikula (ed.), *Justice and Social Interaction.* New York: Springer-Verlag, 1980.

19. Rolf Kroger et al., Are the rules of address universal? *Journal of Cross-Cultural Psychology,* 1979, 10, 395–414.

20. Jacques Maquet, *Power and Society in Africa.* New York: McGraw-Hill, 1971. P. 99.

21. Michael Korda, *Power!* New York: Random House, 1975. Pp. 64–66.

22. Harold D. Lasswell and Merritt B. Fox, *The Signature of Power*. New Brunswick: Transaction Books, 1979.

23. Garrett Hardin, The tragedy of the commons. *Science,* 1968, 162, 1243–48.

24. Kipnis, op. cit., p. 43.

25. Ibid., pp. 97, 99.

26. Ibid., pp. 79, 97, 99.

27. Cf. Uriel G. Foa and Edna B. Foa, *Societal Structures of the Mind.* Springfield, Ill.: Charles C. Thomas, 1974. P. 139.

28. Leonard W. Doob, *The Pursuit of Peace*. Westport: Greenwood, 1981. P. 57.

29. David W. Moore, Foreign policy and empirical democratic theory. *American Political Science Review,* 1974, 68, 1192–97.

30. Peter R. Schneider and Anne L. Schneider, Social mobilization, political institutions, and political violence. *Comparative Political Studies,* 1971, 4, 69–90.

31. Rollo May, *Power and Innocence*. New York: Norton, 1972. P. 191.

32. Gerald S. Leventhal, The distribution of rewards and resources in groups and organizations. In Leonard Berkowitz and Elaine Walster (eds.), *Advances in Experimental Social Psychology*. New York: Academic Press, 1976. Vol. 9, pp. 91–131.

33. Foa and Foa, op. cit., pp. 36–40.

34. U.S.A.: Ninety-six adult males and eighty-six adult females. *Method:* unaware that they were being observed, they could pass along a narrow corridor in a commuter train station of a large city only by invading the space of a tall or a short, a male or a female confederate. *Results:* more persons violated the space of the short than that of the tall confederate, and fewer females than males violated the space of the tall confederate; the sex of the confederate had no significant effect. Marc E. Caplan and Morton Goldman, Personal space violation as a function of height. *Journal of Social Psychology,* 1981, 114, 167–71.

35. U.S.A.: 470 pedestrians. *Method:* unaware that they were being observed, they could deviate from their path or invade the space of one or two confederates standing on the edge of a sidewalk. *Results:* more deviated from two confederates than from one, from a male rather than a female, and from a beautiful rather than an unattractively appearing and attired female confederate. J. M. Dabbs and Neil A. Stokes, III, Beauty is power. *Sociometry,* 1975, 38, 551–57.

36. May, op. cit., p. 31.

37. Leonard W. Doob, *Pathways to People*. New Haven: Yale University Press, 1975. Pp. 131–33.

38. U.S.A.: Twenty pairs of ROTC students and twenty undergraduates, unspecified pairs of ROTC students, sixteen pairs of undergraduates. *Method:* in the first two studies ROTC officers were paired with nonofficers, in the first and the third ordinary undergraduates were paired; in all three one of the pair was given the power to reward while playing a game in the laboratory. *Results:* those subjects lower in a hierarchy (as indicated by status in the ROTC or their power to reward during the game) tended to gaze more frequently or longer than those occupying higher positions while listening to the other person; no differences appeared among the students when speaking in relation to their desire to control their personal existence, but those without such a desire tended to spend more time gazing when listening than those with the desire. Ralph V. Exline,

Steve L. Ellyson, and Barbara Long, Visual behavior as an aspect of power role relationships. In Patricia Pilner, Lester Krames, and Thomas Alloway (eds.), *Nonverbal Communication of Aggression*. New York: Plenum, 1975. Pp. 21–52.

39. U.S.A.: both parents and two children in 367 families. *Method:* the parents were asked "Do you tell your child that God will punish him if he is bad?" and the children "Do you believe that God will punish you when you get angry?" *Results:* The threat was used by one or both parents in two-thirds of the families; in comparison with those not using the threat, more of those using it tended to have lower incomes, to be members in what might be called fundamentalist churches, and to believe that children should obey their parents without question and should be like other children. The number of children replying affirmatively to the question directed to them was higher (a) when both parents and especially mothers used the threat than when neither did, (b) among younger than among older children, (c) among those blaming themselves for their own anger or believing that they should obey their parents without question than among those having the opposite beliefs. *Comment:* for the parents, the investigator suggests that this "coalition with God" occurred when they were relatively "powerless" and were thus seeking some form of "indirect" control over their children. Clyde Z. Nunn, Child control through a "coalition with God." *Child Development*, 1964, 35, 417–32.

40. David V. J. Bell, *Power, Influence, and Authority*. New York: Oxford University Press, 1975. Pp. 37–38.

41. Cf. Don H. Zimmerman and Candace West, Sex roles, interruptions, and silences in conversation. In Barrie Thorne and Nancy Henley (eds.), *Language and Sex*. Rowley, Mass.: Newbury House, 1975. Pp. 105–29.

42. Cf. Barrie Thorne and Nancy Henley, Difference and dominance. In Thorne and Henley (eds.), op. cit., pp. 5–42.

43. Doob, *Pursuit of Peace*, op. cit., pp. 203–209.

44. Eric Berne, *Games People Play*. New York: Grove Press, 1964. P. 33.

45. Cf. H. Giles, Linguistic differentiation in ethnic groups. In Henri Tajfel (ed.), *Differentiation between Social Groups*. London: Academic Press, 1978. Pp. 386–93.

46. Carol Myers Scotton and William Ury, Bilingual strategies. *International Journal of the Sociology of Language*, 1977, 13, 5–20.

47. Cf. Boyd C. Rollins and Stephen J. Bahr, A theory of power relationships in marriage. *Journal of Marriage and the Family*, 1976, 38, 619–27.

48. U.S.A.: Thirty persons who had attempted suicide, thirty who had threatened suicide, and thirty controls who had neither threatened nor attempted suicide. *Method:* a questionnaire concerning powerlessness. *Results:* males but not females who had attempted suicide tended to feel more powerless than those who had threatened; for both sexes, those who threatened and those who attempted suicide tended to feel more powerless than the controls. Friedrich V. Wenz, Subjective powerlessness, sex, and suicide potential. *Psychological Reports*, 1977, 40, 927–28.

49. Cf. Charles Edward Merriam, *Political Power*. New York: McGraw-Hill, 1934. P. 159.

50. Cf. Bernard M. Bass, *Leadership, Psychology, and Organizational Behavior*. New York: Harpers, 1960. Pp. 233–34.

51. Cf. John W. Thibaut and Harold H. Kelley, *The Social Psychology of Groups*. New York: Wiley, 1959. P. 89.

52. Deborah Goleman Wolf, *The Lesbian Community*. Berkeley: University of California, 1979. Pp. 40–43.

53. Cf. Robert Paul Wolff, *In Defense of Anarchism*. New York: Harper & Row, 1970. P. 9. Also Bell, op. cit., p. 59.

54. John Rowan, *The Power of the Group*. London: Davis-Poynter, 1976. P. 30.

55. Cf. John Platt, Social traps. *American Psychologist,* 1973, 28, 641–51.

56. Claude M. Steele, Name-calling and compliance. *Journal of Personality and Social Psychology,* 1975, 31, 361–69.

57. Mauk Mulder, *The Daily Power Game*. Leiden: Martinus Nijhoff, 1977. P. 10.

58. Edward E. Jones, *Ingratiation*. New York: Irvington, 1975. P. 11.

59. India: 165 male executives, mean age ca. forty-two. *Method:* the men were given a "Leadership Style" questionnaire (e.g., "I have affection for my subordinates," "If I do not watch out, there are many people who may pull me down") and another questionnaire asking them to furnish details concerning their work place and subordinates. *Results:* what they believed to be the efficiency, dedication, and esprit of their subordinates as well as of their supposed need for personal care and very careful supervision were related to the leadership styles they ascribed to themselves (whether authoritarian or nurturant) but not to whether they permitted those subordinates to participate in decisions or to enjoy friendly, informal contacts with themselves. J. B. P. Sinha and G. P. Chowdhary, Perception of subordinates as a moderator of leadership effectiveness in India. *Journal of Social Psychology,* 1981, 113, 115–21.

60. Elaine Walster and Jane Allyn Piliavin, Equity and the innocent bystander. *Journal of Social Issues,* 1972, 28, 165–89.

61. Cf. Zartman and Berman, op. cit., pp. 71–73, 205–7.

62. CBS/*New York Times,* news release, November 15, 1980.

10

Outcomes

The analysis has now come full circle or, as in the Guiding Figure, two sets of circles. The outcome both for the observer and the participant can again be simultaneously surveyed, but it is not ordinarily final: "the outcome of every conflict," and every confrontation, "is the possible basis for another struggle" or confrontation.[1] We return to the background and the personality which may have been altered by events, actions, and behavior.

The consequences of a power- or authority-related event are likely to be immediate and long-range. A person is mugged by a more powerful thief: he instantly loses his money or jewelry and then suffers for a long time the effects of the trauma, as a future consequence of which he may avoid walking near the area where the assault and robbery occurred. A tricky power tactic has been called the foot-in-the-door effect: a participant may be more likely to respond to a second more arduous request if he has already responded to one that is less taxing, especially perhaps if he has been praised for complying the first time.[2] Simple praise thus has future consequences enabling the principal, the owner of the foot, to exert power over an unsuspecting subordinate, the door opener; but many subordinates refuse to allow the foot to enter and others do not comply with the second request, divergencies to be accounted for in terms of their previous experiences, the ensuing predispositions, or momentary pressures.

V,5.A *Prediction.* It has been repeatedly emphasized that the links between the predispositions of personality and action or behavior are numerous and complicated, with the result that outcomes of events are difficult to predict. A time factor may also intrude; for example, secret diplomacy between the representatives of nations may lead immediately or later to war or peace; at the time, the details are deliberately concealed. In addition, there may be unexpected, sudden outcomes which are promising candidates for modern catastrophe theory. The name of that theory might suggest that the theorist despairs or is convinced that he cannot anticipate an outcome. In fact, the theory deals with complicated situations aided by sophisticated mathematics. One favorite example appears as an illustration: the attack of an angry dog can be reasonably well predicted from observing his mouth or teeth, the flight of a frightened dog can likewise be anticipated from the position of his ears, but the reactions of an angry, frightened animal are much more difficult to anticipate. The two impulses, if strong, will not cancel each other, rather the dog will either attack or flee. Similar reasoning may often be needed to account for interactions involving authority and power. At a critical moment fraught with danger, a crowd can become either a panic-stricken mob defying authority and exerting violent power *or* a well-coordinated group following the established lines of authority without displaying such power.[3] Once more complexity, whether catastrophic or not, should serve as a warning to the observer and participant to be on guard. The unexpected may be less baffling when it is expected.

To cope with outcomes for which many alternatives appear possible, moreover, perhaps catastrophe theory offers hope, or at least it may becalm the cynics who wish to withdraw from the problem. A salesman who approaches a prospective customer is able to employ various kinds of communications to persuade him or her to buy a product or patronize a service, whereas the customer may be in a position to accept or refuse the proposition. Who becomes the victor in the confrontation depends upon the skill and resources each has at his disposal. The customer may be gullible and buy the glittering, shoddy product; or he may be sophisticated and know beforehand precisely what he would avoid. The salesman may have various devices at his disposal extending from the offer of an alleged bargain to sheer persuasiveness springing from his own experience and skill. Who will turn out to be the more powerful? One bit of field research illustrates how difficult it is to anticipate the outcome of this allegedly simple interaction. No significant relation was found between the actual purchase of insurance and the salesman's pitch defined here as either "expert power" (stressing the salesman's knowledge, information, and skill) or "referent power" (stressing the similarity of goals, interests, and background in order to have the salesman appear attractive).[4]

Instead of despairing, it is better to be pragmatic and to be prepared to cope with the multidimensional nature of power and authority. Knowing that generally—with numerous exceptions, yes—authorities seek to justify their policies even when they have failed, that predispositions always play some role in the outcome, that subordinates are prone to submit to principals with superior resources, or that the final outcome of bargaining sessions may be a verbal or written statement by all participants committing them to perform specified actions may not be a major intellectual achievement, but it can be helpful both to the observer and to some of the participants.[5] Possibly major problems require treatment in their own right, and hence any contribution, whether it be a new theory or new data from a whodunnit approach, is a welcome addition, provided its relation to all other factors or variables is established or discoverable. With some hesitation I would suggest that the reader glance at the War-Peace Figure (note A), at the end of this chapter: it purports to show how those problems can be fruitfully and fully analyzed. If the reader has pursued up to this point the present analysis of power and authority via the Guiding Figure, he will immediately perceive similarities, really identities, between the two figures. In the War-Peace Figure the observer's variables of events, actions, and outcomes and the participant's variables of personality, perception, and judgment reappear. Additional variables are also evident, all of which pertain to groups (reference, decision, and international) and which in the Guiding Figure are subsumed here under ascription and description as well as action. The two figures, in short, are virtually identical, which of course should cause no ripple not because they have emerged from the same writer but because they face similar problems and challenges which have also been portrayed previously in the figures concerned with temporal, communication, and person-perception relationships.

For animate and inanimate forces there are also consequences. Animals learn from experience. Their pecking order may result in part from what has transpired in the past. After a confrontation with human beings, either in a controlling or controlled role, they behave differently in the future. Some natural resources, such as minerals, gradually become exhausted when they are exploited; renewable ones, such as forests and soil, may erode unless they are deliberately conserved. In the confrontation between human beings and animals, an essential feature is the knowledge of the participants which results from experience and ensuing changes. Applied science and engineering enable the consequences of past confrontations to serve as models.

> *Guide:* in spite of surprises and apparent catastrophes, the outcomes of power- and authority-related events or aspects thereof are predictable, within limits.

V,5.B *Short-range.* The tactics of participants, regardless of their roles, are likely to have an immediate effect upon one another. Even the most isolated dictator can be influenced by his followers if only through the intermediaries he designates to report public reactions or restlessness. American citizens, according to two expert pollsters, can and may communicate their views to legislators and other elected officials through the following channels: voting, discussing public issues with others, joining organizations that take stands on such issues, writing or talking with these officials to express their own viewpoints, working for political candidates, contributing money to the candidates or their parties. As might be anticipated, the better educated and the wealthier Americans tended at one time (the late 1940s) to be more active than the remainder of the population on the basis of those criteria. Certainly, as the investigators themselves suggest, political activity of this sort is not equivalent to being influential;[6] yet some relation must be assumed to exist.

Within the last fifty years, samples of participants in Western European countries and in North America have been offered the opportunity to express their views when they have been interrogated by pollsters. That high officials use these surveys to comprehend vox populi has been demonstrated in the United States by the fact that prominent political leaders employ their own pollsters or privately pay a commercial organization to ask politically relevant questions. They keep the results secret so that they and not their opponents can profit from the information. These leaders have confidence in polling data, otherwise they would not invest funds in securing them; and the reductio ad absurdum of such confidence occurred in the presidential election of 1980 when President Carter, on the basis of survey data and preliminary results, conceded defeat before the voting booths had closed on the West coast.

With or without agreement concerning how confrontation can be anticipated by observers or participants,[7] it is self-evident that outcomes can vary between one in which some participants triumph and the others fail completely (a so-called zero-sum outcome) and one in which differences are reconciled to everyone's satisfaction. In between are numerous intermediate compromises. At one extreme, then, are winners and losers: principals and leaders dominate subordinates or followers, particularly when scarce resources are not or cannot be shared.[8] The judge has the authority to sentence the convicted criminal, the jailers and other authorities to execute the sentence. At the other extreme, neither side wins or loses, their strivings are integrated. In any case, the principal decides whether he has succeeded or failed to achieve his objective, the participants whether they have conformed or rebelled; both evaluate the outcome.[9]

When participants avoid the extremes and settle for a compromise, they agree on a contract, as it were, which seems sufficiently though not completely satisfying. They thus avoid the penalties of continuing strife.[10] In democratic societies the procedure usually requires voting, with the result that the majority wins and the minority loses; and the power is thus granted the former and not the latter. In other societies, for example, India[11] and many African societies such as in traditional Somalia, discussion or conflict is prolonged until a consensus is reached: none of the participants presumably believe they have lost appreciable power. Again in the language of exchange theory previously mentioned, one participant relinquishes some of his power or one or more of his own goals so that his opponent feels he too has gained an objective by making what he first judged to be a complete sacrifice.[12] An employer may seek to induce an employee to work overtime by offering him extra pay. He thus incurs the cost of the overtime pay but gains additional production; the employee forgoes whatever he might have been doing during the period when he continues to work in return for the extra pay, provided he does not decide that this pay is insufficient to have him make the sacrifice. In such an interaction, moreover, the leader is affected by the followers as they contemplate the conflicting alternatives for the present and future.

A summary of "social psychological laboratory studies" suggests that the outcome of bargaining, when confrontation assumes that form, depends upon the initial status, the authority, and the power of the participants, especially upon their ability to distribute rewards to one another. Bargaining, moreover, is likely to be effective when the bargainers' "motivational orientation" tends to be cooperative and not individualistic or competitive; when their initial power has been equal rather than unequal; and when, if that power is unequal, the discrepancy is relatively small.[13] The outcome also depends in large part upon the participants' anticipations concerning one another. When they struggle for power, their expectation regarding others may be based upon previous knowledge or it may be a result of information acquired during the confrontation. In either case, the expectation interacts with other predispositions such as established friendships.

The optimistic view may be expressed that all or most conflicts between more or less or equally powerful participants are reconcilable when and if they themselves or through the intervention of a third party are able to peer beneath the verbiage in which their goals are clothed and thus to discover what they "really" seek.[14] Such an ideal is rarely realizable for two principal reasons. First of all, the metaphorical cloth is not easily removed: principals remain fixed upon the demands as they themselves have phrased them, and they frequently are unable to discover their own "real" goals as inferred by an outside observer. Then, secondly, some conflicts are truly intractable. Ever since Marx's time Marxians have been convinced that those who have power, the capitalists, have everything to lose by making concessions to the less powerful proletariat. This, too, has been the policy of the Europeans who have controlled South Africa: they make minor concessions but only in the hope that thereby the seeds of revolt will be uprooted and that they can continue to reign.

Guide: Some conflicts are resolvable in a manner satisfactory to all participants, others are intractable or the resolutions are unsatisfactory to some or most of the participants.

V,5.C

Long-range. It is impossible to imagine events without long-range consequences—unless the participants perish, but then the consequences cease for them but not for the survivors. When a schoolboy demonstrates his power to a peer group, when a lobbyist succeeds in pushing a bill through a legislative body of a democracy, when the military clique of one country reveals its armed strength in what is purported to be only strategic or tactical exercises, such actions may well have consequences beyond the present. Although it is interesting and intriguing to try to discover who has governed in arriving at decisions now gone by, it is equally important to determine whether those making the decisions are able, as a result, to make comparable decisions in succeeding years or in other similar or dissimilar situations; and also of course to ascertain whether the subordinates or followers remain submerged. Attention must be paid, in short, to the benefits and frustrations emerging from the outcomes of past events since they are likely to have profound consequences. Probably the ways in which participants resolve conflicts over power may reflect their predispositions, and then in the future both the method of dealing with the former and the content of the latter may be affected.[15] Perhaps a taste of power or authority resulting from a participant's position in a communication network may have significant repercussions.[16]

V,5.C.1 Both at a given moment and over time, a power or an authority relation may be approved simply because it is part of *tradition*, it is long-standing. Traditions are particularly prominent in all religions, but they also aid powers and authorities in most human activities, whether in Western science or literature.[17] Short-term judgments and actions are the consequences of long-term judgments and actions and thus strengthen or threaten traditions. Anthropological and experimental evidence as well as common sense suggest that long-established practices and procedures, including rationalizations for their exploitation, tend to acquire prestige.[18]

Omnipresent in all societies are forms of patriotism: the attachment to authorities, leaders, fellow countrymen, the land, customs, in fact traditional beliefs and attitudes associated with one's birthplace or country. These beliefs and attitudes are the outcome of innumerable actions in the past that are reinforced in the present. The attitudes of South Tyroleans regarding their country, which have been outlined in Chapter 4, originate in uncountable past experiences, one outcome of which is that these largely peasant peoples have been able to retain their culture and sense of identity in spite of the cruel efforts of Mussolini to change their culture and to expel them and in spite of the fact that since World War II they have remained part of a generous Italy with its benign government focusing on other problems.[19]

V,5.C.2 The essential consequence of tradition is the *stability* which results from adherence to ways of feeling and behaving sanctified and inherited from the past. The society's traditional social structure affects the modal predispositions and behavior of its participants; usually it emerges only after centuries of prior events and changes. Over time the Swiss have evolved a system of decentralization in which the local cantons make most of the decisions so that the country, composed as it is of three major cultural groups and a very small one, is able to function through amicable consensus both within the cantons and for the land as a whole.[20] The evolution of the Swiss system has been the consequence of a series of major and minor decisions, each of which now regulates the distribution of authority and hence power.

The short-range decisions in the past which affect the present are not immediately apparent and generally require empirical investigation. Why, it might be asked, does the chief of a Hausa quarter in the non-Hausa city of Ibadan (Nigeria) exercise so much power over his followers who are traders? That community has undergone various changes historically, but the principal source of authority now rests on a Moslem cult to which all Hausas belong. The sect has created "a new ritual power structure" operating through a chain not of priests but of *malams* (part-time religious functionaries) who, it is thought, can mystically affect the supernatural spirits influencing human affairs. A follower, therefore, "will not undertake any enterprise before asking his malam to divine the prospects for him." In addition, the chief more mundanely determines the credit-worthiness of his followers, he decides who can live in dwellings under his control, and he settles disputes among other activities.[21] The beliefs and attitudes of the Hausa in this community, in short, are an outcome of past developments which make their present actions intelligible.

It is banal to suggest that systems of governance, when once established, have lasting consequences for their participants, but not so banal is the problem of specifying those consequences in general terms that transcend the details of a community such as that of the Hausas in Ibadan. Consider one worthy, typical, statistical attempt to elicit generalities. Governments that effectively allocate power to "functional autonomous legislative, executive, and judicial organs" have been compared with those having "complete dominance of government by one branch or by extra-governmental agency"[22]—in simple language, respectively, democratic or semidemocratic in contrast with authoritarian governments. A total of thirty-four fall into the first category (starting alphabetically with Australia and Austria and ending with Switzerland and Trinidad) and forty-eight into the second (starting with Afghanistan and Albania and ending with what was then South Vietnam and Yugoslavia). The data have been fed into a computer in order to determine in which available respects the two kinds of government differ. Variants of 57 different factors have thus been electronically tested; in this instance, exactly 100 reached the required level of statistical significance: the probability is not more than approximately 5 in 100 and usually even less that the difference is due to chance. For example, 68 percent of those governments allocating power to three branches tend to be more densely populated compared with 4 percent of those not having such an allocation. A sampling of other similarly significant relations conveys the flavor of the computer's output:

> In contrast with nations whose governments are dominated by one branch or an extragovernmental agency, those effectively allocating power to three branches *tend*
>
> to be more highly urbanized,
>
> to concentrate less on agriculture,
>
> to have a higher GNP,
>
> to have a higher economic developmental status,
>
> to have a higher literacy rate,
>
> to permit complete freedom of the press,
>
> to have a larger number of newspapers per capita,
>
> to be linguistically homogeneous,
>
> to have achieved independence before 1914 or 1945,
>
> to be historically Western,
>
> to be less committed ideologically to nationalism as a developmental goal,

to have a constitutional regime,

to have a competitive electoral system,

to tolerate autonomous groups in politics,

to be multiparty states,

to have a nonelitist leadership,

to have leaders with negligible charisma,

to have more effective legislatures and stronger executives,

to have a more modern bureaucracy,

to have a military group whose participation in politics is neutral rather than supportive,

to have police whose political role is not significant,

to be noncommunist.[23]

Such an analysis obviously provides little or no insight into cause-and-effect sequences, it fails completely even to suggest how these attributes interact with one another. But it does indicate the kind of relationships likely to be found in the historical stream as a result of past events when the three branches of government are or are not functionally autonomous with respect to power. Many of these consequences, moreover, result from the forms of government, others affect those forms.

Guide: The past lingers on; in institutions, the influence of tradition is usually as inescapable as the Zeitgeist.

The lingering of the past, however, is not an autonomatic process. The power relations within the society may be reinforced by tactics deliberately adopted to perpetuate the system. Foremost is the use of repression and various forms of violence inflicted upon subordinates who disobey or threaten to do so. The ugly prototype is the authoritarian state in which violence does not need to be actually exercised, and the existence of appropriate apparatus such as the police and military units may suffice to produce obedience. Coercion, moreover, may be disguised or partially disguised. There may be no regulation requiring men and women to seek employment for low wages, but they may work even under almost unendurable conditions when they have no other alternative to survive.

The relation varies between stability and the nontraditional tactics employed to perpetuate the status quo or a change in that status quo. Emperors and colonial governments have remained on top for centuries, decades, or years, but eventually they have been toppled. Perhaps, therefore, tactics affect only the duration of an unequal distribution of power. Powers and authorities often perpetuate their positions in a hierarchy by diminishing their power or authority or by sharing it. Coalition governments in modern times come into existence when principals agree to modify some but not all of their policies and hence at least for the moment seek slightly modified goals. But they are likely to be unstable.

Ultimately, in the short- or long-range, the stability of a system depends upon the satisfactions it brings to all participants. A minimum of satisfaction is required by subordinates if they are not to rebel. That minimum, however, is not likely to be sufficient over time, and therefore both political and ethical challenges arise, topics reserved for the next chapter.

Since participants experience long-range consequences by observ-
V,5.C.3 ing specific powers and authorities, it is essential to consider the
effects of *individuals* on stability. Without subscribing to any version of a great-man theory, it is clear that, just as it can be said that Cézanne exerted influence or power "over a generation of painters,"[24] so truly great leaders, such as those associated with the major religions, affect millions of persons long after their death: their power continues on and on,[25] even though their precise influence cannot be ascertained. Throughout its history, for example, the hierarchy of the Catholic Church has utilized various tactics "to maintain and extend their control over their constituents, specifically the lay elites that participate in the organizational life of the Church at the supradiocesan level." These have ranged from the use of coercive power ("burning at the stake, torture, imprisonment, banishment, blackmail, removal from office, denouncement") at one extreme to the "use of traditional symbols, ritual, ideas, and sentiments" at the other. A Catholic sociologist believes that the use of "coercive or remunerative" tactics has tended to produce "alienation, aggressiveness, and loss of commitment" among its officials. In contrast, nonmanipulative tactics may lead to greater participation in the affairs of the Church and hence to less importance being attributed to the hierarchy.[26] The policy of each pope, therefore, has contributed to the power of the Church.

Above all, as Chapter 2 has previously emphasized, long-range effects result from the power and authority of the various persons responsible for socialization. In the early 1980s a correlational study in the United States asked a sample of Chicano college students to recall (a) how many students, teachers, and administrators had been Chicano in their secondary schools and also (b) various experiences from their school days. More negative experiences from their early youth were recalled by those coming from schools with few Chicanos in positions of power and authority than by those from schools where Chicanos had been more important.[27] The possessors of power and authority in the past thus had long-term consequences even for reminiscences.

The possession of authority has long-range consequences for the leaders themselves. Self-confidence may be increased or decreased as a result of their experiences.[28] They may seek to entrench themselves so that they can remain in power: after the initial victory, more victories are easier to come by, but obviously with exceptions since blunders and changed conditions have their effects. False judgments concerning Russia by both Napoleon and Hitler as they sought to conquer that country had consequences for themselves and the rest of the world. Leaders who would remain in positions of authority seek to establish and strengthen their reputations for honesty, hard work, and an ability to make wise decisions, whether or not they back these attributes with a strong police force or its equivalent.

Guide: The influence of specific principals is ascertainable within limits.

V,5.C.4 In the long run, no person, no group, and no society remains stable; *changes* are inevitable. Ultimately the power and authority of leaders of states depend upon their ability to remain or appear legitimate. Legitimacy, acquired during early socialization and perhaps reinforced less effectively with increasing maturity, may be questioned particularly when followers believe their basic and derived needs are no longer satisfactorily reduced. Whether questioning then produces action, such as a protest, the rejection of a ruling political party, or a revolution, depends both upon the strength of the frustration as well as upon the ability of the regime to maintain itself through persuasion or force. In modern societies, however, as Marxians and others correctly suggest, the varied strata or classes are differentially gratified by those in power, as a result of which they accord the regime correspondingly different legitimacy. Principals and leaders, moreover, may use their authority and positions to create a degree of satisfaction for subordinates and followers which from some standpoints can be considered illusory. The modern era is prone to stimulate rising expectations among those who occupy less favorable positions but who perceive that others are more favorably situated. Followers in an efficient caste system may never imagine they can change their status so that perhaps they accept the authority imposed upon them; but this does not mean that they do not experience frustrations, rather they endure them—at least up to a point.

A follower who is continually frustrated by the decisions or actions of a leader is likely to alter his allegiance when the opportunity presents itself or, if this is the reaction of many followers, when the opportunity is created. In the presidential election of 1980 many American voters shifted from a Democratic president to a Republican candidate because in part they felt that Mr. Reagan, unlike Mr. Carter, might be able to alleviate such problems as inflation and unemployment from which they were suffering. Most voters also hoped that a new president would inspire more trust and confidence than the incumbent. In general, political systems change when the frustrated are organized into groups and become not a loyal opposition but a semiloyal opposition (like the rightist movements in Finland during the 1920s and 1930s) or a disloyal opposition (like political groups in Italy, Germany, and Spain before the fascists there assumed power between the two World Wars).[29]

Changes in the authority of an organization, which means the induction of new leaders in an altered table of organization, have consequences for the participants' predispositions. In 1960 when the lines of authority in an industrial research plant were altered by a new director, for example, employees tended to create "new identity of interests" on the basis of their "relative gains and losses in authority and power,'' but they were not affected uniformly. The new organization produced virtually no change among those satisfied with the plant ''as a hard-hitting organization capable of competing successfully with similar organizations in industry.'' By and large, according to the investigators, modification of authority in industrial organizations results from changes not only in their formal structure but also in the relevant technology and in the values associated with training and interaction.[30]

Changes of any kind are affected by and reflect verbal changes which thus slowly have consequences as they are repeated within and over generations. Some verbal labels or rules are deliberate, others emerge in the give-and-take of normal discourse. In the kibbutzim of Israel, for example, men and women are supposed to share household chores; indeed, with respect to crucial decisions concerning the division of work, the spending of freedom, the family budget, the number of children, and political affiliation, equality has been more or less achieved. But occasionally, contrary to the norm, a wife may be compelled to assume responsibility for those chores, for example, when her husband works long and unusual hours. Such a husband may be ''ridiculed in kibbutz gossip'' by being called ''effendi,'' which is ''Arabic for a feudal landlord who gives orders but does nothing for himself.''[31] Some verbal changes occur so slowly that they are not immediately recognized, in fact it may take a number of years before the appropriate label is produced. Shortly after World War II there was perhaps a shift in the ''American power configuration'' away from the elite who had been called robber barons to more diffuse groups within the society. Those controlling Hollywood, for example, began using ''pre-audience surveys'' because they wished to win the approval of as many persons as possible and thus increase their own profits. These informal groups could be called ''veto groups'' since they affected the decisions of principals and leaders.[32] If that interpretation is correct, then greater sharing of power in the United States has been slowly changing both the practices of the country and their terminology. More than words guide the actions of ruling hierarchies; the words are incorporated into sentences reflecting the consequences of past practices. One of the strongest convictions of White Rhodesians in the late 1950s was the belief that in any kind of situation even well-qualified Africans should never exercise authority over Europeans.[33] That rule could be consciously stated and it produced appropriate action. Elsewhere in southern Africa, according to a psychologist, English-speaking South Africans during the same period consciously expressed mild opposition to the Afrikaner-controlled government, while unconsciously adopting many Afrikaner attitudes and ways of behavior: they realized that government exercised more or less complete power over everyday existence,[34] particularly over ethnic groups. It is also true that the combination of previous experiences giving rise to such attitudes toward and actions regarding authorities are far from uniform, but such a trend suggesting the outcome of the past upon the present is worth noting even though details cannot be anticipated.

Changes take place, but usually slowly, within a group that considers itself inferior and lacks both power and authority. The most radical shift occurs when two groups, as it were, exchange places: this is the revolution described, advocated, and encouraged by Marx for industrial societies. The underprivileged group has less violent alternatives: it may adopt many of the traits of the dominant group (colonial peoples), it may "interpret" some of its own traits so that they are considered attractive or superior rather than unattractive or inferior (American blacks in recent years), or it may create relatively new traits of its own (conversion to a different religion or ideology).[35] Changes of this sort cannot always be traced to specific leaders, although some creative persons can be identified. A kind of collective trial-and-error is evident in the course of which the judgments and decisions of specific individuals culminate in changes for the vast majority.

V,5.C.5 Feelings of *alienation* develop in modern societies as a consequence of another long-term series of events, again not easy to trace. The concept itself is vague and, even when it is operationalized on the basis of clear-cut criteria, it varies tremendously from country to country[36] and from era to era. Often the feelings, unsurprisingly, have been found to be related to other predispositions,[37] yet—just as unsurprisingly—sometimes not.[38] Regardless of the operational definition, the most fruitful, promising conclusion must be that those alienated from conventional authorities—or, for that matter, from the various referents of alienation such as peers, social institutions, the means of production in the Marxian sense, nature, or God[39]—must have had frustrating or unfortunate experiences with such referents, the consequence of which is rejection on the verbal level and possibly in real life. The experiences of each alienated person have been somewhat unique and are not fully or validly revealed by a paper-and-pencil scale or by a series of questions during an interview, techniques that perforce are always latitudinal and not longitudinal. The developmental story is lost in history, even as the source and growth of many social customs is buried in the past; but varied and significant consequences for power and authority linger on.

Perhaps the frequent, low turnout of voters in democratic countries, particularly in the United States, signifies "a sense of powerlessness and a growing skepticism about politics."[40] One provocative analysis seeks to provide an explanation of such a trend. Unspecified persons, presumably those now living in the West, it is said, actually crave authority; but, as a result of frequent deceptions by authorities, they have acquired "a fear of being deceived by authority" and hence struggle to achieve "a freedom to disbelieve in authority." Like little children, they would obey father because he knows best; like maturing adolescents, they would overthrow all authority, especially when they observe widespread tyranny in communist and fascist countries.[41] That bold thesis may be arguable, although undisputed must be the fact that, as a result of past experiences (cf. the name of Nixon among most Americans), each participant at a given moment or in a particular context feels friendly, hostile, or ambivalent toward various authorities and possibly also toward authorities in general.

But leaders and principals still maintain their authority externally as followers and subordinates remain more or less indifferent.

A trend quite the opposite of alienation is also visible in modern society: some participants feel the need for a leader and hence project upon him desirable attributes. Afterwards they may or may not trust the chosen one. Trust is more likely when the participant believes that the goals of the leader are compatible with his own and that this leader is capable of achieving them; distrust, perhaps also alienation, when either of the opposition conditions prevails.[42]

> *Guide:* Power and authority relations are vulnerable to change; plus ça change, plus c'est la même chose?

NOTES

1. Louis Kriesberg, *The Sociology of Social Conflicts*. Englewood Cliffs: Prentice-Hall, 1973. P. 272.
2. Morton Goldman, Mark Seever, and Margaret Seever, Social labelling and the foot-in-the-door effect. *Journal of Social Psychology*, 1982, 117, 19–23.
3. E. C. Zeeman, Catastrophe theory. *Scientific American*, 1976, 234, no. 4, 65–91.
4. Arch G. Woodside and James L. Taylor, Effects on buying behavior of references to expert and referent power. *Journal of Social Psychology*, 1982, 117, 25–31.
5. Thomas McPherson, *Political Obligation*. London: Routledge & Kegan Paul, 1967.
6. Julian L. Woodward and Elmo Roper, Political activity of American citizens. *American Political Science Review*, 1950, 44, 872–85.
7. E.g., Robert A. Dahl, Power. *International Encyclopedia of the Social Sciences*, 1968, 12, 405–15.
8. Cf. John Burton, *Deviance, Terrorism, and War*. Oxford: Martin Robertson, 1979. P. 94.
9. Sanford Dornbusch and W. Richard Scott, *Evaluation and the Exercise of Authority*. San Francisco: Jossey-Bass, 1975. P. 134.
10. Bertram H. Raven and Arie W. Kruglanski, Conflict and power. In Paul Swingle (ed.), *The Structure of Power*. New York: Academic Press, 1970. Pp. 94–96.
11. F. G. Bailey, Decisions by consensus in councils and committees. In Michael Banton (ed.), *Political Systems and the Distribution of Power*. London: Tavistock Publications, 1965. Pp. 1–20.
12. Cf. Michael Parenti, *Power and the Powerless*. New York: St. Martin's Press, 1978. P. 8.
13. Jeffrey Z. Rubin and Bert R. Brown, *The Social Psychology of Bargaining and Negotiation*. New York: Academic Press, 1975. Pp. 198–99.
14. Leonard W. Doob, *The Pursuit of Peace*. Westport: Greenwood, 1981. Pp. 229–42.
15. U.S.A.: eighty-six male graduate students. *Method:* a battery of paper-and-pencil questionnaires attempting to determine the individual's somewhat characteristic mode of resolving conflicts and various values and attitudes. *Results:* in Jungian terms, competition tended to be related to a "thinking" component, accommodation to "feeling,"

A. War-Peace Figure

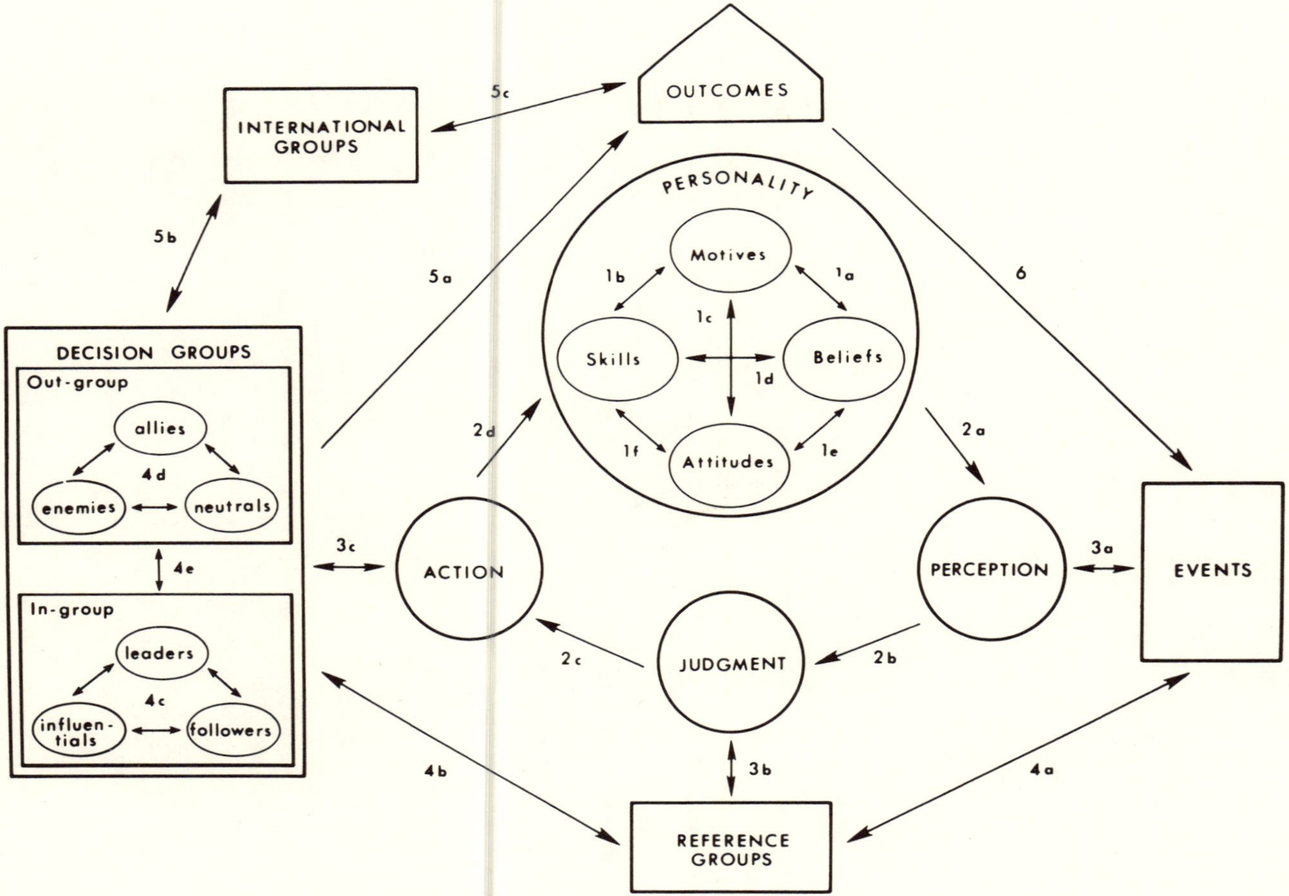

Source: Leonard W. Doob, *The Pursuit of Peace*. Westport, Conn.: Greenwood Press, 1981. P. 9.

collaboration to "extroversion," avoidance to "introversion," and compromise to neutral positions on these psychological categories. *Comment:* presumably resorting to one particular method of conflict resolution may have strengthened an associated predisposition, and the predisposition over time may have affected the preferred method. Ralph H. Kilman and Kenneth W. Thomas, Interpersonal conflict, handling behavior as reflections of Jungian personality dimensions. *Psychological Reports,* 1975, 37, 971–80.

16. U.S.A.: seventy-six undergraduates. *Method:* in groups of four, the students communicated with one another in a bargaining game, with one person assigned a central point in the network; afterwards they rated themselves with respect to power and competence. *Results:* those occupying the central position in this exchange network tended to rate themselves as more powerful and capable than those on the periphery. John F. Stolte, Power structure and personal competence. *Journal of Social Psychology,* 1978, 106, 83–92.

17. Edward Shils, *Tradition.* Chicago: University of Chicago Press, 1981. Especially pp. 94–118, 148–50.

18. Cf. Elaine Walster and G. William Walster, Equity and social justice. *Journal of Social Issues,* 1975, 31, no. 3, 21–43. Also Gerald S. Leventhal, Jurgis Kazura, Jr., and William Rick Fry, Beyond fairness. In Gerold Mikula (ed.), *Justice and Social Interaction.* New York: Springer-Verlag, 1980. Pp. 167–218.

19. Leonard W. Doob, *Patriotism and Nationalism.* Westport: Greenwood, 1976. Pp. 21–22.

20. Jürg Steiner, *Amicable Agreement versus Majority Rule.* Chapel Hill: University of North Carolina Press, 1974.

21. Abner Cohen, *Custom and Politics in Urban Africa.* Berkeley: University of California Press, 1969. Pp. 161–82.

22. Arthur S. Banks and Robert B. Textor, *A Cross-Polity Survey.* Cambridge: MIT Press, 1963. P. 48, div. 48.

23. Ibid., category 167 slightly reworded.

24. Stewart Clegg, *The Theory of Power and Organization.* London: Routledge & Kegan Paul, 1979. P. 43.

25. Cf. James H. and Marge Craig, *Synergic Power.* Berkeley: Proactive Press. P. 41.

26. Jean-Guy Vaillancourt, *Papal Power.* Berkeley: University of California Press, 1980. P. 264.

27. Albert Ramirez and Fernando Soriano, Social power in educational systems. *Journal of Social Psychology,* 1982, 118, 113–19.

28. Cf. Harold D. Lasswell, *Power and Personality.* New York: Viking, 1962.

29. Juan L. Linz, Crisis, breakdown, and reequilibration. In Juan L. Linz and Alfred Stepan (eds.), *The Breakdown of Democratic Regimes.* Baltimore: Johns Hopkins University Press, 1978. Part I.

30. Gene W. Dalton, Louis B. Barnes, and Abraham Zaleznik, *The Distribution of Authority in Formal Organizations.* Cambridge: Harvard University Press, 1968. Pp. 58, 165, 204–12.

31. Lionel Tiger and Joseph Shepher, *Women in the Kibbutz.* New York: Harcourt Brace Jovanovich, 1975. Pp. 4, 23–32.

32. David Riesman, *The Lonely Crowd.* New Haven: Yale University Press, 1950. Pp. 233–55.

33. Cyril A. Rogers and C. Frantz, *Racial Themes in Southern Rhodesia*. New Haven: Yale University Press, 1962. Pp. 172–73.

34. Peter Lambley, *The Psychology of Apartheid*. Athens: University of Georgia Press, 1980. Pp. 50–51.

35. Henri Tajfel, The achievement of group differentiation. In Henri Tajfel (ed.), *Differentiation between Social Groups*. London: Academic Press, 1978. Pp. 77–98.

36. Five modern countries in 1959–60: carefully selected samples, 970 in the U.S.A., 937 in the United Kingdom, 955 in West Germany, 995 in Italy, and 1,008 in Mexico. *Method:* survey schedule administered by native interviewers under the supervision of the authors; a measure of alienation was obtained by singling out those persons who had no or a negative opinion concerning the impact of local government upon their lives and who also were disinterested in politics. *Results:* the samples in the U.S.A. had the lowest percentage of alienated persons, with the United Kingdom and West Germany closely following; the percentages were considerably higher in Italy and Mexico. A quarter of the American sample did not try to influence the national government, again the percentage was slightly higher in the United Kingdom, and the percentages in the other three countries were considerably higher. Gabriel Almond and Sidney Verba, *The Civic Culture*. Princeton: Princeton University Press, 1963. Pp. 99, 203.

37. U.S.A.: 422 adults representing a broad range of eight groups ranging from persons in a "criminally insane" ward and long-term male mental patients to undergraduates and adult-education students. *Method:* a questionnaire, administered individually or in groups, containing sixty items, eighteen of which had a sufficiently strong relation for the investigator to justify calling them a factor of "alienation via rejection" (e.g., "It is hard to figure out whom you can really trust these days," "There's little use writing to public officials because they aren't really interested in the problem of the average man"). *Results:* the alienation scale had a modest statistical relation to other scales the investigator calls emotional distance, authoritarianism, perceived purposelessness, and self-determination. Elmer L. Struening, A factor analytic explanation of the alienation, anomie, and authoritative domain. *American Sociological Review*, 1965, 30, 768–76.

38. Australia: 400 adults. Method: questionnaire measuring alienation in a manner quite similar to the Struening study cited in note 37 above as well as other predispositions. Results: no relation was found between alienation so measured and authoritarianism, and only a moderate relation with anxiety and ethnocentrism. Alan Hughes, *Psychology and the Political Experience*. Cambridge: Cambridge University Press, 1975. P. 66.

39. R. Felix Geyer, *Alienation Theories*. Oxford: Pergamon Press, 1980. P. xvi.

40. Michael Parenti, *Power and the Powerless*. New York: St. Martin's Press, 1978. P. 203.

41. Richard Sennett, *Authority*. New York: Knopf, 1980. Pp. 119, 191.

42. Cf. Morton Deutsch, *The Resolution of Conflict*. New Haven: Yale University Press, 1973. Pp. 164–65.

11

Epilogue

Ethical judgments are unavoidable whenever power and authority are contemplated even in passing. Perhaps, as one writer maintains, people have freed themselves from their "primeval bonds," which include natural forces in the environment as well as their social milieux and their own "animal existence," only to enslave themselves in a web of obligations to newspapers and authorities.[1] Have we therefore improved our lot? Social workers sometimes believe that they alone are "more capable of recognizing what is good" for their clients than the clients themselves,[2] and hence prescribe regimens for them. Should these experts, if they are in fact experts, be encouraged to exercise such power? More generally, it is contended, some form of power is essential whenever no agreement is reached concerning the degree to which equality or zero power is "necessary, practicable, or politically feasible."[3] But probably most persons believe that power should be used as sparingly as possible,[4] and then only in some situations (such as government) but not in others (such as the family).[5] Power, it seems, may be abused either when it is or is not utilized;[6] and who is to make the decision and on what basis?

Who indeed has the right to make crucial decisions for the vast majority? Was Thomas Jefferson espousing an ethical or political truth when he stated that a revolution to overthrow the establishment is needed every now and then? The very notion of authority, especially political authority, has been savagely attacked or conspicuously glorified by writers in the Western tradition.[7] In this context philosophical problems concerning freedom appear throughout the centuries and remain unsolved. Authorities are needed; by definition they then must restrain those who do or must accept them. It might be said that participants freely decide to relinquish part of their freedom to authorities in order to achieve other goals of which they themselves approve. In addition, some power may be needed to exercise what is considered to be one group's freedom, yet at the expense of another group.[8] In an epilogue, reference can be made only to some of the more pressing salient perplexities associated with power and authority.

A *Competency*. The competency of each authority must be judged. In a few instances, as in the control of infectious diseases, obedience is almost automatic and unquestioned: everyone agrees that the diseases are to be avoided and that public health authorities are—or should be—more competent than laymen to select the measures to be adopted in order to avoid those diseases. Doubts begin to be expressed when decisions are made regarding the widespread use of herbicides and pesticides, for here there are conflicting values: getting rid of weeds and pests vs. consequential harm to other plants, animals, and human beings. More serious doubts arise as the relevant knowledge becomes more complex, the most prominent illustration of which is the utilization of nuclear energy. Here the experts contend that only they can make the necessary estimates concerning the risk, whereas lay persons estimate those risks quite differently and maintain that they and not the experts are likely to be victims of disasters. In virtually all fields of human endeavor, ranging from education and government to art and sport, competency is claimed by some authorities and disputed by others.

B *Distribution*. The distribution of power and authority is a perennial problem in any society since unavoidable dependency, beginning with infants and ending with the aged, inevitably results in inequalities. The challenge throughout the ages has been to devise a more perfect system of government and more satisfactory human relationships so that justice and freedom, however defined, somehow can triumph. Just as each human being is solipsistically encased, so participants in a society are trapped in a heritage from the past. The actions of political leaders, the responsibility granted a bureaucracy, the successes and failures of foreign policy, the privileges of the elite, the deprivations of subordinates all result from separate events in the past, leave their traces behind, and cannot easily be undone. Participants lower in the hierarchy are likely to resent their positions, unless they enjoy the evasion or avoidance of responsibility; those toward the upper end are gratified by their location unless they experience guilt or remorse.

C *Curbing Power*. At some point in time or for some participants the critical problem in any organization or group is to uncover the best, the most just way to curb power. Perpetually in the West since classical times good men have debated the various means that have been proposed to achieve that end. In a large country the issue may be that of decentralization according to those who believe that power in government can be more easily abused when it is centralized than when considerable authority is delegated to the province, the region, or the local community. The limitations imposed upon authorities as well as some of the privileges of individual citizens can be embodied in statutes or the equivalent of a bill of rights. Then the privileges and rights must be safeguarded by preventing officials from being overthrown or by a system of courts and enforcement officers. In democracies monopolies and trusts are curbed because, it is believed, the concentration of power prevents subordinates from exercising "free" choice: either they patronize the industry that controls a specific product or service or they deprive themselves of that product or service. The curbing of power in this manner may result in a loss of the efficiency gained through centralization and therefore, in order to gain the advantages of centralization without losing freedom of choice, such enterprises may be regulated by the state. As ever, values must be selected, compromises are likely.

D

Selection. In and outside of traditions men grope for ways to improve their lot which usually means a better way to distribute and control authority and power. Can it be argued, whether in political campaigns or in governments over generations, that the participants, deliberately or otherwise, select the authority and power they truly deserve? In many senses, the question, though not impertinent, is metaphysical since so much depends upon the implicit conception of "deserve." We know that under a totalitarian regime "every authority" is destroyed or made subservient to the state, whereas in a democratic society there is supposed to be a "fundamental reaffirmation of a constitution by the preponderant majority of the people."[9] On a practical level the solution is not that clear-cut. The deeds of Napoleon, Mussolini, and Hitler during their lifetimes are well documented: did the peoples of France, Italy, and Germany merit those regimes? The influence of tyrants lingers on after they have perished. Post–Nazi Germany, for example, has been divided into two countries; but this state of affairs can be only indirectly attributed to Hitler in the sense that division occurred after and as a consequence of the war for which, however, he himself undoubtedly bears significant responsibility. The persistence of neo-Nazis in West Germany can also be ascribed to him in part, and indirectly so can the contemporary reaction against fascism and dictatorship in the country. Whatever consequences can be traced to Hitler, nevertheless, are overlaid in German cultural patterns. Are the German people, then, now enjoying or enduring a state of affairs they have once selected and hence deserve?

The issues of justice and freedom may not arise when the principal is a natural force like a snow storm, although some victims may use the metaphor that nature is unjust, or they may interpret the event as the just or unjust expression of a just or unjust god. The damage caused by a sudden flood, however, may sometimes be ascribed to the failure of human beings to take proper precautions or to greed that has induced them to build and dwell upon submarginal land and thus they have disregarded the natural rise and flow of a river or the sea. The issue may also not arise when animals overpower human beings, although on occasion in other societies and formerly in our own an offending beast has had to stand trial to determine its guilt or innocence; or perhaps responsibility must be traced to persons who were stupidly reckless for some ulterior motive. Thus the issue may reappear even when the subordinate is nonhuman: men are accused of plundering the earth, acting contrary to the laws of nature, or dealing cruelly or stupidly with animals.

A glibly expressed platitude cannot easily be dismissed, in fact it provokes a painful, utopian challenge to whoever would select any form of power or authority: "no political system seems to have evolved and operated to meet all human requirements perfectly" and "perhaps none ever will."[10] The inference must be that in the short run systems satisfy followers or prevent them from rebelling but in the longer run the consequence is change, sometimes drastic change. While it may not be true, for example, that the American Constitution originally responded to the vast majority of people, it is a fact that the founding fathers represented the ruling elite and that the document was approved by the not necessarily representative legislatures of the thirteen states. That Constitution, however, has had to be amended, and decisions of the Supreme Court have to some extent fluctuated with the needs of the time, including among which have been those of the oppressed and the underprivileged. It is, however, not clear whether justice in the abstract or the concrete thus triumphs, for the outcome of change may be a function of the rewards under the control of the contending participants and their retaliative power rather than of their sense of justice.[11]

Decades ago it used to be the custom in the West to sprinkle praise upon the democratic form of government. The major assumption of its proponents was that when power is curbed and distributed widely among citizens by enabling them to vote and otherwise to participate widely in the affairs of state, political leaders will use their authority wisely to diminish inequality. With or without documentation this view is now questioned, in fact sometimes considered a delusion. A careful study, for example, in which social inequality in sixty countries around the middle of the current century was measured through the use of four indices (percentage of adults voting, competitiveness of the party system, electoral irregularity, and freedom of the press) leads to the conclusion that "political democracy has no discernible impact (additive or multiplicative) on social equality, once the degree of economic development is taken into account." It appears, consequently, as if "attaining the legal right to organize for collective action is not the same thing as attaining the practical *capability* to organize."[12] And yet an "empirical study of moral behavior and mentality of rulers and governments," relying upon anecdotal, historical, but usually impressive evidence leads to the generalization that "the greater, more absolute, and coercive the power of rulers, political leaders, and big executives of business, labor and other organizations, and the less freely this power is approved by the ruled population, the more corrupt and criminal such ruling groups and executives tend to be."[13] If this conclusion is correct, it would follow that some form of democratic control, whatever its admitted imperfections, creates fewer risks than when power and authority emanate from an efficient, less controllable set of principals.

According to a competent summary of research available during the 1960s, democratic ideology favors the allocation of "problem-solving and decision-making" to entire work groups rather than to dominating authorities, with the alleged result that decisions by groups secure "higher acceptance" and are "executed efficiently." It is, nevertheless, naive to conclude that acceptance, efficiency, and willingness are always facilitated by group decisions, rather "the relative effectiveness" of any group decision, however made, depends upon the "quality, acceptance, and time variables and on differences in amount of these outcomes resulting from these methods, neither of which is invariant from one situation to another."[14] Cultural factors may also play a role; thus in Japanese companies, workers are not discharged during a recession because, according to a spokesman for a large corporation, "when we select someone, the person becomes part" of that company's "family."[15]

Justice. The final problem is the most important of all and hence
E is unavoidable. While it may be true that "the justice motive with
its various forms" can be considered "a central theme around which considerable interaction is organized,"[16] and that "ideas as to what is considered just and unjust are found embedded in every aspect of culture and personality,"[17] the "various forms" and the "ideas as to what is considered" to be just action are so varied and culture-bound that guiding criteria of a universal nature are not easy to locate.[18] One of a thousand illustrations, in this instance, is a quotation from a native of Sardinia: "The providence of God being merciful to all his creatures, how would he allow it that the shepherds of Gallura possess 500, 800, or 1000 sheep, while we have little flocks of a hundred? Wherefore, if we, through deceit or bravery can steal from them some hundreds, we help, at least in part, to effect distributive justice."[19]

As indicated in effect when the bases for his decisions concerning justice were suggested in Chapter 8, the participant compares what he has contributed or will contribute in a given situation (his inputs) with the rewards he has received or will receive (the outcomes for him); and the results of the comparison in turn are compared with those of other participants. The first comparison is thus a judgment concerning the self, the second a judgment of others; and the outcome is affected by some guiding principle. Over and above the issue of justice is a possible conflict between the welfare of the participant and that of his community. Here arises the challenge of what has been called "the tragedy of the commons": literally there is immediate gain from allowing one's cattle to graze freely on public grassland, but there is also the belief that overgrazing and subsequent loss of that grassland are inevitable when others do likewise.[20] This tragedy requires just solutions for everyone in the community, yet most participants find it easier to think in individual terms. Perhaps North Americans deal with persons they consider the victims of powers or forces by seeking to compensate them or by judging that for some reason or other they deserve their present plight.[21] But such rectification or rationalization will not save the commons. Wisdom may begin when the present or incipient tragedy is recognized: how can the inequalities that exist in the world, whether within a country (rich vs. poor, palaces vs. slums) or between countries (developed vs. developing) be justified and, more important, altered? The tragedy of the commons is simpler because the penalty from overgrazing presumably is experienced by every participant during his life time, but it may be only the descendants of those now profiting from inequalities and inequities who will suffer; hence the incentive of the powers to introduce effective changes is not great—unless they guide themselves with a compelling moral principle or unless they show genuine concern for those descendants.

There is, therefore, no final solution to the problems of justice—or freedom. We know only that neither can be absolute from society to society nor from person to person. Inexperienced young children must obey their parents. Citizens of all states are required not only to perform or not perform certain actions formalized in legal codes but also to do "whatever some specified persons tell them to do."[22] Over the ages a strong bias has emerged which affirms that each participant, regardless of his status within a hierarchy, should be treated equally and without prejudice when confronted with authorities. They should have access to competent legal advice if and when they are accused of breaking a law. They should have similarly equal opportunities to influence authorities through voting and other pressures—and we realize that this utopian situation exists nowhere, not in the West, not in communist countries, and not in traditional societies. Similarly we know that in a "free democracy" there must be "a two-directional process of communication between the government and the governed, each influencing and stimulating the other";[23] but we also know this ideal can be only approximated. Finally, it seems certain that, when people seek freedom—and not everyone does in all respects—they wish to achieve whatever goals they seek and they are convinced that they themselves should select those goals.[24] If their self-belief is internally oriented, they may be convinced that they are thus free: their achievements depend upon their own efforts and they themselves are at liberty to follow whatever paths seem attractive.

But, but, but—how can one be optimistic when we view the evil in which we dwell in large part because of severe defects in our power and authority structures: disease, poverty, malnourishment, and above all war? In our struggles to mitigate, possibly to eliminate these evils, we in effect must find ways to prevent leaders from exercising their authority and power ruthlessly. In their verbal utterances, therefore, even the most entrenched rulers contend they rule by the consent of the governed; and the principle of consent—or the pious hope—has permeated English and hence American political ideology for centuries.[25] Periodic elections are supposed to enable vox populi to be heard. The American Constitution contains a widely known form of restraint, viz., the separation of powers through the system of checks and balances, whereby the three branches of government interact and presumably prevent each other from usurping all the power.[26] It is clear, however, that the distribution among the three branches shifts over time, in large part as a result of the particular principals who occupy positions in the White House, the Congress, and the Supreme Court. Writers who find fault with the American system forever complain about the ways in which it functions in practice, they decry what they consider to be the "unaccountability" of government as a whole to the American people.[27] Again, it must be emphasized, both groups and governments require organization, and organization demands allocation of authority and power, which inevitably produces some inequality.[28] Short of utopia, is it possible for everyone, all participants, principals as well as subordinates, leaders as well as followers, to exist in the midst of authority and power and yet enjoy the necessities as well as the spiritual values they crave? I wonder, yes—alas—I wonder.

NOTES

1. Herbert Rosinski, *Power and Human Destiny*. New York: Praeger, 1969. Pp. 9–23.

2. Adolf Guggenbühl-Craig, *Power in the Helping Professions*. New York: Spring Publications, 1971. P. 1.

3. D. A. Simmons, *Economic Power*. Northold, Middlesex: Gemini Books, 1976. P. 3.

4. Cf. Samuel DuBois Cook, Coercion and social change. In J. Roland Pennock and John Chapman (eds.), *Coercion*. Chicago: Aldine-Atherton, 1972. Pp. 107–43.

5. Ronald V. Sampson, *The Psychology of Power*. New York: Random House 1966. P. 15.

6. Betty H. Zisk, *Local Interest Politics*. Indianapolis: Bobbs-Merrill, 1973. P. 3.

7. Cf. Carl J. Friedrich, *Tradition and Authority*. New York: Praeger, 1972. Pp. 45–56.

8. Cf. ibid., p. 83.

9. Theodor Eschenburg, *Über Autorität*. Frankfurt: Suhrkamp Verlag, 1965. P. 168.

10. Hadley Cantril, *Human Nature and Political Systems*. New Brunswick: Rutgers University Press, 1961. P. 6.

11. Cf. U.S.A.: 160 male undergraduates. *Method:* in pairs but in separate rooms each subject performed a clerical task and was informed that he had done twice as well as the other student; then each was told to divide a fixed reward under varying conditions, so that he thought the coworker had contributed less. *Results:* there was a tendency for "justice" to prevail among equally powerful coworkers, "self-interest" when the other person was less powerful and the reward was impressive. *Comment:* according to the investigator, "humanitarian behavior can override maintenance of social justice norms under conditions in which social exchange between persons of unequal power is reciprocal and reward value is high enough for those persons' responses to have discernible effect on others." Jerald Greenberg, Effects of reward value and retaliative power on allocation decisions. *Journal of Personality and Social Psychology*, 1978, 36, 367–79.

12. Robert W. Jackman, *Politics and Social Equality*. New York: Wiley, 1975. Pp. 61–89, italics his.

13. Pitirim A. Sorokin and Walter A. Lunden, *Power and Mortality*. Boston: Porter Sargent, 1959. P. 37.

14. Victor H. Vroom, Industrial social psychology. In Gardner Lindzey and Elliot Aronson (eds.), *Handbook of Social Psychology*. Reading: Addison-Wesley, 1969. Vol. 5, pp. 196–268.

15. Steve Lohr, Overhauling America's business management. *New York Times*, January 4, 1981, section 6, pp. 14–17, 42–45, 51, 53, 58, 62.

16. Melvin J. Lerner, The justice motive. *Journal of Personality,* 45, 1977, 1–52.

17. Laura Nader, Forums for justice. *Journal of Social Issues,* 1975, 31, no. 3, 151–70.

18. Cf. Morton Deutsch, Equity, equality, and need, *Journal of Social Issues,* 1975, 31, no. 3, 137–49.

19. Nader, op. cit.

20. Garrett Hardin, The tragedy of the commons. *Science,* 1968, 162, 1243–48.

21. Cf. Melvin J. Lerner, Dale T. Miller, and John G. Holmes, Deserving and the emergence of forms of justice. In Leonard Berkowitz and Elaine Walster (eds.), *Advances in Experimental Social Psychology.* New York: Academic Press, 1976. Vol. 9, pp. 134–62.

22. Charles E. Lindblom, *The Policy-Making Process.* Englewood Cliffs: Prentice-Hall, 1968. P. 36.

23. Wilhelm Geiger, Authority and freedom in modern western democracy. In George N. Shuster (ed.), *Freedom and Authority in the West.* Notre Dame: Notre Dame Press, 1967. Pp. 55–68.

24. Ivan D. Steiner, Perceived freedom. In Berkowitz (ed.), op. cit., 1970. Vol. 5, pp. 187–248.

25. Lord Radcliffe of Werneth, *The Problem of Power.* London: Secker and Warburg, 1952. P. 44.

26. Cf. Arnold A. Rogow and Harold D. Lasswell, *Power, Corruption, and Rectitude.* Englewood Cliffs: Prentice-Hall, 1963. P. 29.

27. Cf. Morton Mintz and Jerome S. Cohen, *Power, Inc.* New York: Viking, 1976. P. xix.

28. Cf. Peter Schneider, *Recht und Macht.* Mainz: v. Hase & Koehler, 1970. P. 17.

Recommended Readings

Alfred Adler. *Understanding Human Nature*. New York: Greenberg, 1927.

The renowned defense, for better or worse, of the proposition that most of human behavior can be traced to a craving for power, with psychoanalytic attention concentrated on possible resulting pathologies.

T. W. Adorno, Else Frenkel-Brunswik, David J. Levinson, and R. Nevitt Sanford. *The Authoritarian Personality*. New York: Harper, 1950.

The holocaust-inspired study which related fascism and anti-Semitism or prejudice in general to personality traits among Americans; the relation subsequently has been sometimes confirmed and sometimes not in scores of similar investigations elsewhere in the Western world.

Gordon W. Allport. *Patterns and Growth in Personality*. New York: Holt, 1961.

A humanistic, yet sufficiently scientific analysis of the subtle ways in which human beings come to be organized and often even integrated.

Hoyt Alverson. *Mind in the Heart of Darkness*. New Haven: Yale University Press, 1978.

A stirring tribute to the Tswana, a people living in Southern Africa, who, whether dominated by the harsh conditions of the desert in which they live or the mines of South Africa in which many of the men toil, do not appear to have the "scars of bondage" usually associated with powerful forces but instead find meaning in their own existence and have pride in themselves.

Marc Augé. *Pouvoirs de Vie, Pouvoirs de Mort*. Paris: Flammarion, 1976.

A delicate description of the conflict between the power of life and of death with the inevitable reference to what in this instance is called "an anthropology of repression."

Robert F. Bales and Stephen P. Cohen. *Symlog*. New York: Free Press, 1979.

A schema for recording with maximum precision and reliability the interactions of members of small groups and hence producing a most detailed description of how power and authority are associated with such situations.

James David Barber. *Power in Committees*. Chicago: Rand McNally, 1966.

An empirical description and then a dissection of how thirteen finance boards in the United States reached decisions, thus revealing how the "elements of power" function in face-to-face situations created by omnipresent committees.

Ruth Benedict. *Patterns of Culture*. Boston: Houghton Mifflin, 1934.

One of the first clear-cut if somewhat simplified demonstrations that, although cultures are most diverse, each of them is integrated and organized around values and modes of acting.

Peter M. Blau. *Exchange and Power in Social Life*. New York: Wiley, 1964.
A first-rate account of how sociologists both conceptualize and empirically relate power to social structure.

John Burton. *Deviance, Terrorism, and War*. Oxford: Martin Robertson, 1979.
A model seeking to embody not only the three phenomena in the book's title but also the role of power and authority therein, including the author's own practical attempts to find solutions to political disputes.

Dorwin Cartwright (ed.). *Studies in Social Power*. Ann Arbor: Research Center for Group Dynamics, 1959.
An astute collection of laboratory and real-life studies as well as theoretical formulations whose very lack of unity can inspire an attempt to produce a more coherent theory of power.

Abner Cohen. *The Politics of Elite Cultures*. Berkeley: University of California Press, 1981.
A stimulating, provocative conception of power and symbolism derived in large part from an account of the patterning of power among the Creole population of Sierra Leone.

James S. Coleman. *The Asymmetric Society*. Syracuse: Syracuse University Press, 1982.
A sober, heterogeneous collection of essays suggesting the largely disadvantageous effects of the concentration of power in American corporations, government, and education.

Robert A. Dahl. *Who Governs?* New Haven: Yale University Press, 1961.
A microscopic analysis of the groups and leaders who determined the distribution of political, economic, educational, and social power in New Haven, Connecticut, from its founding and up to the middle of the twentieth century.

Theodor Eschenburg. *Über Autorität*. Frankfurt: Suhrkamp Verlag, 1965.
A readable (for those knowing German) historical account of how the concept of authority has been used and abused from classical times to contemporary West Germany and consequently has reflected somewhat the societies in which the speakers and writers lived.

Mary Parker Follett. *Dynamic Administration*. New York: Harper, 1942.
An optimistic discussion of the power struggles in modern industry based largely on the author's own experience and skill.

R. Felix Geyer. *Alienation Theories*. Oxford: Pergamon Press, 1980.
An admittedly one-sided, but stimulating defense of "General Systems Theory" (closely related to cybernetics), in the course of which emerges a sufficiently clear exposition of current alienation theories whose central concern is usually a sense of powerlessness.

Fred I. Greenstein. *Children and Politics*. New Haven: Yale University Press, 1965.
A detailed description, based upon interviews and questionnaires, of how a sample of American children gradually had become aware of the power and authority associated with local, state, and national governments.

P. H. Gulliver. *Disputes and Negotiations*. New York: Academic Press, 1979.
An anthropological analysis of the two components inherent in conflicts over power and authority, illustrated by a detailed examination of one dispute between tribesmen in Tanzania and another in American industry.

Stanley S. Guterman. *The Machiavellians*. Lincoln: University of Nebraska Press, 1970.
The relation of (a) scores derived from a paper-and-pencil schedule seeking to

measure "an amoral, manipulative attitude toward other individuals, combined with a cynical view of men's motives and of their character" to (b) miscellaneous demographic, social, psychological, and moral attributes of Americans.

Fritz Heider. *The Psychology of Interpersonal Relations*. New York: Wiley, 1958.
The embodiment of power in an eclectic system of psychology which features the numerous factors affecting and being affected by the individual, perforce in his daily contacts with friendly and unfriendly peers and other human beings.

Adolf Hitler. *Mein Kampf* (My Struggle). Any English or German edition; originally published in 1925–27.
The rambling, emotional, nonintellectual basis for the rise of the Nazis and their evil acts, and consequently an important reminder of how power can be seized and perpetrated.

Thomas Hobbes. *Leviathan*. Any unabridged edition; originally published in 1651.
A deliberate, and ever-challenging discussion of power and sovereignty, with considerable attention given to the alleged nature of human nature.

Robert W. Jackman. *Politics and Social Equality*. New York: Wiley, 1975.
An impressive, statistical approach, not easily comprehended, to the problem of "the inequality of within-nation distribution of material goods" and hence of the power those goods represent.

Irving L. Janis, George F. Mahl, Jerome Kagan, and Robert R. Holt. *Personality*. New York: Harcourt, Brace & World, 1969.
An encyclopedic, eclectic but organized handbook-type collection of facts, theories, and fancies concerning the ways in which behavioral scientists in the Western world describe and investigate their subjects, clients, and ordinary people.

Edward E. Jones. *Ingratiation*. New York: Irvington, 1975.
A successful attempt to sensitize any literate person to the power involved in eliciting and responding to this not always harmless form of behavior.

Bertrand de Jouvenel. *The Pure Theory of Politics*. New Haven: Yale University Press, 1963.
A civilized, almost philosophical dissection of politics viewed historically and also through shrewd observations.

David Kipnis. *The Powerholders*. Chicago: University of Chicago Press, 1976.
Another global approach to those in positions of power, containing many illuminating instances of their strategies and tactics.

Hans and Shulamith Kreitler. *Cognitive Orientation and Behavior*. New York: Springer-Verlag, 1976.
An impressive conceptual model, fortified by a variety of experiments performed in Israel and the United States, which demonstrates a solid connection between what people wish or intend, provided they are asked the proper questions, and what they actually have done or then do.

David D. Laitin. *Politics, Language, and Thought*. Chicago: University of Chicago Press, 1977.
An account (a) of a power struggle concerning which of three scripts should become the official one for transcribing the previously unwritten language of the Somalis and also (b) the effects that language's structure and vocabulary have upon the thought processes of its speakers.

Harold D. Lasswell and Abraham Kaplan. *Power and Society*. New Haven: Yale University Press, 1950.

A "framework for political inquiry" that carefully defines and both sufficiently and eruditely illustrates the concepts and propositions considered here to be the basic concern of political science.

Thomas Lemaitre. *L'Art de Commander et l'Art d'Obéir*. Avignon: Editions Aubaniel, 1969.

A wide-sweeping discussion of obedience ranging from helpless children to law and religion.

V. I. Lenin. *The State and Revolution*. Any unabridged edition; originally published in 1918.

Like the *Communist Manifesto* of Marx and Engels, another highly influential document that, if only implicitly in the present day, affects the strategy employed by many orthodox communists as they seek to possess or retain power.

Charles E. Lindblom. *The Policy-Making Process*. Englewood Cliffs: Prentice-Hall, 1968.

A valiant but admittedly partially fruitless effort to comprehend the rationale and underlying processes of public policy decisions, consequently an antidote to glib generalizations.

William W. Lowrence. *Of Acceptable Risk*. Los Altos, California: William Kaufman, 1976.

An objective exposition of the implications that "a thing is safe if its risks are judged to be acceptable," a thesis relevant to many of the prescriptions, decisions, and plans emanating from powerful authorities and affecting most persons.

David C. McClelland. *Power: The Inner Experience*. New York: Irvington, 1975.

The relation between "power motivation" as measured by spontaneous stories inspired by standardized drawings (a form of the Thematic Apperception Test, or TAT) and a variety of phenomena: psychological traits, sex differences, developmental stages, the drinking of alcohol, and cultural expressions.

Thomas Mann. *Buddenbrooks*. Original German edition, 1904. (English translation) New York: Knopf, 1924 et seq.

The tortuous but always intriguing history of the rise and fall of a North German family of merchants who worried about power within their society and community as well as among themselves.

Karl Mannheim. *Ideology and Utopia*. New York: Harcourt, Brace, 1936.

The definitive, very Germanic but intelligible treatise which is the basis for what is now called the sociology of knowledge, viz., tracing ideas to the social or class position of their sponsors.

Jacques Maquet. *Power and Society in Africa*. New York: McGraw-Hill, 1971.

The numerous forms of power in traditional African societies, with special emphasis upon kinship and economic networks as well as upon the symbols associated therewith.

Karl Marx and Friedrich Engels. *The Communist Manifesto*. Any unabridged edition; originally published in 1848.

Perhaps the best summary of Marxist philosophy and economic or historical determinism which continues to play a prominent role in the thinking of powerful leaders and many of their followers.

Philip Mason. *Patterns of Dominance*. London: Oxford University Press, 1970.

An historical and contemporary account of how and why ethnic groups, particularly colonial and semicolonial peoples, have been dominated by those in power and eventually have secured what they hoped to be freedom for themselves.

Augustine Kobina Ebow Mensah. *Autoritätskonzept und Autoritätswandel in Ghana, Nigeria, und Uganda*. Munich: Kurfürsten-Druck, 1970.

An interesting dissection of the concept of authority followed by an application of the resulting theoretical view to the Ashanti in Ghana, the Baganda in Uganda, and the Hausa-Fulani and Yoruba in Nigeria.

John Middleton and David Tait (eds.). *Tribes without Rulers*. London: Routledge & Kegan Paul, 1958.

The skillful delineation of traditional devices in six African societies enabling them to maintain social order mandated, by and large, through lineages.

Stanley Milgram. *Obedience to Authority*. New York: Harper & Row, 1974.

A series of impressive, depressing experiments, some famous beyond academic circles, which demonstrate that many but not all ordinary persons are willing ostensibly to hurt other human beings in order to obey someone they believe to be an authority.

C. Wright Mills. *The Power Elite*. New York: Oxford University Press, 1956.

A stimulating tour de force, rich in anecdotes and assertions, which maintains that the United States tends to be dominated by an interlocking directorate of persons seeking, possessing, and determined to wield power.

Ashley Montagu (ed.). *Learning Non-Aggression*. New York: Oxford University Press, 1978.

Seven case studies of traditional societies which train their children in various but dissimilar ways to emerge as relatively nonaggressive adults who seem to dwell in harmony with their own authorities and with one another.

William Ker Muir, Jr. *Police: Streetcorner Politicians*. Chicago: University of Chicago Press, 1977.

A demonstration, derived in part from observing and testing twenty-eight officers in an American city, that police exercise their designated authority through the use not only of clubs and guns but also of persuasion and diplomacy.

Geraint Parry. *Political Elites*. London: Allen & Unwin, 1969.

A back-and-forth and hence a balanced discussion of the eternal, perhaps undocumentable question as to whether or to what extent power in the West is concentrated among the very few, the somewhat numerous, or the many.

Plato. *The Republic, Book IV*. Any unabridged edition; from the fourth century B.C.

An early and everlasting challenge to powerful leaders and the powers of the state.

Nelson W. Polsby. *Community Power and Political Theory*. New Haven: Yale University Press, 1963.

A review of the studies and hypotheses concerning power in American communities which is so sensible that it provides good reasons for not leaping to conclusions about other cities on the basis of experience in one of them.

Fredrick C. Redlich and Daniel X. Freedman. *The Theory and Practice of Psychiatry*. New York: Basic Books, 1966.

A large volume that begins by relating the history of psychiatry and eventually includes comprehensive presentations of the numerous psychiatric theories and syndromes of mental disorders.

Amaury de Riencourt. *Sex and Power in History*. New York: David McKay, 1974.

An original historical account of the relative statuses of the two sexes, couched in nonsexist, nonpropagandistic terms and offering a balanced exposition of the hypotheses and hunches concerning the significance of the differences.

David Riesman. *The Lonely Crowd.* New Haven: Yale University Press, 1950.

The justly appealing interpretation of the allegedly modal orientations toward other persons and ourselves and hence toward obedience and authority which are said to have shifted from era to era in Western society.

Bertrand Russell. *Power.* New York: Norton, 1938.

A wide-ranging, creative plunge by a faustian guide into the powers inherent in societies, religion, economics, and science.

Jonathan Schell. *The Fate of the Earth.* New York: Knopf, 1982.

The epoch-making assemblage of hard facts and sagacious speculation concerning the not remote possibility, maybe even the probability, that mankind can destroy itself or a good portion of the earth if nuclear warfare were to occur.

Richard Sennett. *Authority.* New York: Knopf, 1980.

A graceful, largely historical essay raising the question as to whether it is true that modern men and women, while apparently seeking power, in fact are afraid of authority and hence rebel against authorities.

Gene Sharp. *The Politics of Nonviolent Action.* Boston: Porter Sargent, 1973.

A description of 198—yes, 198—nonviolent methods that have been or could be employed to protest and rebel against power or authority that is considered unjust or unjustified.

Guy E. Swanson. *The Birth of the Gods.* Ann Arbor: University of Michigan Press, 1960.

A scholarly, systematically developed thesis that the kinds and numbers of powerful gods and other religious beliefs have some relation to the structure of the society in which the believers dwell.

James T. Tedeschi (ed.). *Perspectives on Social Power.* Chicago: Aldine, 1974.

A useful miscellany of views offered by American professors on the exercise of power, usually buttressed with experimental or empirical data.

Leo Tolstoy. *War and Peace.* Any unabridged edition; originally published in 1869.

The novel providing the best way to sharpen one's wits concerning the power inherent in simple bickerings, love affairs, domestic policies of the state, and of course international conflicts.

Max Weber. *On Charisma and Institution Building.* Chicago: University of Chicago Press, 1968.

A selection of the diverse, coherent, erudite papers written by the influential, very Germanic sociologist who gave the word "charisma" a prominent place in his intellectual arsenal but who, since he used the term quite consistently, should not be held responsible for its current popularity as a sloppy buzz word.

Robert Paul Wolff. *In Defense of Anarchism.* New York: Harper & Row, 1970.

A careful discussion of power, obedience, and authority oriented toward many of the ethical issues and dilemmas of our time.

I. William Zartman and Maureen R. Berman. *The Practical Negotiator.* New Haven: Yale University Press, 1982.

A courageous attempt to suggest that recent international negotiations can be loosely characterized by a series of almost inevitable phases during which satisfactory or unsatisfactory resolutions are achieved.

Index

The page numbers in *italics* indicate the text pages on which a note reference is made without mentioning the author's name.

ABOUT THE AUTHOR

Leonard W. Doob is a Senior Research Associate of the Institution of Social and Policy Studies, Associate Director of the South African Research Program, and Sterling Professor Emeritus of Psychology at Yale University. His published writings include *"Ezra Pound Speaking"* (Greenwood Press, 1978), *Panorama of Evil* (Greenwood Press, 1978), *The Pursuit of Peace* (Greenwood Press, 1981), *Becoming More Civilized, Patriotism and Nationalism, Communication in Africa*, and *Patterning of Time*.

AUG 28 1987			
OCT 14 1987			
NOV 24 1987			
APR 19 1988			
DEC 4 1989			
NOV 4 1990			
FEB 08 1992			
AUG 11 1994			
[illegible] 09 1995			
DEC 10 2001			